In the Name
of the
Working Class

In the Name of the Working Class

The Inside Story of the Hungarian Revolution

Sandor Kopacsi

Translated by DANIEL *and* JUDY STOFFMAN
With a foreword by GEORGE JONAS

GROVE PRESS • New York

Published by Grove Press, Inc.
920 Broadway
New York, N.Y. 10010

First English-language edition published in Canada 1987 by Lester &
Orpen Dennys Ltd., Toronto

Library of Congress Cataloging-in-Publication Data

Kopácsi, Sándor, 1922–
    "In the name of the working class."

    Translation of: Au nom de la classe ouvrière.
    Bibliography: p.
    1. Hungary—History—Revolution, 1956—Personal narratives.
2. Kopácsi, Sándor, 1922–
3. Police chiefs—Hungary—Biography. I. Title.
DB957.K6613   1987   943.9′053′0924   87–271
ISBN 0–802–10010–4

Manufactured in the United States of America
First Edition 1987

10 9 8 7 6 5 4 3 2 1

The author wishes to thank Tybor Tardos for his work in shaping the original Hungarian manuscript into the book that was originally published as *Au nom de la classe ouvrière*. Thanks go also to Tibor Meray for his valuable information and advice.

■ *Foreword*

It is next to fraudulent to hold any opinions about the nature of the Soviet system without knowing certain facts. This knowledge can be acquired through first-hand experience or — rather less painfully — by reading a dozen or so seminal books. Sandor Kopacsi's autobiography, *In the Name of the Working Class*, is one. The others (to name only a few) include Milovan Djilas' *Conversations with Stalin*, George Faludy's *My Happy Days in Hell*, and Alexandr I. Solzhenitsyn's *The Gulag Archipelago*.

In the Name of the Working Class fills a particularly important gap in our understanding of the post-Stalin era. As an upper-middle echelon member of what Milovan Djilas termed "the new class" — the ruling Communist bureaucracy — Colonel Sandor Kopacsi, police chief of Budapest until November 1956, was in a unique position to observe the causes and effects of de-Stalinization throughout the Soviet bloc. As far as I know, his book is not just the first but the only one to date to give an accurate analysis of the Hungarian Revolution of 1956.

It is unnecessary to belabour the significance of 1956. Small-scale uprisings within the Soviet bloc had occurred in previous years, notably in East Germany in 1953. Attempts at moderating the most tyrannical aspects of the system had been made in Gomulka's Poland and, very importantly, in the Soviet Union itself, under Khrushchev, at least two years before the first guns were fired outside the building of Radio Budapest on the evening of October 23, 1956. But it was the events of the next two or three weeks that demonstrated to the world, unmistakably and for the first time, the inability of totalitarian socialism to respond to real political change with anything but brutal repression.

Many years before the term "reform-communism" gained currency in the dictionary of international politics, the revolution in Hungary was an expression of it. The students, writers, workers, politicians, and soldiers who created the climate, laid the groundwork, set forth the political demands, and eventually precipitated the armed struggle were, with almost no exceptions, Communists. Far from aiming at the restoration of the old semi-feudal regime in Hungary — as the Soviets and their apologists were to claim after the uprising was crushed — they did not even aim at the creation of a liberal, free-enterprise democracy. All they wanted was "Communism with a human face" — a clear indication that it had no human face before — and, as Hungarians, a degree of national sovereignty. Their mistake, for which many of them paid with their lives, was that they believed both to be possible. If they had not been Communists, they would have had no such illusions. In the end they were betrayed solely by their own faith.

Colonel Kopacsi's book makes it evident that the Hungarian Revolution was a Communist uprising initially, begun not to deny but to fulfil what its participants believed to be true Marxist-Leninist ideals. It is hard to say whether the originators of the uprising realized that events might carry political reform in Hungary much further, not in the direction of "fascism" — this was simply not in the cards in 1956 — but in the direction of liberal democracy. It is hard to say whether the reformists considered at the time (as the Kremlin certainly did) that if the revolution succeeded Hungary could end up as a genuinely non-aligned parliamentary democracy whose freely elected governments might include no Marxist parties at all. Without doubt, such a result would have dismayed Colonel Kopacsi and his fellow reform-communists. However, as honest idealists and patriots they might have preferred it to Communism, the regime of their own ideological choice, being maintained at the point of bayonets — especially foreign bayonets. It is also likely that (perhaps naively) they could not imagine the people of Hungary ever rejecting a social system in which they themselves passionately believed. After all, with its Stalinist errors rectified and returned to its pure Marxist-Leninist origins it was, in their opinion, the best and most humane system in the world. The workers, peasants, and students wouldn't turn it down.

The Kremlin of 1956 — that is, Premier Khrushchev and Ambassador Andropov, as he then was — wasn't so sure. Perhaps more ix

realistically than any of the reform-communists then or since, Khrushchev and company saw "democratic Communism" as a contradiction in terms. They knew that Communism and real political freedom are incompatible, for the simple reason that, if free to choose, people (at least people in European countries such as Hungary) are not likely to choose Communism. The Soviets were certainly not willing to risk it — or to risk even an independent Communist regime, a kind of precursor to Euro-communism, whose subservience to Moscow's political aims would forever be in doubt. For the Politburo's rulers, one Tito was already one too many.

Nevertheless — as Kopacsi's account makes clear — the seeds of the Hungarian Revolution were sown in Khrushchev's Soviet Union by the very powers that came to repress three years later. After Stalin's death the Kremlin's ascendant bureaucracy did want some degree of reform. In June 1953, long before his famous speech denouncing Stalin's crimes to the 20th Party Congress, Khrushchev had already pressured Hungary's Stalinist dictator Matthias Rakosi into yielding leadership to the reform-communist Imre Nagy. Khrushchev probably wanted no fundamental changes, and certainly none that might jeopardize the Communist Party's monopoly on power or the Soviet Union's supremacy over its satellites. But Stalin's paranoid dictatorship had taken a fearsome toll within the ranks of the Party itself. Khrushchev's de-Stalinization essentially aimed at making the Communist world safe for its own ruling elite.

Orthodox Communists objected to Khrushchev's reforms on the basis that, once begun, the process of "liberalization" could not be contained. Remove the worst repression, they argued, give people an inch of democracy and freedom, and they would take a mile. Stalinists feared that such a thaw might melt the foundation of the Party's exclusive power and perhaps the very basis of a centrally planned socialist state.

It would be simplistic to suggest that in opposing any modification of the strictest dictatorship old-fashioned Stalinists were worried only about the loss of their own privileges. No doubt some were, but many had an equal concern about endangering a historic mission which, as true believers, they felt sure would ultimately benefit mankind. Khrushchev seemed to them to be playing with fire.

Idealist reform-communists like Imre Nagy also feared for the survival of the planned socialist system, but they identified the dangers differently. They argued that a thaw was needed precisely to avert a complete popular rejection of the Communist model. In the case of Nagy and his collaborators it may be no exaggeration to say that they supported an uprising in Hungary in order to prevent one.

In a confidential memorandum which Nagy circulated among members of the Central Committee of the Party in Hungary in early 1956 — he even left a copy addressed to Andropov at the Soviet Embassy — Nagy argued that "There is still time for [the Soviet bloc countries] to prevent a general crisis for their regimes by taking energetic measures of democratization. Tomorrow? If these measures are too late in coming, it could happen that the very principle of a state-controlled structure will come under question."

Reform-communists like Nagy believed, or were at any rate hopeful, that the men at the helm of the new-style Kremlin, the men who toppled Stalin from his pedestal, who acknowledged his "mistakes" (the word "crimes" was not yet in use then) and who had reined in orthodox Stalinists like Rakosi, might allow fundamental reforms in Moscow's subject states. They did not see that Khrushchev's reforms were mainly aimed at keeping the ruling bureaucracy from destroying itself in Stalin's gulag, without changing the principles of the gulag-state. They did not see — as it did not accord with their own honest beliefs — that totalitarian socialism is incapable of any self-adjustment more fundamental than a palace-revolution.

Nagy and his followers wanted to rescue the system. They believed that allowing events to take their course along the clear desires of Hungarian students, workers, soldiers, and intellectuals was the best way to rescue it. They also hoped that the Soviet Union might permit this to happen. They were probably wrong in their first belief, and undoubtedly wrong in the second. The Soviet tanks rolled in, and within two years Imre Nagy and some of his colleagues were hanged by the Marxist state they had tried to save.

Had Moscow not sent in the tanks, would Nagy and his colleagues have succeeded in saving the Communist regime? Almost certainly not in the short run. As a purely practical matter of the immediate preservation of a Soviet-style system in Hungary, Khrushchev's method was better. But it also proved that tanks and the hangman's noose are not merely a perversion of Marxist-Leninist statecraft but its essence — with Stalin, or without him. The reform-communism of Imre Nagy (or of Dubcek in Czechoslovakia twelve years later) would have proved the opposite. The reform-communists might not have been able to rescue the system, but they would have proved that it might be worth rescuing.

Still, if the Soviet Union drew the line for Hungary — as it later did for Czechoslovakia and Poland — Hungary also drew a line for the Soviet Union. Having to repress a full-scale revolution turned out to be a costly business for the Kremlin. Its rulers were not keen to provoke another one. The compromise at which they arrived with Janos Kadar's government (which they installed and which rules Hungary to this day) had to include at least some of the hopes and promises of October 1956. Kadar, himself a cautious reform-communist and a former victim of Rakosi's torture-chambers, prevented the re-emergence of the worst features of the totalitarian state. Today no country in the Communist world is better off than Hungary. In this sense, the sacrifice of Imre Nagy and his fellow patriots has not been in vain.

There were changes in the Soviet Union itself relative to Stalin's days. To go no further, under Stalin all of Nagy's followers would have been executed but under Khrushchev many, like Kopacsi, were allowed to live. Having survived, he could become a witness.

In the Name of the Working Class is best described as a statement of direct evidence. A military man rather than a writer or philosopher, Kopacsi sets forth in plain words what he was in a position to observe. He indulges in no theorizing and no changes of stance through hindsight. He does not attempt to appear wiser or braver than he was. He offers explanations but no excuses. It is this that makes his book so rare: the testimony of a trustworthy witness sufficiently well placed to see, and sufficiently honest to tell.

In our century the cause of the Marxist-Leninist state — unlike fascism or other totalitarian movements — succeeded in attracting many humane and intelligent people such as Colonel Kopacsi or Imre Nagy. In a sense, therein lies the tragedy of Communism; in a sense, therein lies its danger. But in another sense, perhaps, this also provides the only hope for the people and nations in its grip.

George Jonas
August 1986

■ Translators' Preface

This book has a curious history. It started life as a Hungarian manuscript of more than a thousand pages, which was edited and translated into French by Tybor Tardos, a Hungarian journalist, himself imprisoned when the Hungarian revolution was crushed, and now living in Paris. *Au nom de la classe ouvrière* was published in Paris by Robert Laffont in 1979 and later translated into German, Italian, Dutch, Swedish, and Japanese.

We came across the book soon after its publication while spending a year in France. We were intrigued to discover that this memoir, so favourably reviewed in the press and excerpted in *Lire* magazine, its author invited to appear on the celebrated *Apostrophes* television program, was written by a Toronto janitor we had never heard of, a man who had been the police chief of Budapest during the turbulent events of 1956. Upon our return to Toronto, we sought out the author for an interview, which appeared in the *Toronto Star*. It was the beginning of a friendship with Ibolya and Sandor Kopacsi that we've come to treasure. The two of them have seen much, suffered much, and have had their courage and loyalty tested more severely than it's possible for most Canadians to imagine, living as we do in a country where politics is not a matter of life and death. Yet these brutal experiences have left them not embittered and reactionary in their views, but tolerant and humane and with an enormous capacity for enjoying the life they came so close to losing.

We are pleased to have been able to prepare the English edition of this book, the first published version that the author is able to read and understand. Working with Sandor, we have corrected the few inaccuracies that had crept into the French edition and added new material to produce, we hope, the definitive version.

Daniel Stoffman
Judy Stoffman
July 1986

■ *Contents*

1	"General Memory"	1
2	Andropov and "Budapest by Night"	11
3	"You'll Finish Too High"	19
4	In the Old Man's Service	28
5	"You Are Innocent, But...."	32
6	Internment Director	39
7	Police Chief and Colonel	48
8	The Strange Lieutenant Dohany	54
9	"Stalin Is Dead: *Nichevo*"	60
10	"Your Uniform Doesn't Become You"	66
11	Imre Nagy and Janos Kadar	74
12	Tito's Revenge	83
13	From Demonstration to Riot	95
14	A Nasty Blow	109
15	"Civil War"	120
16	On a Plywood Chair	136
17	Operation Sunday	150
18	Continue as if Nothing Were Wrong	165
19	Farewell to Our Dreams	174
20	To Parliament	185
21	"Men Sprout Like Weeds"	199
22	The Man with a Skeleton's Fingers	207
23	Operation Scapegoat	217
24	General Serov's Sentence	227
25	Assassination of an "Unpresentable" Prisoner	238
26	In the Labyrinth	247
27	"You Will Be a Witness"	257
28	"In the Name of the Working Class"	271
29	Seven Years of Darkness	287
30	*"Isten Hozott"*	293

■ *"General Memory"*

As the acacia trees of Budapest were bursting into bloom in the spring of 1975, it suddenly became fashionable to speak of human rights. The European nations, both East and West, were preparing for a conference on human rights in Helsinki, where they would sign a historic agreement guaranteeing the free exchange of ideas — and the free movement of people — across international borders.

Reading about all this in the *Tass* dispatches in our Budapest newspapers set my wife Ibolya to thinking. She put down the paper, turned to me, and said, "Maybe you should start again."

"Start what again?" I was thinking of other things. It wasn't easy to rid myself of the memories that haunted me, night and day.

"If you are going to see someone influential to press your request to be struck off the list, this might be a good time...."

I had been condemned in 1958 to life imprisonment as one of eight leaders of the Budapest insurrection. A general amnesty in 1963 gave me my freedom, but I had never regained my civil rights. I was still on the list of those whose judicial files carried the damaging phrase *condemned to lifelong detention*. In Hungary, a person with a file like that need not waste his time looking for a good job. He'd probably find himself led out between two policemen — an unhappy predicament for a former police chief like me.

Before plunging into politics and police work, I had been a metalworker, like my father and grandfather before me. On my release from prison, friends got me a job practising my old trade in a Budapest factory. The authorities had no objection, nor did they interfere when, in 1969, to finish studies begun before I was jailed, I presented my thesis at the law faculty of Eotvos Lorand University.

The thesis received first-class honours and, after I completed some additional courses, I had my degree in industrial law. But my right to practise was denied.

So here I was, an ex-jailbird pushing fifty. If I was ever to start my career as a lawyer, it would have to be soon. Time was running out. But, as regular as clockwork, my requests came back, red-pencilled with the word: "REFUSED".

Feeling helpless, I went to see the dean of my faculty.

"What do you think of my case?" I asked him.

"That you have a perfect right to practise. Your penalty should have been cancelled right after the amnesty. What's their motive in refusing?"

"There isn't one."

"That's impossible. There's a reason for every refusal."

The dean had never run into a case like mine. "In your place," he said, "I would do everything I could to find out more about this craziness."

One morning, before I left for work, my wife pushed me towards the telephone. "Now you're going to ask for a meeting with Mihaly," she said.

Mihaly Korom was Minister of Justice and a former comrade. The last time I had seen him was before the uprising.

"You talk as if he's going to see me. He won't have anything to do with an ex-con."

"Try anyway. We'll see."

My wife was right. The audience was quickly granted. On a beautiful morning, I arrived at the ministry, a large baroque building with a statue of blindfolded justice on top. The secretary came to get me in the corridor.

"Sandor Kopacsi? This way please. Comrade Minister is waiting for you."

In his spacious, sunlit office, Mihaly greeted me with a smile.

"Sandor! I'm happy to see you again. How is your family?"

"Fine, thanks."

He asked the secretary to bring us some coffee. We had never been close friends, although our studies had brought us together. Of working-class stock like me, he was a native of Budapest, while I came from the north. For five years, we had attended the same law seminar; I was police chief at the time, while he was a member of the Central Committee charged with responsibility for the armed forces and police. After seminars or exams we used to return to my place to eat with my wife, who is a first-class cook.

"What's Ibolya doing?"

"She has a job, nothing much, a bookkeeper for a co-operative."

"And your little girl? You do have a little girl?"

"Yes, but now she's big. She just got married. She's living with her husband in Canada."

There was a short silence. I took advantage of it to get to the object of my visit. The minister's face took on a pained expression.

"I'm going to speak frankly to you, Sandor. I supported your first request to be struck off the list. To my great astonishment, the council of the Praesidium turned it down. It was the first time I had been overruled in that way. As you can imagine, I did not push the matter further."

"But I can't be refused the right to live like everybody else. I've been amnestied."

"I know that very well...."

"At least give me the reasons for the refusal. The 'considerations', to use the jargon of the trade."

He looked at me. Then he grabbed a pencil and a notebook and wrote a few words on a piece of paper.

"Go to this address. I'm truly sorry, Sandor. Your case is outside my sphere of influence."

The address was that of the Supreme Court. The office indicated on the paper was on the second floor, Room 51.

A young female employee was waiting for me.

"Sandor Kopacsi? I've been expecting you. If you'd be so good as to follow me."

She chose one from a bunch of keys and opened a door. We crossed an empty room. She chose a second key and opened a second door that led into a cramped, windowless space. She turned on a light, revealing a table and chair in the middle of the room. The walls and door were of steel.

"Sit down. You're going to read the text concerning you."

She took a thin folder from a drawer, opened it, and placed it before me. I found a page covered in pencilled scribbling, poorly organized and full of words scratched out and added.

Most of the manuscript was given over to various details: reference numbers, dates, registration numbers. In the middle of the page, a few lines resembled an explanation. "The verdict pronounced having been life imprisonment, the subject cannot be granted any reduction in the penalty."

I thought I was dreaming.

"Miss?"

"Yes?"

"What I've just read makes no sense."

"I beg your pardon?"

"My sentence was commuted to fifteen years in prison. The sentence is fifteen years. That's the stipulation I currently fall under."

She listened to me with a neutral air. "I'm only the employee in charge of the records."

"Will you let me take this document?"

"That's impossible."

"May I have a photocopy?"

"We're not equipped for that."

"May I take notes?"

"That's not allowed."

The time was up. She put the paper back in the folder and the folder back in the drawer. She triple-locked the steel door behind us.

I was out on the street, completely bewildered. The authorities were covering up their motives for refusing to normalize my status. They were making certain that I couldn't put my finger on the slightest proof of illegality. Yet this was a period of reconciliation in which the Hungarian government had stopped persecuting former revolutionaries. Unlike myself, the other surviving leaders of the insurrection were quietly practising their professions.

Suddenly, I saw the light. The authorities themselves were cornered. With a view to keeping me in a precarious position indefinitely, a higher power obliged them to commit a series of illegalities, a practice the government itself found repugnant.

I took a week of sick leave from work and spent it racking my brains. Obviously, this was the work of the Allamvedelmi Osztaly (AVO), the Hungarian security police. Without the personal intervention of Janos Kadar, the head of the Hungarian state, I would have been hanged in 1958, together with Prime Minister Imre Nagy and Minister of Defence Paul Maleter. The AVO had never reconciled itself to my continued existence.

What could I do? How could I get free of these piranhas of

the Danube? In despair, I decided to ask the help of a childhood friend of my father's, a man who was highly placed but outside the obvious circles of power.

The man did not appear to have aged in the twelve years since I had last seen him, which had been at the state funeral for my father. He had stood next to the casket, accompanied by some Soviet dignitaries who had come to pay their last respects to a distinguished Second World War Resistance fighter. The funeral took place one day after my release from prison, and my father's friend had had tears in his eyes. I remember wondering whether the tears were because of my father or because of me and deciding that they were probably for both of us.

"Well, Sandor, I hear that you are intent on regaining your right to vote."

I told him I wanted much more than that. I wanted the AVO off my back.

"Let's go for a walk."

He made a gesture toward the door leading to his garden. Even this man, who was above all suspicion, preferred to talk outside his own walls.

"Sandor, the secret police have nothing to do with your problem. I've looked into it. Your files have disappeared. There's not a trace of your case in the archives.

"Have you heard of someone called 'The Memory'?" he continued, ignoring my surprise. "He's probably the one who's got your files."

I knew the man. At the Ministry of the Interior we had given that nickname to General Ichtchenko, a senior officer of the Soviet secret service. If he had my file, it was because the Russians hadn't pardoned me. It looked as though I was headed for the firing squad or the gulag.

My friend looked at me impatiently. "Poor Sandor. You didn't inherit your father's realism, that's the least I can say. Times have changed. The Memory no longer gets involved in such trifles. He has become someone whose opinion is highly valued. If he's interested in your case, it's because the Russians are *keeping you in reserve.*"

Apparently the role I had played during the insurrection could be significant in more ways than one. As a former member of the Hungarian Communist Party Politburo and a companion of Nagy, the martyred prime minister, I had a background that could be useful to Moscow in a moment of crisis. It would not have been the first time Moscow made use of a formerly disgraced politician to put a new face on the government of one of its satellites.

"The ways of diplomacy are unfathomable. If the case arises, a man like you could be catapulted into one of the highest offices in the country."

I'd heard the suggestion before. In 1956, in the dying days of the uprising, I had been invited to join in the new group that was going to run Hungary, a Hungary once again safely inside the Soviet camp. A senior Soviet official had told me I might even become a minister. I had refused. Holding power meant being willing to sign your friends' death warrants, and I wasn't capable of that.

"Returning to power doesn't interest me," I said. "I'd rather end it all."

He walked several steps, without looking at me. "Do I talk of ending it?" he murmured in a barely audible voice.

Toward the end of the meeting, he told me his impressions of a recent trip to Moscow, of how Brezhnev was more and more impatient to see his Helsinki gamble on improved relations with the West succeed. He turned toward me.

"There perhaps is a door...a narrow door for you to escape through."

He talked about the writers and other dissidents expelled to the West by Moscow on the heels of Solzhenitsyn. Of course, there had not yet been a military man among them. Even a very active and annoying one like General Grigorenko was kept in a psychiatric hospital. But perhaps, if things were organized very precisely....

"Would you be ready to take a big risk to emigrate?"

I was ready to do anything. My daughter was waiting for us in Canada. I didn't want to live the rest of my life manipulated like a puppet by the regime.

He put his hands on my shoulders. "I'll give you a sign. Meanwhile, not a word, to anybody."

A few days later, in the middle of the night, the telephone rang. Drunk with sleep, I picked it up. I heard a voice say: "Kiss Jozsi's granddaughter for me."

Click, the caller hung up. Jozsi, the diminutive of Joseph, was my father's name. His granddaughter was my Judith. My father's comrade was telling me that he judged the moment right if we meant to leave the country. But that didn't mean it would be easy. "Ibolya, there's some news. Maybe we're going to see our child again — in Canada."

As I expected, the day after I submitted my request to emigrate, I lost my job. The chief engineer at the plant, a man who had been greatly helped by my father in years gone by, was compelled to sign a declaration claiming I had infringed the labour regulations and must be fired without compensation. The man was so distressed by having to take part in this falsehood, that he suffered a heart attack.

A second ordeal awaited us at the Canadian consulate. The consul wasn't at all sure that his country could give asylum to someone as deeply involved as I in political affairs.

"I'm not promising anything. I'm going to investigate. You'll have to come back...."

This first visit to the Canadian consulate propelled the AVO into action. They emptied a whole floor of the building across the street from ours by arresting the regular tenants, high-class whores who did a lively business with foreigners thereby earning valuable hard currency for Hungary.

The apartment's new tenants lived behind closed blinds. From the moment we left our apartment, two men, or a man and a woman, tailed us. What did they hope to discover? My wife and I liked to go for walks, as a way of not dictating our conversations directly into the microphones hidden in our apartment. When our walk was a long one, the security police on our tail would be relieved by fresh operatives. They weren't very good at their jobs. If I had used such incompetent personnel when I was police chief, I would have been quickly fired — which would have saved me a lot of trouble later.

Five or six days after this surveillance began, I was almost run over by a moving van, when it broke the chain separating the sidewalk from the street. If it hadn't been for the quick reflexes of Ibolya, who pulled me out of the way, I would have stayed on that sidewalk.

"Hey, you! Murderer!" Ibolya screamed.

The van backed up off the sidewalk, gunned its engine, and roared off. No head was visible through the window, and for an instant I had the insane idea that the vehicle was driverless.

The next day, the same thing happened, this time the moment we stepped out of our building. I was ready and leapt out of harm's way. The van knocked over the garbage pails lined up in front of the building and sped away.

We raced back up to our apartment, closed the curtains, and decided that I wouldn't go out again. We phoned all our friends and declared that we were starting a hunger strike that would last until we were granted permission to leave the country.

Two days later, a visitor rang the doorbell. He introduced himself to my wife as an emissary of the Minister of the Interior. The director of the passport bureau wanted to see me urgently.

"What guarantee do you give me that you won't detain my husband?"

"Really, madam, 'detain', in the time that we live in — how can you imagine such a thing?"

"In any case," Ibolya retorted, "you are warned: if my husband isn't back in two hours, the phone lines to Canada will be very busy and the Western newspapers will know everything."

"But, madam —"

"There is no 'But, madam'. In your own interest, give my message to the minister."

At the passport office, I was received by a friendly young man, handsome and tanned, who said he was the minister's private secretary.

"Comrade Kopacsi (nobody had called me Comrade since my imprisonment), I've got two pieces of news for you, one good and one bad. The bad news is this: your request for expatriation has not been granted. It has become unnecessary. The good news will explain why. Comrade Kopacsi, yes, we have infringed your rights. We admit our mistake. Beginning tomorrow, you will have access to a job that corresponds to your qualifications."

"Does that mean that from this moment on I've got a clean record?"

The young man cleared his throat. "Well...no, not right away."

"Ah."

"But I'm making a note, you see: I'm noting your request on this paper: 'clean record', right? I'm going to refer this to the minister. In the meantime, he asks you to please speak to madam...to the comrade...to your wife."

"Speak?"

"To have a little bit more confidence and patience. To abandon this idea of emigration, to accommodate herself to the very desirable conditions that we are offering you...that you will have very soon."

Back at the house, we went over what they had told me with a fine-tooth comb. A job offer from the Minister of the Interior. The meaning of that was clear. I would be working for the AVO. And what if, at the last minute, the minister decided to play a dirty trick? In light of the current international situation, the government would be embarrassed if it had to deny my request to leave. But if I withdrew the request, I lost my leverage. I might never get my clean record.

We phoned the Canadian consulate. "Have you any news of our visas?"

"You've changed your mind?"

"Changed our mind? We certainly have not changed our mind."

The consul was completely taken aback. "There's a little game going on here that I don't understand. The Hungarian diplomatic representative in Ottawa has just officially informed the Canadian government that the Kopacsis have renounced their application for permission to immigrate."

"Absolutely false!"

Truly, our leaders took us for cretins. But they were playing with fire. I was sure they hadn't told The Memory of these manoeuvres. In the current international context, they were courting trouble.

At 10:00 p.m., my daughter called from Canada. The conversation was interrupted twice. But before the line was cut, we understood that our friends on the other side of the Atlantic had decided to step up the pressure. In Canada, there was a large Hungarian community and I had personal friends among them, from the days of the Resistance as well as from my time as police chief. My case was going to be publicized on television. Journalists had interviewed my daughter, who was running a genuine propaganda office. She and her husband, Peter, maintained contact with some well-known people, including the humourist George Mikes, who broadcast on Radio Free Europe under the pseudonym "Gallicus", and Otto Habsburg, the last of the dynasty that had ruled Austria and Hungary, who had become an influential member of the European Parliament. Radio Free Europe and the Voice of America had already announced a series of programs entitled *In Favour of Kopacsi*. The case was being discussed in newspapers and on Radio Free Europe as a "bad omen for the Helsinki conference".

The reaction took a few days, but when it came it was brusque. The doorbell rang. An AVO soldier presented himself as the personal emissary of the Minister of the Interior. "The Comrade

Minister invites you to come to his office."

This time we took no precautions. We knew we didn't have to because it was clear that we had won. We were received at 9:00 a.m., not by the minister but by his administrative assistant. Without a word of explanation, he handed us a large sheet and a receipt book for our signatures. The large sheet was our "Emigrés' Passport". (In our country, this document was a sort of expulsion order, written on a single sheet for a whole family.) No "comrade", no extended hand, not even "goodbye and good luck".

As we left, we landed nose to nose with the minister, flanked by two uniformed Soviet generals. The minister gave no sign that he knew us well, which he did; instead he pretended to be very absorbed in conversation. When we were out of the building, my wife pinched my arm. "Did you recognize the one on the right, the elder of the two?" She was speaking of the two Soviet generals.

"I wasn't paying much attention."

"It was him."

"Who?"

"General Ichtchenko. The Memory. I'd recognize him in a crowd of a thousand people, from the look in his eye."

The Memory had come to make sure that the Kremlin's order had been executed and that the Hungarian state had truly rid itself of the very troublesome Kopacsis.

Andropov and "Budapest by Night"

The first time we met The Memory was at the very end of 1955, during a small New Year's Eve party for the Soviet advisers attached to the Ministry of the Interior. It was nine months before the Budapest uprising.

My wife and I were invited out of the blue. We had decided to spend New Year's Eve at home when, at 11:00 p.m., the telephone rang. At the other end of the line I could hear snatches of music. A merry voice with a strong foreign accent said, "It's Petofi."

Petofi was the greatest Hungarian poet of the nineteenth century. It was also the pseudonym of one of the two Soviet advisers who worked with me at police headquarters. (The other called himself "Magyar-Miska" or "Miska the Hungarian"; their papers carried phoney identities, to the consternation of the guard at police headquarters whom they forced each morning to inspect their entry passes.)

"Comrade Colonel, we wanting you and Missis...come here... I beg you."

He didn't have an interpreter with him. As I spoke Russian poorly and Petofi's Hungarian was so bad as to be non-existent, the negotiations were difficult. We thought he was inviting us to have a drink with him and his wife. He was a friendly man, especially to us. Whenever he returned from Moscow, he remembered to bring a small gift for Ibolya — some European-style eau-de-Cologne (she hated the Russian patchouli) or a box of chocolates from one of their co-operatives, something you couldn't find in the regular stores.

"We can't refuse," whispered Ibolya. "Let's go, just for an hour."
I put on my uniform, my wife slipped on a skirt and blouse, and
we left.

We found forty of them sitting at tables, the men in dark suits,
the women in full-length evening dresses. All the senior Soviet
advisers attached to the Ministry of the Interior were there but, except
for us, not a single Hungarian was present. Ibolya, in her skirt and
blouse, was nearly in tears from embarrassment.

Petofi ran up to greet us and introduced us to the other guests:
"Comrade Kopacsi, the police chief of Budapest, and Mrs. Kopacsi,
both of them partisans in the Carpathians with the Red Army."
(Actually, we had been in the Bukk Mountains, south of the
Carpathians.)

Smiling faces greeted us. We sat down and accepted filled glasses.
At that moment, ten violins and five double-bass fiddles broke into
a tune frequently used to accompany ovations. "Long live our beloved
chief and his charming lady!" exclaimed a voice in Hungarian. I
knew at once that it must be Jaroka, the leader of "my" gipsy
orchestra. I hadn't noticed his band, which was hidden from view
behind a screen. Several years before, when these musicians were
out of work, I had included them among the personnel at police
headquarters. Jaroka became a lieutenant, his second violin a sub-
lieutenant, and so on, right down to the fifth double-bass fiddler
who became a simple police constable. For some time, the Soviets
had been borrowing them from me for their parties.

"How are you doing, Jaroka?" I asked him during a break in the
music.

"Comrade Colonel, this is a great day for the whole band."

"Why is that?"

"We pissed in a washroom made of black marble." (The toilets
were superb in the advisers' club, which had been the home of the
eldest son of Admiral Horthy, regent of Hungary before the Second
World War.)

The dinner, which must have come from the kitchen of one of
Budapest's best restaurants, was as fine as the surroundings. Although
the atmosphere was formal, the guests were amiable, almost shy.
Looking uncomfortable in their unfashionably cut suits, the men
chatted quietly. These men and their fleshy wives, squeezed tightly
into flowery evening dresses, their hair in braids wrapped around
their heads, resembled nothing so much as a party of prosperous

citizens in a northern Hungarian town before the war. My wife and I ate in silence.

It was Jaroka with his inimitable violin who livened things up. He played tunes known to gipsies the world over, singing to us of the Volga boatmen and of the coachman dying by his horses in the middle of the icy steppes. Filled with emotion, the guests began to hum along. I gave them a surprise when, signalling to Jaroka, I began to sing:

> *Vyezhayut rastisnye*
> *Stenky Razina chelny.* . . .
>
> (The painted boats of
> Stenka Razine sail on. . . .)

It was a seventeenth-century Russian song, taught to me by Soviet soldiers to whom my father and I gave shelter in our mountain hideout during the Resistance.

"*Encore,* Colonel. *Encore.*"

I knew several of these old Russian soldiers' songs, perhaps more than these senior Soviet bureaucrats knew. They were delighted to hear a Hungarian officer perform folk music from their own country.

. Jaroka wasn't one to linger too long over any single facet of his art. A glance at the room told him that the time had come for dancing. First he played a few tangos and fox-trots, the only Western dances known to this particular gathering. The men's trouser legs, as wide as those of sailors during the Russian Revolution, floated around the ladies' too-high-heeled evening slippers. My wife and I danced with everybody in turn. We taught them a Hungarian csardas; they taught us their exhausting and very athletic gopak. It wasn't yet midnight and the party was going full blast.

I was the first to notice two new arrivals. The first was a staff officer with a Prussian crew cut. He stepped aside near the entrance to let a civilian pass. The civilian was slim and elegant, dressed by the best tailor in Budapest, his hair touched with silver. This was Yuri Vladimirovitch Andropov, Soviet ambassador to Hungary, who would go on to become head of the KGB and, finally, to succeed Leonid Brezhnev as head of the Communist Party of the U.S.S.R. I had met him several times.

Andropov gazed affably at the dancers. The first violinist motioned to the band, which once again struck up the ovation music while Jaroka bowed reverently. The dancing stopped and the dancers turned towards Andropov and bowed, as Jaroka had done. These officials, including some of very high rank, venerated in Andropov someone who was more than an ambassador. This civilian with the elegant manners was also, in all probability, in charge of the KGB's operations in Hungary. That meant he was the real boss — both officially and unofficially.

"Please continue," said the ambassador.

Petofi grabbed me by the sleeve and pulled me over to the newcomers.

"Comrade Colonel Kopacsi, police chief of Budapest."

Andropov shook my hand and said amicably that he knew me. He kissed my wife's hand with a grace that any French aristocrat would have envied.

The staff officer with the crew cut shook my hand and introduced himself: "Ichtchenko." His eyes glistened like steel. This was the chief of all the Soviet advisers in Hungary, the man the Hungarians called "The Memory".

The gipsies started up again, louder than ever. Moments later, my wife drew Andropov into the liveliest csardas of the year that was ending. (The year that was beginning — 1956 — was going to treat us to some "dances" that would be more feverish still.) An hour later, the dance team of Ibolya and Andropov was still at it, in the middle of a circle of singers who were clapping rhythmically.

The next day was dawning when I finally had a chance to ask my wife what she and Andropov could possibly have found to talk about for so long. "We talked about international politics," she answered. When I persisted, she finally admitted, "Andropov told me I had beautiful eyes...He repeated, *'Ochi chornye, ochi chornye.'* " Then I understood why the ambassador had tormented Jaroka by making him play, at least a dozen times, a popular Russian song called "Black Eyes".

A few days later, at three o'clock in the morning, I was in a Budapest slum, slumped at a table in a dive called the Three Hussars, with Major-General Iemelianov, instructor general of the Soviet police attached to the Hungarian Ministry of the Interior, and his interpreter.

"So, Kopacsi, I hear you've been up to some mischief."

"What do you mean, 'Comrade Major-General?"

"You didn't tell me you were planning to give a recital."

"But...."

"Or that your wife planned a dance marathon with Andropov."

"I thought you were in Moscow for New Year's."

"You really are a great sleuth."

He looked at me warmly. "For having enough talent and charm to amuse my compatriots, let me offer you a little souvenir of Moscow."

He handed me a stunning cigarette case in solid gold with my initials engraved inside. The eyes of twenty thugs were instantly riveted on the glittering item.

"Thank you. This must have set you back plenty. But are you sure you picked the right spot to give me this precious object?"

Iemelianov looked up and noticed the hungry eyes of the vagrants and prostitutes fastened on his gift. He roared with laughter and fell back in his seat, pounding his thighs.

"To Budapest by night!" He lifted his glass as if to toast all the slums and all the crooks in the world.

I was delighted to be with Iemelianov again. This was a man who loved good food and gipsy music and who liked to get official matters done with quickly so that the real exchange of views could begin. I listened to his slow discourse, translated by his personal interpreter, who resembled him like a brother, on war, on the Stalinist period — which he had known very well during the despot's final years — on women, on love, and on the pleasures of travel and nature. It may be odd to say this of a Soviet policeman, but I'm convinced that he loved people because he loved life.

Our nocturnal outing had come about under curious circumstances. One of the new party directors, a handsome fellow named Bela Szalai (the Hungarian Politburo had just received an infusion of young blood at the urging of Khrushchev) had decided it was his duty to meet the masses. At an intersection where two important boulevards meet, he had sent his chauffeur home and taken a few steps down the adjacent street.

He had stumbled into the traditional hangout of Budapest's most hardened prostitutes. Before he had taken ten steps, the young man was accosted and practically dragged by force in the direction of a furnished house. I do not know if he succumbed. But I do know that early the next morning, he was on the phone.

"Comrade Kopacsi, are you aware of the presence of prostitutes in Budapest?"

"Uh...yes."

"But in great numbers...?"

"Just a minute, Comrade Szalai, I've got the register right here. There are, let's see, five thousand listed here."

"Five thousand! As many as that? Are you certain?"

"Let me finish. There are also fifteen thousand who aren't registered."

He was outraged. "Comrade Kopacsi, in accordance with socialist morality, we have closed the brothels. We have guaranteed these poor girls an opportunity to be integrated into society. There are retraining programs all over the country to allow them to become decent workers, cab drivers, nurses. This is a scandal! I just don't understand."

It was true that many prostitutes had become cab drivers. These talented chauffeurs often earned two fares from one client; once when they drove him to the park and the second after they arrived.

"What do you expect, Comrade Szalai? It's not easy to suppress the world's oldest profession from one day to the next."

"That's what you think. I consider this a serious matter and I'm going to bring it before the Politburo."

Several days later, the K line, the red ministerial phone, rang. It was my boss, the Minister of the Interior.

"Kopacsi, you've got us into a fine fix."

"Why, Comrade Minister?"

"The Politburo wants a report on the night life of the capital. They want it based on first-hand research."

"I understand, Comrade Minister."

"This is all your fault. And worse still, the principal Soviet advisers insist on being part of this nocturnal escapade. What'll I do if someone bumps them off?"

"No one will bump them off."

The minister gave a worried sigh. "Do the best you can. We're coming tonight. And understand that Iemelianov will be there. All we need is for someone to touch a hair on his head and we're all bound for Siberia."

The minister could indulge in such jokes on the K line; if there was a tap on the line, it would be accessible only to his own staff.

Towards 8:00 p.m., a dozen senior Hungarian and Russian dignitaries showed up at police headquarters. These were the very top law-enforcement brass, with the minister leading the way.

"How many men are you taking with you?" he asked me.
"None."
"What? Have you already posted men in the places we're going to inspect?"
"I haven't posted anybody anywhere. I thought that, without escort and unarmed, you would be in a better position to observe."
"Without escort and unarmed! You don't know what you're saying. We've got senior Soviet comrades with us."
The interpreters translated. Iemelianov listened, smiling. He said: "I agree with Comrade Kopacsi. I'm going to recommend that all the Soviet advisers leave their guns here."
Our first visit was to a disreputable pub, a big place not far from the stadium. At 9:00 p.m., it was overflowing with drunks. I had the head of the criminal section with me. He was immediately accosted by the manager, a retired wrestler with cauliflower ears.
"Good evening, Superintendent, I'm happy to have you with us — "
Before he could finish his sentence, a brawl started. Bottles and chairs flew through the air, and the pushing and shoving flattened us against the wall.
The manager seemed unconcerned. In a commanding tone, but without raising his voice, he ordered the troublemakers out. And out they went. They knew that if they tried to stay, he would dispatch them himself, bruising a few ribs in the process.
"Comrade Iemelianov, you're not scandalized?" I asked.
The Soviet officer smiled. "Budapest by night is nothing compared to what we lived through in Moscow in 1927: a pitched battle with guns for fifteen days in the sewers against the hoodlums."
The last stop, at about 2:30 a.m., brought us to the Three Hussars, which stayed open later than any other dive in Budapest. We ordered soup and smoked sausage. Suddenly, the minister cried out, "Look, under the table, this is disgraceful, what are they doing, those two? You'd think they were copulating...."
That's exactly what they were doing. And they weren't the only ones. At 3:00 a.m., when there are drunks and prostitutes around, certain things are inevitable. Even in socialist countries.
Of course, our little tour did nothing to raise the tone of such establishments or to stamp out prostitution, which continued to flourish in Budapest as it always had.
"To be a cop," Iemelianov remarked over a cup of coffee as day

was breaking, "isn't to persecute people. It's to know everything and understand everything."

▌ "You'll Finish Too High"

It had never been my childhood ambition to become a Budapest cop. I was perfectly content with my life as a metalworker in Diosgyor, my home town in the foothills of the Bukk Mountains in northern Hungary. Diosgyor is the industrial suburb of Miskolc, a seedbed of Hungarian nationalism and radicalism. The streetcar used to rattle along its long main street, carrying passengers from the Tisza train station through the suburb of Uj Diosgyor, all the way to the end of the line in Diosgyor.

The Diosgyor metalworks were huge, spread over thirty hectares and employing 20,000 workers. Iron ore would arrive at one end and come out the other in the form of railway track, heavy machinery, tanks, and other finished products. At night, the fire from the enormous furnaces was visible from twenty kilometres away. The steam locomotives that provided connecting links between the work sites screeched and vomited smoke. The great steel mill was redolent with the odour of sulphur, evoking the descriptions of hell I had read in fairy tales. It was a forbidding place, but to me it was home. I loved our beautiful factory; in winter the soot from its smokestacks turned newly fallen snow black in hours, but in summer the extra carbon dioxide it poured into the atmosphere produced the tastiest fruit I've ever eaten.

As a three-year-old, I looked forward eagerly to visiting the steel mill with my grandfather, who had worked there for forty years.

"Lubri... lubri... lubricant!"

The ends of my grandfather's big moustache shook rhythmically

as he pushed his wheelbarrow with its barrel of lubricants. "Lubri...
Lubriii!"

The workers grabbed their oil cans and grease guns and gathered
around my grandfather as if he were Santa Claus.

"Who does the kid belong to?"

"My son."

"The one who works at Machine Tools Number Four? I can see
the resemblance. Kid, I hope you're going to be a worker, like us."

The worker at Machine Tools Number Four was my father, Joseph.
He was dark-haired, hard, just, and for me an irreplaceable model.
When it was time, he introduced me to factory life: "Here's my
young Sandor. Make him a metal turner like me." With the same
ease, he introduced me to the workers' movement to which he and
my grandfather had long belonged as members of the metalworkers'
union.

My father's radicalism was forged in his youth. Hungary had a
short-lived Communist government in 1919 under the leadership of
Bela Kun, who was ousted in the course of a counter-revolution led
by Admiral Miklos Horthy. During the Kun regime, the Czech Army
took advantage of the internal turmoil to invade northern Hungary,
hoping to annex this industrial area. My father was one of a group
of northern metalworkers who sneaked across the line to join the
Hungarian Red Army. When the Communist government fell, the
Romanian Army occupied Budapest, decimating the captured
soldiers. Although my father escaped death, he was brutally beaten.

These events tied him for life to left-wing causes, and in 1924
he joined the Social Democratic Party. Politics was a big part of
our home life. As a five-year-old, I was already listening to Radio
Moscow's Hungarian-language broadcasts in the company of family
friends who were awestruck by the Komintern's transmitter, said to
be the world's most powerful.

But childhood wasn't all politics and visits to the steelworks. It
was also summers at my grandfather's little cottage on the banks
of the Sajo River. Tied to the weeping willow and rocking gently
in the water was a rowboat named "Ica" after my mother. My
cousins, Luke, Gabor, and Geza Simon, often joined us there. Luke,
the eldest, read us James Fenimore Cooper's stories of Indians. We
decorated ourselves with mud and chalk and fought mock battles
with bows and arrows. We occupied islands and repelled invaders.

As I grew into the workers' movement, I always kept something of this playful childhood spirit. I never saw struggle as an occasion for hate and bitterness. At age eleven, I accomplished my first mission: accompanying a jolly, blond young man named Willy to the station. He was an escapee from the workers' uprising in Vienna, and was seeking refuge in Hungary while waiting to cross into Czechoslovakia.

I wasn't yet fifteen when I was shot at for the first time by fascists, the bullet lodging in my right thigh. It happened at nightfall. We were seven or eight young workers operating under the direction of my father, who was an official of the youth movement of the Social Democratic Party. Our task was to criss-cross the town distributing tracts ridiculing the Arrow Cross, the nascent fascist party. At 9:00 p.m., we had almost finished our deliveries when one of our men accidentally opened the door of the fascists' headquarters.

All hell broke loose. My father and I, who had already passed the door, raced back, and my father jumped into the battle with me right behind him. From the opposite side of the yard, in an explosion of bright orange, came the first shot, then the second, and the third. At the fourth shot, I felt a sharp burning in my thigh and cried out: "Pa, they've got me!" Gripping a gatepost with both hands, I slid slowly down to the pavement.

The bullet, which hadn't touched the bone, was extracted at the hospital while two cops waited to talk to me.

"How old are you?"

"Almost fifteen."

"Tell us what happened."

"My father and I were taking a walk. We heard some shooting. A stray bullet injured me in the thigh. That's all I know."

The cops looked at one another. They didn't believe my story for a minute. One of them, a sly old fox, looked me right in the eye. "Watch out, kid. If you start too soon, you'll finish too high."

"Too high" meant on the gallows. The fox had intuition.

My father stayed at my bedside. It was left to my mother to take revenge. The next day, she showed up at the hospital, her dress torn and her forehead covered with bruises. With fifty young social democrat workers, she had raided the fascists' headquarters. The wretches called the police, but that didn't stop my mother's troops. Eighteen mounted cops were injured, mostly by electric light bulbs filled with tar, the "Molotov cocktail" of the day.

At the age of eighteen, I completed a course in metalworking, a skill that came naturally to me. But my attention was quickly captured by the violent historical events then in progress. Hitler had attacked the Soviet Union, and in June 1941, Hungary followed suit by declaring war on the Soviets. In December, Great Britain declared war against Hungary and, under strong German pressure, Hungary declared war on the United States. Thus the country was drawn into a conflict that, in the next four years, would cost it more than 300,000 men, the flower of its younger generation, and more than 400,000 of its Jewish citizens.

The youth wing of the Social Democratic Party, to which my father and I belonged, decided to organize a demonstration for peace. The plans were made, as usual, in the sewing-machine repair shop that belonged to my father's comrade Sandor Fried; during the Commune of 1919, the two men had fought in the Hungarian Red Army. This sewing-machine repairman had a beautiful daughter, a brunette named Ibolya.

Ibolya had big mischievous eyes and, beneath her sweet exterior, was a determined supporter of the workers' movement. We fell in love. She was determined to love the gangling boy that I was at the time, thin enough to make a mother cry. The years have given me a few more pounds, and also some gumption, but even today, I never take a decision without first consulting Ibolya.

We were only two children — I was nineteen at the time and Ibolya was seventeen — but we were old enough to fight. The social democrat youth in our area were renowned for their demonstrations, for distributing leaflets and tracts, and for the theft and destruction of industrial designs and machines destined for the German war effort. Hand in hand, Ibolya and I struggled for our ideals.

In September 1944, the Soviet Army crossed our country's border. A month later, the Hungarian government attempted to make a separate peace with the Soviets, much to the displeasure of Germany. A preliminary armistice was signed, but almost immediately the government was overthrown in a German-backed *putsch* by the Arrow Cross Party. What followed was a period of fascist terror, the bloodiest in Hungarian history. Along with Ibolya and fourteen comrades from the factory, the Kopacsi family joined the underground.

On November 17, 1944, I was in the middle of heavy bargaining with a Hungarian soldier who was part of a Wehrmacht unit that was withdrawing westward. He had a superb German rifle for sale

for 200 pengoes, the equivalent of a month's salary for a worker.
"Listen, if you were a patriot, you'd give it to us for nothing."
"Are you nuts? How do you expect me to eat during the trip [to
Germany]?"

Finally, I had the rifle for 150 pengoes, and the soldier threw in
700 cartridges. I had just finished loading my new weapon when
I heard a tremendous racket from near the factory. Ibolya arrived
on the run at the hideout in the Bukk Mountains.

"The Red Army is here!"

Ten minutes later, we descended the mountain to the village. The
German garrison was retreating, but it was no rout. My father gave
us a signal to hide in the bushes and keep quiet. A German detachment passed. When the Germans were twenty metres away, we threw
our grenades and let loose with all of the limited firepower at our
disposal. I aimed at one of the cavalrymen, a blond youth. He collapsed on the neck of his horse and, as if in slow motion, toppled
to the ground. A few seconds later, twenty artillerymen in uniforms
we had never seen before appeared and set up an anti-tank gun.
We ran up, shouting, *"Zdravstvuyte!"* which was Russian for hello.

Ibolya and I embraced and told each other that the nightmare was
over, that now we were free, for life.

Captain Ustinov, commander of the artillery unit, examined our
papers, which were made out in Hungarian and Russian, and stated
that we were part of the Mokan, a broad-based organization whose
members included socialists, Communists, army defectors, soldiers
loyal to Horthy, and young army cadets, as well as ordinary citizens.

(This corps of irregulars was engaged in sabotaging shipments
to Germany of war materiel produced in Hungarian factories and
in doing reconnaissance work for the Soviets, giving them the loca-
tions of German installations so that bombs could be dropped
strategically. The Mokan also had its own press, which churned out
thousands of anti-fascist pamphlets.

So effective was the Mokan that Otto Klatt, the German
commander in our region, estimated its strength at 20,000. In fact,
we numbered no more than 500.)

Captain Ustinov called his interpreter, who translated, "In the name
of the Soviet Army, I congratulate you."

We, in turn, congratulated the Soviet Army.

"We'll operate side by side," said the captain. "How many are
you?"

When he learned that our unit contained only fourteen and that our comrades, who were fighting on the other side of the valley, numbered no more than fifty, his face darkened.

"Not a single shot. You are forbidden to use your rifles," he said. "The Germans are still in the area; we've only just started to dislodge them. Your role will be to stay in contact with us and do reconnaissance."

A few days later, the Germans regrouped and counterattacked. Ustinov's small unit of scouts was wiped out, and the streets of Miskolc were strewn with the corpses of Russian and German soldiers. The Germans buried their dead, but they wouldn't let us do the same for the Russian victims.

The prisoners were shot, though I helped one Russian escape the carnage. He was Piotr Petrov Annikievitch, a forty-one-year-old peasant from a kolkhoz (collective farm) in central Russia. He had been hiding in the hayloft of a house belonging to one of our friends, and the friend asked me to take him to safety. I brought him workmen's clothes and an identification tag from the steel mill. Carrying a basket of potatoes, he walked out of town with me and I led him to our mountain hideout, where he stayed until December 3, the day the German Army evacuated the area.

A high-ranking Russian officer moved down the main street of Miskolc. He wore a uniform cut of English cloth and boots fashioned of the finest kid. He smoked through a long cigarette-holder. The ladies couldn't help but stare after him, this major-general of the Second Ukrainian Front of the Carpathian Military District. His name was Leonid Brezhnev. He was thirty-eight years old at the time and didn't yet wear a moustache.

"Comrade Major-General, let me introduce you to a young underground fighter of this mountain, Sandor Kopacsi. He's going to marry my cousin, Ibolya, who is right here."

Ibolya's black eyes sparkled with pleasure while Major-General Leonid Brezhnev paid her a compliment. Cousin Fazekas, whom we had feared dead, had become a captain in the Soviet Army. He smiled as he translated: "Comrade Brezhnev says you are the most beautiful little partisan he has seen since the war began."

We watched Brezhnev mount his horse and soar over the wall of the barracks. We weren't the only ones watching. The actresses of the Moscow Soldiers' Theatre were also there, swooning with pleasure at the exploits of the handsomest officer in the army. The future ruler of the Soviet Union stayed in our city for fourteen days.

All the underground fighters of the Mokan group were rearmed and became part of the law-enforcement apparatus of the new Republic of Hungary that was just being born. That's how I became a cop.

The first four years of my service at Diosgyor were marked by disappointment. In the resistance, social democrats and Communists had marched together. But when the war was over, the Communists in charge of the political section of the police (the forerunner of the AVO secret police) persecuted the social democrats. They arrested Paul Popradi, who had struggled at my father's side for twenty years in the workers' movement, and then Lajos Dancza, another social democrat leader. The political section didn't bother finding pretexts; it was always the same refrain: those charged had "collaborated with Horthy's police". I asked for a meeting with my chief.

"Listen: my father and I know Paul Popradi. He's devoted to the cause of the workers' movement. As for Dancza, he risked his life hiding a Soviet soldier the Germans were looking for."

The response was: "Mind your own business. We've got proof."

A delegation was formed, made up of fifteen officers and resistance fighters. Major Kecskes, commander of the political section, had them disarmed and put under arrest. That was too much. A group of ex-Mokan fighters, myself among them, occupied a wing of the police station and phoned the commander: "We're on strike until our comrades are liberated."

"A rebellion? You'll pay dearly for this."

We expected an attack by the political section at any second. Through it all, we could hear our arrested comrades singing the Internationale. After an hour or two, Kecskes and his friends backed down. Our comrades were freed, but not the social democrat leaders. I was transferred to a post in the country, about fifty kilometres away.

In the summer of 1946, I was recalled to Miskolc where I had an opportunity to meet some of the most important leaders of the country. Unfortunately, the circumstances weren't the best. Hungry and desperate, the coal miners of the region had lynched a miller who had sold flour on the black market. The police arrested and tortured several miners. News of the torture soon became public. Two days later, 20,000 miners surrounded the police station and demanded the torturers' heads. Negotiations got nowhere. The crowd invaded the station, killed Captain Fogarasi, chief of the political section, and then headed toward the house of an officer named Borus who had allegedly assisted Fogarasi in abusing the miners. But Borus had gone into hiding and couldn't be found.

Weakened by malnutrition from postwar shortages, I had been bedridden for several weeks with pneumonia. Suddenly, our apartment door burst open, and a woman entered with a boy, who looked about eight. Both of them were very pale.

"I'm Captain Borus's wife. I beg you to protect us."

Ibolya took them into the bedroom while I phoned the station and asked for weapons. One of my comrades came, accompanied by two soldiers. They were armed with rifles and grenades.

The crowd began to gather around the apartment building, and shouts rose up from the street: "Kopacsi, you're hiding the wife and kid of that Borus bastard. Send them out or you'll have us to deal with."

"Have you gone crazy? The wife and child aren't guilty of anything."

"Don't try to outsmart us. At the station, we got Fogarasi. The miners are with us. If you don't send out the woman and the kid, they'll throw their dynamite at your house and you'll all be killed."

Ibolya tried to calm the woman and child, who were green with fear. She got a rifle and a grenade and we took up positions behind the windows. I couldn't let them get close to the building, where they might try to set off their only weapon, dynamite taken from the mines, so I made a little speech.

"Listen. You people know me. You know I tell the truth. I'm sheltering an innocent woman and child. The first person who sets foot on the sidewalk, I'll blow him away."

The suspense mounted. Some of the crowd left and were replaced by others. There were at least a hundred of them. We knew that the first shot would probably set off a massacre. I looked at Ibolya. Were our lives to be over so quickly? The "beautiful days in the Resistance", the hardship when the war was over, and now, death over a minor incident like this? Ibolya began to cry, but her grip on her gun was steady.

Gradually, the crowd began to dwindle. People decided it made more sense to concern themselves with something other than a cruel and useless vengeance. For another hour or so, groups of gawkers hung about the house, but it was no longer an angry mob. Toward 3:00 p.m., to the sound of a bugle, a police commando from Budapest arrived to rescue us.

I fell back into bed with a temperature of 40°C. Gabor Peter, head of the National Security Service, interrogated me at my bedside. He was accompanied by a bold young leader named Laszlo Rajk and a tall thin fellow named Janos Kadar. They came to me for information, in preparation for a big meeting the miners had organized for the next day.

I don't know what they said at the meeting but it was a raucous affair and, according to reports, Kadar had his face slapped by a furious miner.

In the Old Man's Service

Early in the spring of 1949, I was transferred to Budapest, directly to the centre of power: the headquarters of the Central Committee of the Communist Party, which included the most important leaders in the country, among them the head of the party, Matthias Rakosi. My immediate superior was Colonel Joseph Szilagyi, a robust, strapping fellow with square shoulders and an open expression. The son of a poor peasant from eastern Hungary, he had finished his legal studies with first-class honours and become a member of the Communist Party when the party was illegal. For being a subversive, Szilagyi had served three years in the infamous Szeged prison during the war. We young officers admired him; he was our ideal, a legendary hero, but one whom we could rub shoulders with every day.

Szilagyi took a liking to me. He questioned me about my life as a metalworker in the industrial north. When he found out that Ibolya and I were having a hard time finding an apartment for ourselves and our three-year-old daughter, he went out of his way to help us and wouldn't listen to our expressions of gratitude.

"I owe it to you," he said with a charming smile. "You are working-class people."

He knew his Marxism-Leninism backwards and forwards. To listen to him talking about the class struggle, peasant revolts, the French Revolution, or the role of the state after the period of the dictatorship of the proletariat was like being in a university course.

Szilagyi introduced me to the mysteries of the antiquated building on Akademia Street that was Central Committee headquarters. He wanted to make me his second in command.

One day, toward noon, he took me aside. "I have to leave soon. At noon, a file has to be taken to the old man."

The old man! Matthias Rakosi himself! I thought that the ground was opening up under my feet. I knew very well that the first secretary of the party, this legendary hero, came to work every morning in his office, but I had never seen him. He had spent sixteen years in Horthy's jails. Stalin's favourite, the most celebrated man of all the Communist parties! I was going to meet him.

The file, which contained a report on Communists in the police force, shook in my hands as I carried it to Rakosi.

The Hungarian Stalin didn't live in splendour. His secretariat consisted of a sort of labyrinth where, among shelves reaching to the ceiling, I found Jolan Simon, an ethereal-looking, soft-spoken young woman who was married to Gabor Peter, the head of the security police.

Rakosi's private office had a padded door in front of which the secretary hesitated an instant.

"You are. . . ?"

"Captain Kopacsi. I'm bringing the file on. . . ." At that point, words failed me.

Jolan Simon smiled. (What a touching smile she had. Later, when Rakosi threw her to the secret police to try — without any success — to get an accusation against her husband, she was tortured in the style of Torquemada, suspended on pulleys, her spindly limbs weighted down.)

"I was expecting you, Captain," she said. She opened the door and ushered me in. "The report on the police, Comrade Rakosi."

The man seated behind his desk raised his nose from a paper. He had a strange, round, bald head, pushed well into his shoulders. But he was powerfully built, and his handsome hazel eyes regarded me reassuringly.

"Ah! The report. Put it here, Comrade. Thank you. What is your name?"

"Sandor."

Rakosi looked amused.

"Well, then, Sandor. . . ."

He rose (I was astounded at how small he was), went toward the coffee table on which there was a tray with several plates, then placed his small, fleshy hand on the latch of a hidden door that led to a toilet. He turned toward me: "Where do you come from? Miskolc-Diosgyor, I'll wager."

"Why yes, Comrade Rakosi!"

I was stunned by his astuteness: from the merest hint of my slight northern accent he had guessed precisely where I came from.

"You fought with the Soviet Army in the northern mountains, I suppose."

"Yes, Comrade Rakosi."

Truly, this man could guess everything.

He had gone to wash his hands, but from the small washroom, he continued to question me.

"You wouldn't have run into a certain Major-General Brezhnev? A real ladies' man?"

Then I understood that someone had informed him about me, down to the smallest detail.

"Yes, Comrade Rakosi, I met that officer."

"He was only a minor member of the Ukrainian delegation when I was placed to the right of Comrade Stalin at the victory banquet. But —"

Rakosi came out of the washroom, a towel in his hand. He winked at me.

"— I hear that that particular officer loved the little ladies. Especially the comic actresses...."

So that was it. That damned Szilagyi had repeated all my confidences to Rakosi. I smiled uncomfortably.

"That's what they say, Comrade Rakosi."

The victory banquet! To the right of the great Stalin. I was dazzled. Rakosi looked at me piercingly. The subject of my background had been exhausted. He indicated that I should leave and began eating his modest lunch.

Every day from then on, I saw Rakosi, who was known as "The Brain", and his second in command, the ascetic and half-starved Erno Gero, former commissar of the GPU (the forerunner of the KGB) in the Spanish Civil War and now chief Hungarian agent of the KGB in Budapest. Their offices occupied the so-called presidential wing of the old Akademia building, close to those of the two other leading lights of the Politburo: the sadistic Mihaly Farkas, a pot-bellied stutterer, who was commander-in-chief of all the armed forces of the country; and Joseph Revai, chief party ideologue, who hid behind the thick spectacles of a scholar. These "four coachmen" as they were called, all of whom had once emigrated to the Soviet Union, ran the country. Laszlo Rajk, who had stayed in Hungary to lead the Communist Party when the party was illegal, and Janos Kadar, a leader of working-class origin like myself, cut no ice with the Soviets compared to these Muscovites.

Another wing of the Central Committee headquarters overlooked an adjacent street. It contained the offices of less important figures, including Imre Nagy, another member of the Politburo, also a Moscow emigré, who was hardly known outside the field of socialist agriculture. Since the war, he had alternately been Minister of Agriculture or the minister responsible for "agricultural deliveries". These deliveries were actually taxes in kind. In certain periods they were nothing less than armed robbery.

Nagy showed up rarely. He was the only one among the top-ranking leaders who didn't seem like a mixture of ecclesiastic and journalist. Instead, he resembled a Hungarian farmer (which he was), but a farmer who had consecrated his life to study (which he had). His massive body, his drooping moustache, his direct manners, his country accent: all that was the common side of him. His pince-nez and a long past in the research institutes of Moscow (he was one of the fervent disciples of Bukharin, the famous Bolshevik theoretician and comrade in arms of Lenin) belonged to the professorial side. This man, swept along in the whirlwind of history, would reach a prominence he had never sought before his life ended in a bloody martyrdom.

■ "You Are Innocent, But...."

Overnight and for no apparent reason, the atmosphere in Akademia Street became oppressive. I couldn't help but notice that the sudden disappearance from sight of Laszlo Rajk, the Minister of the Interior who had recently been named Minister of Foreign Affairs, coincided with the change in atmosphere. Other comrades of the Central Committee, people we were used to seeing every day, also departed "on a trip." Szonyi, chief of the cadres section, a young comrade of upright bearing and conduct, with the manners of a soldier, stopped coming to work in the morning, as did his assistant, Szalay, a sort of saint with long, curved eyelashes and a soothing way of speaking. At the same time, certain individuals we had never seen before, busy and vindictive in manner, passed through the corridors. Gabor Peter, the chief of the security police, the AVO, turned up every day in Rakosi's office accompanied by high-ranking officers.

One fine day, we were all confined to the "small wing". Only Szilagyi was admitted to the "presidential" corridor.

That night, I asked him: "Who has arrived?"

Morosely, he replied: "Some comrades."

As I had observed the arrival and departure of a series of cars from the diplomatic corps, I asked if some Soviet comrades had been visiting the Central Committee headquarters. Szilagyi looked at me angrily and, speaking to me for the first time in a belligerent, wounding tone, replied: "Why don't you clean up your own act instead of butting into what doesn't concern you? Look at your boots, those aren't boots, they're shit!"

One morning, we were called to the ministry for an ultra-secret meeting. Once the doors of the room were bolted, we learned, amid deathly silence, of "the treason of Laszlo Rajk and his band", vulgar agents and spies of Tito and the imperialists, police informers since their adolescence, organizers of a plot to assassinate Comrade Rakosi and topple the government.

I was sitting next to Szilagyi. Before the reading of the communiqué was finished, he leaned close to me and whispered, "Sandor, not a word of this is true."

I almost jumped out of my seat and was about to ask him a question when he signalled me sternly to keep quiet.

"After. We'll talk about it after. But first, promise me never to repeat what I'm going to tell you. Except, of course, after I'm dead."

I promised.

"Rajk isn't guilty. This is a cabal of the Soviet security and their Hungarian colleagues."

"What are you talking about?"

"Comrade Rakosi has been shamefully taken advantage of. As no one else has done it, I'm going to warn him."

That was the first time that I had heard a good Communist cast doubt on the infallibility of the party, the first time I had heard a distinction made between Soviet comrades, the security services, and the party.

"That's impossible!"

Szilagyi looked at me sadly. "My information is reliable," he said. "It comes from my childhood friend Laszlo Angyal, one of the directors of the AVO. He has been responsible for the inquest into the Rajk affair. On the orders of General Bielkin, emissary of Soviet security, all the prisoners have been horribly tortured. Not one of them knew what was wanted of him, Comrade Rajk less than the others."

For me, all this was absurd. Szilagyi continued: "It happens like this, always in the same way. After several months of terrible torture, they change the tone. On Bielkin's orders, our AVO officers take the mutilated prisoners aside, almost mad with suffering, and say to them: 'The party knows that you are innocent. The party asks you to understand the gravity of the international situation. You have to take the blame for the crimes you've been charged with. You have to admit publicly that you are Tito's agents. Afterwards, you will be condemned to death. But instead of being executed, in recognition of the services you will have rendered, the Soviet Union will welcome you to a rest home in the Crimea where you will enjoy a peaceful existence to the end of your days, in the company of your whole family.'"

Szilagyi sighed deeply. "It's all a lie. Bielkin has had scaffolds erected, coffins readied, and quicklime piled up in a cellar. The Soviets have ordered that the principal ones charged are not to come out of their trials alive."

I listened, dumbfounded, not understanding anything. (In retrospect, it all seems clear; the "Moscow" Communists, led by Rakosi, were conducting a purge of the "national" Communists, led by Rajk. But for me it took six years, a magisterial lesson in history, and my own involvement in the same process, to believe it.)

Szilagyi looked at me harshly. "My friend Angyal decided to shoot himself with his service revolver this morning. I spoke with him last night. His reasoning was that our ideal, the Communist ideal, is simple and pure. There's no room in it for assassinations and deceit. Comrades' lives can't be used as currency. If *that* is the Communist Party, life isn't worth living any more. That was his conclusion. Me, I see things differently."

I listened, fascinated. Szilagyi continued: "The party has been fooled. Comrade Rakosi isn't clued in. I'm going to write him a memo and deliver it in person."

Szilagyi did so the same day. The next day, our group at the Central Committee headquarters was dissolved. The Rajk trial was over. Those accused were hanged, then thrown in quicklime.

Szilagyi was transferred away from Budapest. Before he left, he came to find me in the lodgings he had obtained for me several months earlier. With a peculiar expression on his face, he said, "My ideas...maybe that was just a figment of my imagination."

That's what I thought, but didn't dare to say it.

"You, Sandor," he continued. "You're young, you've got a long career ahead of you. Try to do the maximum of good and the minimum of evil to people."

"I promise."

We shook hands, and he left. Through the window, I watched his large, peasant's body disappear in the darkness. It was six years before I saw him again.

Janos Kadar, the new Minister of the Interior, passed us in review, as if on a military parade. He stopped in front of me.

"They tell me you were a worker, like me."

Colonel Szucs of the AVO, in whose company the minister was examining the files, thought it necessary to answer for me: "Comrade Kopacsi, metalworker, like his father and grandfather, has been in the workers' movement since his childhood. He comes from Diosgyor."

Kadar looked at me. "I remember you. Stay with the Ministry of the Interior. We need people like you."

That's how my future was decided by the man whose own fate, at that moment, had already been determined: in the series of unjust trials started by the Rajk affair, he was to succeed Rajk, not only in the ministerial chair but also in the torture chamber.

I was appointed a permanent member of the party organization in the ministry. In this centre of national power, my northern bumpkin's eyes watched stupefied as the finest people in the government disappeared one after another. It all happened with incredible speed. Bela Korondy, a police colonel and former member of the underground, and Colonel Kalman Revay, our "centaur", the finest horseman in the country and also a former Resistance fighter, were executed along with several army generals.

The secretary of the party organization had this explanation: "These officers of the old regime were all traitors to the cause of the workers."

Then it was Kadar's turn to be arrested.

"But why? How? A great leader like that and of working-class stock to boot."

"Traitors exist everywhere, even in the heart of the working class."

Young and inexperienced as I was — I was only twenty-six — I accepted the official explanations. The menacing international situation made the idea of a conspiracy all the more believable. Tito, "the mad dog of imperialism", was thumbing his nose at us across the border. The West Germans, we were told, might trigger a new world war at any moment. It was natural that such a charged atmosphere would lead to trouble.

I hoped that smoother sailing lay ahead. The new Minister of the Interior was a mild-mannered, level-headed young academic with a penetrating stare: Sandor Zold. He came from the same village as my former commander and friend, Szilagyi, and they had known each other from childhood. One day, during a meeting at the minister's office, I asked him, "Any news of Szilagyi?"

His face darkened. "I'm wondering if our friend Joska [a diminutive of Joseph] isn't a bit touched. I asked him to return to service here, and he replied, 'I prefer to cultivate the land in our village.' But there's no shortage of farmers. It's a shame. Joska has an intelligence and honesty that one finds only in the best comrades."

A few weeks later, Sandor Zold didn't appear at his office. We thought he was sick. But when several other leaders disappeared at the same time, it started us thinking. The Minister of Foreign Affairs was arrested (the son of a shoemaker in eastern Hungary, he was a member of the highest authority of the party). Geza Losonczy, editor-in-chief of the party's daily paper and a young and dynamic leader, also disappeared. We wondered if our minister, tied to these young traitors, hadn't also tumbled into some monstrous trap.

The answer was yes. The special AVO commando in charge of arrests of important comrades inside the party apparatus made daily raids on our offices.

On one occasion I saw them go up to Colonel Benko's office. Benko, who was in charge of professional instruction of the police, was very intelligent, a tanned and handsome man, always dressed to kill. In the anteroom of his office, there was a tailor's mannequin, which held his colonel's tunic. No one had ever seen a crease on that tunic.

The head of the commando turned Benko's doorknob, but the door didn't open. He shouted the customary, "In the name of the law, open!"

Inside, nothing moved.

A hard kick and the door gave way. There was no one in the anteroom and no one in the private office. Facing the door was the famous mannequin and on the mannequin, as always, the colonel's tunic, this time decorated with all his medals: his Resistance medal, the Red Star, the Medal of Merit, and the insignia of the Model Worker. There were so many medals it sparkled. Across the medals, held in place by a pin, was a piece of paper bearing the words: "ALL THIS WASN'T ENOUGH FOR YOU?"

Benko had guessed the night before that he was going to be arrested. Inventing an inspection tour of the posts along the Austrian border, he had crossed the Iron Curtain that same night. (It's said he's still alive, somewhere in the United States.)

Things turned out differently for Juhasz, a brilliant counter-espionage officer, the son of poor peasants from eastern Hungary, the most backward part of the country. Previously party secretary in a large metallurgic factory, he joined us and immediately vaulted to the top of one of the most important services. The man had the physique of a James Bond — perhaps not quite so handsome, but he made up for it in virility. He had a way about him that captivated us.

At 3:00 a.m., when the commando turned up at his apartment, James Bond was in bed. He slid into his pants and boots, and was out on the balcony before his visitors could force the door. He descended six floors from balcony to balcony, hopped into the street, and disappeared into the alleys.

AVO forces combed not only the capital but the entire country looking for him. Two days later, Juhasz was spotted, fifty kilometres from Budapest, in the marshes of Lake Venice. A full-scale search began, using small craft, dogs, and amphibious vehicles. Juhasz had his service pistol with him, with seven bullets in the magazine. He killed six of his pursuers and unloaded the last bullet into his own head.

And the fate of our minister, Sandor Zold, he of the soft words and all the promise of youth? Of course, he got wind of the operation that was being mounted against him. The horrible precedents of Rajk and the others demonstrated clearly what physical and mental suffering awaited him and probably his family as well. (Rajk's wife had been imprisoned and his child had disappeared.)* Accompanied by his young wife, Zold went out to talk things over with her on a public bench. His house, like those of almost all the leaders, was well-equipped with hidden microphones.

The couple could come up with only one solution. That very night they killed themselves, their two young children, and Mrs. Zold's mother. The commando found only their corpses. Zold was declared a spy for the French.

Colonel Szucs of the AVO (the same man who had, only a few months earlier, introduced me to Kadar) was seized with doubts about the wisdom of all this carnage and, on his own initiative, went to

---

* Laszlo Rajk, Jr., lived his childhood in foster homes under an assumed name until 1954 when his mother, Julia, was released from jail and tracked him down. Today he is an architect in Budapest and an outspoken opponent of the current regime.

Moscow to tell Stalin personally that he was being misled by General Bielkin. He returned to Budapest to be butchered by a mixed Soviet-Hungarian commando while his only brother, also a security officer, was beaten to death in the cellars beneath AVO headquarters.

General Bielkin was decorated with the highest honours of both Hungary and the Soviet Union. His Hungarian counterpart, Gabor Peter of the AVO, was also decorated.

Matthias Rakosi, first secretary of the Hungarian Communist Party, was officially declared the best "student" of Comrade Stalin among the leaders of the popular democracies and had the place of honour, on Stalin's right, at the great chief's seventieth birthday celebration.

Today, the victims rest in a cemetery for eminent leaders of the party. Bielkin was executed, under his real name of Abakumov, the name by which, as Beria's second in command in the KGB, he sent millions to the gulag. (The Russians seemed to think that having this man operate under the "cover" of an assumed name, pretending that he was not really the deputy head of the KGB, would somehow make his activities in central Europe less obnoxious to the citizens of those countries.) General Peter directs a garment manufacturing co-operative in Budapest. Rakosi was banished to a collective farm in Soviet Asia where he died.

■ Internment Director

Toward the middle of 1949, Joseph Veres, the Secretary of State in the Ministry of the Interior, called me to his office. "Starting tomorrow," he informed me, "you are Director of Internment Affairs."

I knew that internment camps existed in Hungary. They were places to put people who had never been convicted but whom the authorities didn't want walking about. As a student at the police academy where we had learned notions of law, I was opposed to this institution. Why shouldn't the courts rule on all these matters? But since the party asked me, I took the job.

I had to sign all the decisions although they were taken by a committee of three. The two other members of this late unlamented "troika" were Gyula Decsy, a lawyer with the rank of colonel on the staff of the AVO, and Steven Bodonyi, a lawyer specializing in administrative affairs whose service in the ministry went back to pre-Communist days.

The troika's meetings were simple and always the same. The orderly brought us the dossiers, which had been prepared by police detachments in the city districts and provincial departments. For the most part, the cases dealt with theft, especially rural pilfering of poultry and crops. The camps were populated with workers and unsuccessful farmers, as well as a few from social classes declared hostile to the regime. The troika's task was simple: to prolong, usually by six months, the internment of those detained.

The AVO colonel would take a document and, without showing it to us, read: "Denes Kovacs. Engineer. Spy for the English. In view of the confidential nature of the affair, I'm leaving out the

details. Six months' prolongation. Agreed?"
We agreed.
"Peter Kiss. Spy for the French. Six months' prolongation. Agreed?"
Timidly, I asked: "The spies — why leave them stewing in a camp? Wouldn't it be better to send them before a court and have them convicted of espionage?"

The old specialist inherited from the former regime smiled under his moustache. He knew what the AVO colonel was going to reply, which he proceeded to do in a slightly irritated tone: "Please, Captain. There isn't enough proof yet to get a conviction. We know what we have to do. Let's move on to the next case. Zoltan Job. Trotskyist. Six months' internment. Objection?"

There were no objections. That's how we dealt with the dossiers of the "Demeny faction" (an illegal group of Communists opposed to the official party), adherents of the "Justus wing" (the pro-Communist wing of the Social Democratic Party, which had been legal under the previous regime), and others who were characterized simply as "reactionary elements" or "pro-fascists" or "pro-former regime", without a shadow of genuine proof.

Six months of internment. Or six months of prolongation. Obviously, this was a far cry from the ten- or fifteen-year extensions that were the norm in Siberia. Nevertheless, internment was internment, and those who received one six-month extension after another did not enjoy greater liberty than those whom the Soviets treated to between fifteen and twenty-five years in Siberia.

We didn't get many letters or petitions because most of the internees' families didn't know our administration existed or where it was located. But some did. I'll never forget the case of "Ginette", the wife of an engineer accused of being a French spy.

"Ginette" was skin and bones. She looked like an Auschwitz inmate, the result, undoubtedly, of her anguish over her husband. "Ginette" was Hungarian; we called her by a French name because of her husband's alleged employment by the French espionage service. She sent petitions and complaints to every possible address without ever receiving the slightest response.

One morning when I arrived at the ministry, my way was blocked by this living skeleton. It was a terrible scene — in tears, her hands joined together, she knelt before me on the sidewalk. "Have mercy on my husband. Mercy!"

"Madam, I don't know who you are. Please follow me to my office where you can tell me calmly what you want."

She sat down, like a broom laid against a chair. I think her husband was called Lucas. He was an unimportant engineer with a job in an unimportant nationalized enterprise. He had never been to France or anywhere else; he was involved in nothing but his work and his love for his wife, a love that was reciprocated in full.

"How long have you been married?"

"For ten years, sir, and it's like the first day, the first day...."

Until then, her manner had been overwrought, full of exclamations and tears. But as soon as I told her that I didn't have the authority over the case but that I would speak to Mr. Decsy about it as soon as possible, a glimmer appeared in her unhappy eyes.

"What name was that?"

"Mr. Gyula Decsy, a colonel in the AVO. He's the one with the power of decision in your husband's case."

Suddenly, "Ginette" was calm. She wiped her eyes, got up, thanked me with simple dignity, and left.

Fifteen days later, the troika gathered for its regular meeting. At the mention of engineer Lucas's name, Colonel Decsy lifted his hand.

"Wait a minute. This man is a gangster and a low-born bastard. He not only deserves internment camp, he deserves the scaffold. Can you imagine, this criminal's wife, who is a walking cadaver, somehow got hold of my name and address and now, every morning, she pesters me in the most outrageous fashion."

"That's unbelievable."

"Listen to this. As soon as I leave the building where I live, she throws herself on her knees in front of me and backs up, still on her knees, until I get in the car. Before the chauffeur can start the ignition, she's already flat on her stomach on the road, in front of the wheels. The neighbours are there every day to watch the show. I can't take any more. You hear me, gentlemen, I can't take any more. My nerves are shot."

He paused. The old specialist and I expected to hear, "Do what has to be done. Arrest this nut case." But no. Decsy wiped his forehead and blurted out, "Release her gangster of a husband. The minute I see that woman's shadow, I'm sick to my stomach. Send him home as quickly as possible. Do you agree?"

That's when I truly understood the meaning of the term, "war of nerves". And the greatness of the power of love.

One of the first things I did in my new position was to inspect Kistarcsa, an internment camp in the countryside. The camp, which covered an immense area surrounded by barbed wire, consisted of both permanent buildings and shacks and was similar to those in descriptions by Solzhenitsyn and others of the gulag camps.

I walked down the yards one by one. They were packed with detainees. Whenever I stopped near one, he would stand at attention and formally introduce himself. One old peasant, whose moustache reminded me of my grandfather, the carrier of lubricants at the factory, told me he was under detention for having put aside thirty kilos of corn from the co-operative lands for his own use. I couldn't believe anyone would be put behind barbed wire for such a trifle.

Another peasant, this one a young man, piped up: "Captain, it was the same thing with me, except I only took ten kilos."

"Get serious. Nobody gets put in prison for months or for years over ten kilos of stolen corn."

"Sir, I have the honour to tell you that they do, especially when they are disliked, as I was, by the mayor's secretary."

There was a camp within the camp, a sort of purgatory, smaller and guarded by the AVO. Here the prisoners were in individual cells. In the first, I met a man who had been a Communist before the party was legalized. He had been a member during the war of the famous Demeny faction. Like us, these patriots had fought against the Germans, and like us they had seen the Soviet Union as the best hope of the workers. Hundreds of Communists had been trained in the Demeny "school". Their only crime was that they belonged to a network other than the one directed by Rakosi's people.

"I've been a Communist since 1941! I demand to be interrogated. I've been here for months without even knowing why."

Next door, an emaciated man threw himself against the open cell window shouting, "I'm a member of the *Polish* Resistance. It's me, the celebrated Tadeusz Kosciusko [a Polish poet who had been dead for a century]!"

The man had been driven mad by his captivity. As for the others, seeing a police uniform made them mad with hope; it was the first time they had seen anything but the discouraging khaki of the AVO. "Listen to us!" they cried. "Come to see us. You must learn the truth."

I met people whose sole crime had been to take part, before the merger in 1948 of the Social Democratic and Communist parties, in seminars directed by Paul Justus, one of the best minds among the social democrats and in the entire workers' movement.

"Listen to us! Write down what we tell you. It's impossible that we are imprisoned here, without being judged, for nothing."

When I returned to the ministry, I called my assistant. "Istvan, I spent three days at Kistarcsa. Here is a list of 150 names. Bring me their files, on the double."

An hour later, we were seated behind a mountain of papers. For the most part, the records confirmed the detainees' stories. Thirty kilos of corn for this one. A sheep killed for this one. Killing a pig that hadn't reached the legal weight (it was too light by five kilos) was the crime of a third. And so on, right down the list.

The worst of it was that in a state where power was supposed to belong to the workers and peasants most of the detainees were workers and peasants. Something wasn't right. These wrongs had to be remedied. Hadn't I been put in this post by the party — and hadn't it given me full power to act?

"Do I call the committee, Captain?"

"For this? Not necessary. Get a pencil, we're going to strike out the names of those I'm going to liberate."

Ninety-five of the 150 were released the next day, by a simple decision signed by me. Several days passed. The telephone rang. The ministry's secretary of state, Veres, wanted to see me urgently. He was a hard, pitiless man, with the manners not of a soldier but of a tyrant.

"Comrade Kopacsi, what have you done at Camp Kistarcsa?"

"Comrade Veres, I've liberated ninety-five detainees."

"How dare you?"

"Comrade Veres, the number of admissions at this camp was more than allowed under the regulations."

"That was the only reason?"

"No, Comrade Veres. There was another reason as well."

"Which was?"

"These people had done nothing to justify being interned."

I handed him the ninety-five decisions containing the reasons for releasing the detainees.

Without even glancing at them, he threw the papers on his desk.

"I put you at the head of an important department and at the end of a few weeks you botch it up. Obviously, you're too young and too damn stupid."

Young I no doubt was. To be director of internment affairs for the Ministry of the Interior was a brilliant success for a twenty-seven-year-old. As for being stupid, well, it's true that I was naive. I didn't understand that "director of internment" meant simply "overseer of suffering", even if I "made exceptions" or ventured into "humanitarianism".

One month later I was dismissed from the ministry and admitted for two years to the party school — the school for automatons. This was considered an honour and I was surprised to receive it. "Why me?" I asked. "You have made mistakes but you have a good background and are capable of being reformed," I was told. Furthermore, as I was conveniently out of a job, my schooling would not create a bureaucratic vacancy.

The school was in a large convent on the edge of the municipal woods. The building hadn't been used as a convent since liberation, but the priests of the new order maintained the repressive spirit of the old. Sex was outlawed. For a kiss exchanged in a corner, students had been expelled. Yet these students weren't children. They were functionaries in training who, although still young, were already important to the party and to the state.

Much of the instruction was military. The school possessed a large arsenal, of which I was made the overseer; the students soon were as familiar with automatic weapons as with Hegelian dialectic. Several major manoeuvres were organized, including some using real weapons. These were attended by members of the Central Committee and the Politburo.

Much more difficult and dangerous than the fire of automatic weapons was the struggle of "criticism and self-criticism" that lasted throughout the course. This fearsome procedure involved creating among the students an atmosphere of suspicion, in which moral judgement was encouraged. The director of the school, Elizabeth Andics, a woman of Hungarian origin but with Soviet citizenship, excelled at organizing investigations and counter-investigations. The slightest bad-mouthing was a pretext for an inquisition. Day after day, the students concentrated on "affairs to be cleared up" in which certain students, through no wish of their own, were dangerously implicated, as I was in the "Chimney Sweep affair".

One day, the director assembled all the students in the meeting hall to discuss "a particularly serious affair". She informed us that "certain of our students have been overheard in a public place [the Chimney Sweep pub near the school] repeating confidential political information. A Communist waitress in the establishment in question has given us a word-for-word account of these conversations. This is the most serious possible transgression. It would behoove those students who have committed it to make themselves known voluntarily and to admit their mistake, which is unworthy of a Communist."

No one responded. A commission of inquiry, made up of teachers and students, was named. We looked at each other, and the blood froze in our veins. In the company of a small group of friends, I myself frequented the pub and the members of the commission knew it. We were questioned. Finally, five of us found ourselves under suspicion. We flatly denied any wrongdoing. "At the pub, you talk like a worker after his shift: jokes, remarks about women, pulling each other's leg, family problems. But never politics."

Three weeks passed in an atmosphere of mortal suspicion, with one inquest and interrogation after another. There was talk of expelling the "chimney sweeps" from the school and even from the party.

Suddenly, I came to a decision. As a policeman, I was going to clear up this nonsensical business. I began in the school dining-hall, by speaking with a waitress I'd seen once at the Chimney Sweep.

"What do you think of all this, Manci?"

The young woman smiled. "I get a laugh out of you people and your investigations. Are you playing detective too? Listen, if you want to know all about it, I'll go to see the cook at the Chimney Sweep."

That's how I found out that this cook hated her job and wanted a change at any price. She would have welcomed a position in the school's kitchen. A few jocular words with the Chimney Sweep cook, who was called Olga, then another conversation with Manci, and I was at the bottom of the intrigue. To have a trump card up her sleeve, the cook had invented the story of the talkative students. She thought that after an act of such benevolent vigilance her request for employment in the school dining-room couldn't help but succeed.

"Olga, didn't you think of the consequences of your little plan? The whole school has been turned upside down."

Olga wasn't a bad sort. She admitted everything to the director. The affair was silenced and the commission of inquiry was dissolved with no explanation to the students. At the next party meeting, I spoke.

"Comrade Andics, the Chimney Sweep affair is apparently over. But there are five of us here who have been under suspicion for the past three weeks. We were on the brink of being excluded from the party. Shouldn't it now be stated that the 'chimney sweeps' are innocent? Don't you think that the correct step now for a Communist director would be to *rehabilitate* us?"

It never happened.

The party is infallible. It is the "collective conscience"; it never makes a mistake. And if it does have the misfortune to make a mistake, one had better keep quiet about it. Infallibility is the guiding principle of a Communist regime and to question it is considered unseemly.

My second year at the school was like a second honeymoon with Ibolya because I was actually allowed to sleep at home. (During the first year, as in the military, the students had to live at the school and only rarely got leave.) My wife and I realized that we couldn't live apart, even for a day. As adults, and after having done so much and seen so much, we rediscovered each other like two abandoned children.

Towards the end of 1951, my second year at the party school, the emphasis on military instruction became stronger (we sat for the same exams as reserve officers), and I became one of the instructors in my group. I wore an army uniform while my friends were arrayed in the school outfit of navy blue trousers, white shirt and red tie. One day, marching in a row, we were returning from a theatre where we had seen a Soviet film when a strange *accident* happened in the street.

I was at the head of the column; we were on the right side of the street, with the traffic on our left. Suddenly I heard a terrible cry behind me. It was an inarticulate shout, like nothing I had ever heard, as if a man had screamed, "Mother!"

I turned around and saw one of the first-year students rush headlong into the traffic and throw himself under a bus that was coming from the other direction. The driver swerved but couldn't avoid him. The man was crushed; the huge wheels smashed his thighs and blood spurted from his body as he lost consciousness. One of us phoned for an ambulance, which took him to hospital.

What followed was more sinister than the "accident", which was clearly a deliberate act. The previous night, the student had been in a class in which the instructor had spoken of an espionage trial in Czechoslovakia, organized, like those in Hungary, by Bielkin. The student, a thirty-five-year-old man named Elek, had been a member during the war of the Slovakian underground, on Hungary's northern border. He had known both Rudolf Slansky, a leader of the Czech party who had just been executed, and Husak, who runs Czechoslovakia to this day, but who at the time was involved in the "affair" and sentenced to twenty years in prison.

Undoubtedly, news of the trial of the former comrade had frightened Elek, and this fear had provoked his suicide.

After the "accident", we learned, AVO agents tried to extract a bedside confession from him. It was a waste of time. He was delirious, tearing off his bandages, and after six weeks of agony, he died without admitting anything.

The whole school was seized with horror and we were in a state of shock for a long time afterwards. Curiously, it wasn't the personal drama of Elek that had the greatest impact on us, but rather the imminence and ubiquitousness of the danger that surrounded us. Think of it: hundreds of future functionaries, carefully chosen, brought together in a place that was thoroughly regimented and policed, and yet completely open to an "agent" who was directly linked to "the worst enemies of the movement". Innocents that we were, we fully believed this at the time.

The death of this man (who, as would later become clear, was completely innocent) was a timely reminder to us at the end of the school year of the vigilance under which we must live, we the future leaders of the Communist Party.

Police Chief and Colonel

"Is your candidate tall?"

"Six feet, Comrade Rakosi."

"And...how should I put it? Is he *Aryan?*"

The Minister of the Interior, "Aryan" himself, couldn't believe his ears. Rakosi, a Jew, had asked a question worthy of a Nazi. It was so scandalous it couldn't be answered directly.

"He's a metalworker from the north, Comrade Rakosi. His father was a metalworker too. And his grandfather." (In Hungary at that time Jews didn't have factory jobs.)

Pensively, Rakosi examined the file. The other members of the Politburo exchanged smiles, thinking to themselves, "Here we go again, the old man and his complexes about being small and Jewish...."

"It seems to me I've met this man," he said, examining my photograph.

Suddenly, he exclaimed: "I know. It's Sandor."

Another smile from the Politburo members, with the same thought running through their minds: "That's the old man, all right. He's one of a kind. What a memory." Rakosi remembered every person, every face, he had ever seen.

"So, you propose to make him police chief of Budapest. Me, I've got nothing against it. But let's make him a colonel at least."

According to the eyewitness report of my boss, Arpad Hazi, who was Minister of the Interior at the time, that is how, in April of 1952, I became a chief of police.

They needed a working-class chief, but the reign of my predecessor, a certain Moravetz, like me a former metalworker, had been a total disaster. One of poor Rajk's so-called "crimes" had been to "leave the comrades of working-class origin out in the cold". To correct this, the director of the AVO had taken Moravetz, who was a corporal on his force, made him a colonel, then a major-general, and finally police chief of Budapest. It may have been good politics, but it was hell for the Budapest police.

Moravetz was at the station practically twenty-four hours a day. His watchwords were vigilance and internal purification. Budapest's criminals breathed a sigh of relief because there was no more surveillance, no more tailing, no more raids, and no more arrests. There was no room for crooks in the police cells because they were filled with cops. Under Moravetz, the police were an arm of the AVO and, on the direct order of the AVO chief, prisoners were jailed without hope of release.

At police headquarters, everyone spied on his neighbour and kept a little overnight case ready because nobody knew which policeman would be arrested next.

Moravetz fell flat on his face on the occasion of the annual April 4 military parade celebrating Hungary's liberation by the Soviet Army at the end of the war. Instead of deploying enough police to keep order along the parade route, he used several armed battalions to surround the Yugoslav Embassy, which stood directly across from the stand on which Hungarian and Soviet dignitaries would review the parade. According to Moravetz, this step was necessary because Yugoslav "enemies" might attack our leaders.

Unfortunately for Moravetz, the crowd spilled through the police lines, causing a series of rear-end collisions in a parade of tanks. On the reviewing stand, the Soviets scratched their heads in amazement while the Western military attachés laughed up their sleeves. Farkas, the Hungarian defence minister, was beside himself.

That same day, Moravetz was fired and installed in a new job as party secretary in a third-rate factory. Since the former chief had made a mess of April 4, my first job was to ensure the success of the May 1 celebrations.

"Comrades, as a greenhorn fresh from the bush, I'm not going to try to impress you with my vast knowledge. Experienced policemen know their jobs a hundred times better than someone who has just arrived. I need your help. For my part, I can guarantee you a calm atmosphere at headquarters. As for the unnecessary overtime, that's finished. And I'm going to review the files of everyone who's been detained. The cells are for criminals, not for policemen."

I was careful to speak in a neutral tone; the last thing I wanted was an ovation, which would have accomplished nothing. But I could feel some of the tension go out of the atmosphere. It became positively friendly when I brought up the question of bonus money. Part of the police budget was set aside to pay bonuses to staff members whose performance was outstanding. Moravetz had found none of his 5,000 employees worthy of receiving a bonus.

"On arriving at headquarters," I continued, "I found the reward cashbox full. I have ordered that these funds be dispensed to the best organizers of the crowd-control contingents for May 1. I hope that many of you will receive a bonus. Now, comrades, I wish you good luck. I'm off to take a look at the cells."

In three days, the cells were emptied, and I had affairs at police headquarters solidly in hand. May 1 was a success for the police. My modest reforms had been obtained thanks to my good relations with the minister. Arpad Hazi had a terrible reputation as a stubborn dogmatist. (At the time, we didn't yet say "Stalinist".) Dogmatist or Stalinist, this old comrade understood human psychology and hated bureaucracy. For him, my working-class background wasn't just good public relations, as it was for Rakosi. Hazi truly believed that the working classes harboured treasures of talent and energy. I don't say this for myself; I'm thinking of the numerous people of humble origin with whom this old Stalinist surrounded himself and to whom he accorded his complete confidence during his short career as a minister.

He was the one who introduced me to Iemelianov.

"Come here, Kopacsi. Let me present Comrade Kopacsi, our worker police chief. This is Comrade Iemelianov, principal counsellor to the Ministry of the Interior for the Soviet Union."

I looked at the old Soviet officer and the old Hungarian functionary. Side by side, they looked like two brothers. During their long lives, they had survived the same storms, grappled with the same difficult decisions, and assumed responsibility for thousands of people under their orders.

"*Tovarishch* Kopacsi," said the Soviet officer, using the Russian word for comrade, "I've sent you two very good counsellors."

"Thank you, Comrade Iemelianov. I've only been there a few days and I haven't met them yet."

"You've got time. They're not ultra-modern types, perhaps, but their hearts are in the right place. You'll see for yourself."

"Petofi" and "Magyar-Miska" were most certainly not "ultra-modern". They were both colonels, but whether in the Soviet secret police or the regular police I never learned. Their offices were side by side on the seventh floor, overlooking the street. You could tell Petofi's from a hundred metres away because the two windows were always wide open. During the interminable siege of Leningrad, Petofi had contracted a disease that made his blood pressure climb to incredible levels; the Soviets called this the "Leningrad disease" and, according to the colonel, thousands of people suffered from it. Because of his blood pressure, Petofi had a purplish complexion and couldn't stand the slightest heat, even in winter. His specialty was criminology.

"*Tovarishch* Kopacsi, I really must give a talk on the use of photography in criminology."

"But of course, *Tovarishch* Colonel. My men and myself are most interested in the progress made in this field by the Soviet Union."

I said this without the slightest irony. How could I have known what Petofi was going to tell us? At that time, we had excellent teams of criminologists, partly inherited from the pre-Communist regime and including, as well, young researchers versed in literature on criminology imported from the West and secretly translated.

We listened silently to his long-winded discourse on the role of photography in police work. But the audience began to stir when Petofi showed us the photos he had made in Leningrad on the occasion of this or that crime. One of the superintendents leaned toward me and whispered, "We were making them like that back in the thirties."

I was only an amateur photographer myself, but I was astonished to see negatives and prints obtained by such obviously outdated methods. We used cameras imported from East Germany and some excellent Japanese equipment, illegally purchased by the police soccer team on a tour of Western countries.

"*Tovarishch* Colonel, what make of camera do you use?"

Petofi plunged his hand to the bottom of an enormous leather sack and pulled out an object that he held up for all to see.

"This camera is the latest thing, the basis for the avant-garde technique of Soviet criminology."

We had to bite our lips to keep from laughing. The thing obviously predated the Russian Revolution.

Petofi began to sense that we weren't quite as impressed as he had expected; he looked at us sternly and said, "Don't you know what make this is? Don't you see the initials FED on the side?"

None of us knew the significance of the initials FED. "FED" the colonel informed us, "are the initials of Felix Edmondovitch Djerjinski, the creator and incomparable director of our first Cheka, the prototype for every revolutionary police force in the world. He was the one who created this kind of camera to facilitate the pursuit of criminals in the Soviet Union."

We all knew who Djerjinski was. His bearded portrait decorated the walls in most of our offices. But we also knew that the great chief of the Cheka had succumbed to tuberculosis in 1926.

We listened to the rest of the talk in silence. When it was over, I said, "We thank the comrade colonel for his excellent talk, which has been most informative. On this occasion, my photo lab team invites him for a visit as a way of completing together this remarkable survey of the field."

If Petofi was impressed by our equipment, which, unlike his, did not date from well before the war, he didn't let on. He had nothing at all to say. Even this timid initiative of mine was noted and found its way into my file. It would be used against me at the time of the trial in 1958 as evidence of "a skeptical attitude *vis-à-vis* the avant-garde techniques of the Soviet Union".

Nevertheless, I passed some delightful hours in Petofi's company. He, his interpreter and I would spend long, calm summer afternoons either in his office or in mine, discussing the war over cups of herb tea (he never touched alcohol or coffee). He would describe Leningrad during the siege. I would talk about the big factory in Diosgyor under the Germans, about the meeting with the Red Army in the northern mountains, and about friendships formed with the Russians in the underground. War is what men like to talk about in countries where wars have been fought. And in our two countries we had fought our share.

The other Soviet adviser, Magyar-Miska, was an innocent little man from the heart of the central-Russian steppes. At the beginning, with his imperturbable professional conscience, he had given several lectures on "bandits in the forest" and other matters that were still relevant to police work in the Soviet Union but had not concerned Hungarian police for more than a hundred years. We listened politely. After a while, he stopped giving lectures. This was his first urban posting and, realizing he was out of his depth, he made up his mind to keep his eyes and ears open and to give advice only when asked.

On the other hand, Magyar-Miska and Petofi took part in all our meetings, with their interpreters summarizing the essential points in Russian. In the evening, they went to the Ministry of the Interior where they met with their superiors, probably to give their reports. Afterwards, they would be driven to their homes in the residential neighbourhood of Buda, where in pre-Communist days cabinet ministers had lived. There, they had their private clubs, sports fields, and schools for their children.

The Strange Lieutenant Dohany

One evening, some time after I became police chief, I noticed a rhythmic noise that seemed to come from the upper floors. Normally, no one was in that part of the building at night. As I climbed the stairs the noise grew louder. There was no doubt: at this late hour, someone had arrived unannounced and uninvited to do construction work in the building.

In the middle of the corridor on the top floor, I found two soldiers installing the uprights for a steel door. Two other soldiers, clutching automatic rifles, stood by.

"What's this for?" I asked.

One of the armed soldiers turned toward me. "What are you looking for here?"

I was in civilian clothes as usual. "I'm Colonel Kopacsi, chief of police." My explanation didn't have the expected effect.

"Your papers."

Happily, I had my card on me. The soldier examined it.

"Comrade Colonel, do you have a summons?"

"A summons? No."

"Without a summons, nobody is allowed in this corridor."

I was at a loss as to how to react.

The soldier gave me a moment to think. While I did so, he pointedly rested his hand on the breech of his automatic rifle ("in case the supposed enemy tries to pass to the attack," as military regulations put it).

The soldiers' caps bore the wide blue stripe of the AVO, the

Hungarian security force. They were part of an elite recruited according to criteria almost as precise as the racial guidelines of the Nazis: descendants of workers or poor peasants, with membership in the Communist Youth, good references from local authorities, and so on. But that did nothing to reduce my annoyance at their behaviour.

"Stop hammering a moment while I talk to you."

A young man appeared from behind a padded door and curtly asked the reason for my presence.

I stated my identity. Instead of inviting me in, he said, "Comrade Colonel, I had planned to see you tomorrow."

"But...who are you?"

"Zoltan Dohany, lieutenant of the Security of the State, commander of the counter-espionage detachment attached to the headquarters of the Budapest police."

As he addressed me curtly, I replied in kind. "I would have preferred you to introduce yourself before moving in, Lieutenant."

He looked at me arrogantly. "Why?"

"Oh, I don't know. Out of common courtesy, perhaps?"

He stared at me, as if he'd understood none of what I'd said.

The next day, in the middle of the afternoon, someone pushed open my office door. It was Lieutenant Dohany.

"Hello, Comrade Colonel. I have a request."

I thought to myself, "What a fine idea. He's decided to discuss the installation of his offices behind the steel door." But that wasn't it at all.

"I need a secretary."

"Very well. I'll tell the personnel officer."

He looked at me oddly. "Comrade?"

"Yes?"

"The AVO is a very special organization."

That morning, I had made my own small investigation of Dohany. The first thing he had found to do upon his arrival had been to trumpet to our drivers that "the AVO is the spearhead of the working class" and that an "AVO brigadier is more important than a police colonel".

"And?"

"I need a secretary in whom complete trust can be placed."

"You will have a choice among five hundred secretaries, all very carefully selected."

"I've already made my choice."

"Bravo. Who is the lucky one?"

"Your private secretary."

I've never been one to fly off the handle quickly and so I replied calmly, "You have hundreds of secretaries and stenographers to choose from. As for my private secretary, I'm keeping her."

The lieutenant got up (he had sat down uninvited) and said, "Comrade Colonel, you're deluding yourself. What I've decided goes. It's too bad, but that's the way it is."

He turned his back and left.

I asked to see the minister, Arpad Hazi, who received me the same evening.

"So, my little Kopacsi, the AVO is making your life miserable?"

"This young man has offended hundreds of secretaries on our staff by stating that none of them is 'worthy of confidence' except one."

"Yes. But you know very well that I can't intervene directly."

"You can talk to Comrade Peter."

General Peter was the very famous president of the AVO.

The minister thought for a moment. "Yes, I could," he said. "But before doing that, I want to ask you to do something for me. Go home and reflect on all this. Tomorrow, we'll decide together what course to follow."

The next morning, I called Hazi, and told him, "Comrade Minister, let's drop it."

I hadn't slept all night. I had understood. The choice of a secretary counted for nothing. I was involved here in a test of strength. Hazi's use of the word "reflect" had opened my eyes. The AVO really was sovereign, so far above the party and the state that an old comrade like Hazi, a member of the Central Committee and a minister, had to "reflect" before intervening. What Dohany had trumpeted to the drivers was true: an AVO brigadier was indeed powerful, even more powerful than a minister.

It was sad, but one had to resign oneself. As the saying of the day had it, "Beautiful or not, a fiancée is made to be laid."

My relations with Lieutenant Dohany remained strained. It couldn't be otherwise. His little detachment was constantly trying to pin something on my officers. Without advancing the slightest proof, they were capable of announcing that they were on the verge of uncovering a vast conspiracy.

"But that's horrible," I said to Dohany. "Let me see your reports."

"Impossible," he replied dryly. "State secrets."

"Give me a few names at least. Surely you don't want me to remain surrounded by spies."

"I'm sorry, but the investigation is in progress."

He had requisitioned several cells in the basement, which were guarded by his men. What secret things happened there?

One day, I was visited by the wife of an excellent officer based in a suburban station.

"Comrade Kopacsi, they've taken my husband."

"They? Who are 'they'?"

"Why, your security people."

"My security people? My poor friend, they're not mine, they're against me."

The officer in question had a high rank despite his youth, and he was none other than the grandson of a famous minister of the Hungarian Commune of 1919. I asked Dohany to come to see me.

"You've arrested Commander N?"

"There is no Commander N. There is only the traitor N, an agent for years for British intelligence."

"This officer is the pride of our workers' movement, the grandson of a minister of the Commune, a favourite of the Central Committee. What have you got against him? Let him go."

Dohany threw back his shoulders, stuck his chin in the air, and retorted, "For us, there are no grandsons of famous people, or any favourite sons of the movement, there are only the innocent and the guilty."

The man's wife spent months going from door to door before rescuing her husband from Dohany's clutches.

Dohany wandered into my office at will, never asking for an appointment or having himself announced.

"One of your chief inspectors is involved in a serious anti-Soviet provocation. He's been picked to dynamite the monument honouring the Soviet Army."

"The son of a bitch. I hope that, with the overwhelming evidence you've no doubt got, you'll drag him into court before it's too late."

Dohany avoided looking me in the eye. "There is proof, but it's not all compiled yet. In the meantime, this man should be sent out of Budapest."

"Reflect," the minister had told me. I gave ground once more. Under some silly pretext, I sent one of my best inspectors away.

Naturally, Dohany was never able to prove the existence of any plot.

One day when Dohany pushed open my office door, as usual without having himself announced, I reached my limit. It was two years since Dohany had first shown up at police headquarters and during that time the political climate had changed. Imre Nagy was in power and the AVO's excesses were being curbed.

"Comrade Kopacsi, I've come for...."

"Get out, Comrade Lieutenant."

"I beg your pardon?"

"Turn around, go and see my secretary, and ask her to announce you. If I have time to receive you, then you will come in, stand at attention, and say, as the regulations require, 'Comrade Colonel, I present my respects and ask permission to report.' Is that understood?"

White as a sheet, Dohany backed out without a word. During that day and the ones that followed, he took pains to avoid me.

He must have "reflected" just as I had. The next time, he had himself announced as the rules required.

To finish my portrait of Dohany, I should add that this working-class boy, saddled with an unpleasant personality and no education beyond a short course in administration, underwent a spectacular transformation in the spring of 1956. Dohany and a good number of his colleagues were sent, as undercover AVO agents, to infiltrate the meetings of the Petofi Circle, the activist wing of the Young Communists. This group was hostile to Matthias Rakosi and instead favoured the reformist Imre Nagy. Rakosi was counting on the AVO reports as a basis on which to charge the most enthusiastic participants in the debates. The secret agents noted the arguments developed by the speakers, among whom were the best scientists, historians, philosophers, writers, and journalists in the country.

As the investigation proceeded, the agents became more and more susceptible to the reformist ideas they were supposed to expose.

A scandal erupted at AVO headquarters. A majority of the informers announced that they agreed with what they had heard at the Petofi Circle and drew up a memorandum declaring their solidarity with the ideas of the party's young reformers.

Rakosi was outraged and demanded immediate action. Those who had signed the memorandum were called one by one before the president of the AVO. Every single one of them caved in and withdrew his signature. Except one. His name was Zoltan Dohany. He came to see me to say goodbye, having himself announced as the regulations required. "It's over," he said. "I'm not a lieutenant any more."

"What are you going to do, Dohany?"

"No problem, Comrade Colonel. I'm going back to my workbench at the factory. I never should have left it."

We never saw each other again.

▋ "Stalin Is Dead: Nichevo"

It was three o'clock in the morning. Elbows on knees, head on hands, a thirty-year-old beanpole in a crumpled uniform, I was sobbing all alone in my office. Stalin, the liberator of my country, was dead.

An hour earlier, I had been awakened at home by a call from the minister. "Get down to headquarters. There's a second-degree state of alert."

The corridors were empty, my deputies hadn't yet arrived, and my office smelled of freshly waxed floors and the stale smoke of yesterday's cigarettes. I left the door open and collapsed in the chair.

Abruptly, I sensed someone present. I raised my head and saw Iemelianov, the principal counsellor of the Soviet Union for the Ministry of the Interior. He was alone, without his interpreter.

"Cognac? Do you have cognac?"

I had some in a cupboard. A bit embarrassed that my eyes were reddened with tears, I filled a glass and handed it to him. He made a gesture of refusal.

"You. Yes, you. Drink." He was speaking a simple Russian he knew I could understand.

I drained the glass.

He laid a hand on my shoulder. "Stalin is dead," he said, then added: *"Nichevo."*

I didn't believe my ears. *"Nichevo"* means "It doesn't matter; it's nothing."

Yet to me it was obvious that the death of Comrade Stalin was a terrible calamity for everyone, a tragedy for mankind. I told him so, but the officer shook his head obstinately. "No."

He looked me in the eyes, then brought out his pocket handker-chief, an old-fashioned one with big checks, and handed it to me. "We are living, *da?* Life goes on."

He left my office. Several minutes later, I watched through the window as he got into his car and departed. He had come to tell me not to despair. Or...to pass along also, perhaps, *another message?...* Who knew?

The crowd is a force of nature, like the sea. The chief of police who doesn't know its laws and its moods is as lost as the captain of a ship without a compass.

With their order, "Everybody to Stalin's statue" for the commem-orative service, the party organizations risked channelling 100,000 people to the edge of the municipal park.

Rakosi was in Moscow for the burial, and Gero, his usual replace-ment, was in charge in Budapest. He demanded that the statue be roped off to protect the party leaders in case the crowd surged forward. We tried to dissuade him.

"Even the heaviest ropes won't keep the crowd out. Nobody will see them except the people who are right up against them. We're risking big trouble."

Gero was nervous, as he often was. Since his youth, he had suffered from gastritis and severe stomach ulcers.

"Do as I say. The statue has to be roped off."

It was a dismal day. The wind blew up a storm. Instead of the 100,000 we had expected, more than 300,000 showed up. The leaders were staggering about inside the roped-off area. Elizabeth Andics, director of the party school, dressed all in black, was in a state of collapse, as if she had lost her husband. The defence minister, Farkas, supported her the way one supports a widow. More emaciated and sinister-looking than ever, Gero spoke. But about what? Because of the wind, the crowd couldn't hear a thing.

The pushing started at the back of the crowd, and a strange, terrifying eddying began. As 300,000 people surged forward, the ones who were up against the ropes began to be crushed. They screamed; women by the hundreds fainted. Injuries and deaths — many injuries and deaths — were inevitable.

His wire spectacles resting on his nose, Gero continued his oration. I turned to my minister.

"Comrade Hazi, if we don't do something, it'll be a catastrophe."

"What do you want to do?"

"Save the people who are being crushed against the ropes, of course. Let's use bayonets to cut the ropes."

"Kopacsi, you're crazy. They're too heavy to cut, and even if we could our leaders risk being trampled by the crowd."

"Let them climb up on the statue."

There was no more time to lose. The screaming was becoming ever shriller and a whole row of victims was hanging unconscious over the ropes. I motioned to my officers and, with our bayonet points, we began feverishly trying to sever the ropes. After several minutes of frenzied labour, the ropes began to yield.

The pushing crowd finished the job. A tremendous cry rose up and the crowd invaded the reserved area.

As we felt the tension ease, we rushed to pick up the wounded. Gero, Farkas, Elizabeth Andics, and the others trembled as they stared at the human tidal wave, the people of Budapest, swirling around them. I really think it was the first time they had seen the people at such close quarters. It was a shock to them, but nothing worse.

That night, I learned that in Moscow the KGB had faced the same problem but had resolved it differently. They had charged the unruly crowd with tanks, leaving hundreds dead.

Three months after Stalin's death, a childhood friend of mine who had become an officer in the AVO invited me for a drink and then suggested that we go for a walk on the secluded trails of Margaret Island.

"Something crazy has happened to me, Sandor. I've got to talk to you about it in absolute secrecy."

"It's that serious?"

"You'll judge for yourself. I've just got back from Moscow where I was accompanying Rakosi."

He paused. "Now, get ready for this: Stalin is no longer God and Rakosi is no longer prime minister of Hungary."

I needed to find something to hang on to. Or at least find a bench to sit on. We chose one in the shade. In a low voice, with constant glances to right and left, my friend recounted one of the historic events of the century.

On the way there, the Hungarian delegation didn't suspect a thing.

Curled up in a corner of his lounge car, Rakosi was busy consulting his notes. The president of the Republic, Steven Dobi, as usual divided his time between drinking and sleeping; a former member of the Smallholders' Party, he was an alcoholic and a totally passive individual. (During this period, a non-Communist always played this ceremonial role.) Gero and Farkas, Rakosi's right and left arms, whispered secretively; they always acted like that. Imre Nagy, meanwhile, talked with my friend.

"He asked me questions about life in the country, which I know a lot about because of my position. He listened to me carefully. It was like talking to an old friend. He's not like the other leaders."

On arrival in Moscow, the delegation was taken before the highest body in the Soviet Union: the Praesidium of the Supreme Soviet. All the top leaders were there — Malenkov, Stalin's designated successor; Khrushchev, the party chief; Mikoyan, Khrushchev's right-hand man — as were all the survivors of Stalin's celebrated team: Molotov, Beria, Bulganin, Suslov, Kaganovich, Vorochilov.

The atmosphere was extremely tense. After having coldly welcomed the Hungarians, Malenkov addressed Rakosi. "What is your position in Hungary?" he asked, as if he didn't know that Rakosi was both first secretary of the Hungarian party and prime minister. Grudgingly, Rakosi stated his titles.

"Only twice head of the country?" asked Malenkov. "You're sure you're not also president of the Republic?"

Dobi, feverishly following the translation of Malenkov's words, exclaimed: "No, the president of the Republic, that's me."

This slightly cheered up those present.

"Listen, Rakosi, let's get serious," Malenkov continued. "In Hungary, things are going from bad to worse. You've overstepped the mark. In your industrial centres, in Csepel, Ozd, Diosgyor, there is serious turmoil."

Rakosi launched into a lengthy self-defence laced with statistics. The Russian leaders began to yawn and Mikoyan interrupted: "You're drowning us in numbers. We've got statistics too and they're different from yours. In the field of industrialization, you're guilty of unbridled adventurism. You built a new town for iron and steel manufacturing without an ounce of coke. You've started building an incredibly expensive subway when you haven't even got enough food to feed the workers. Your farmers, forcibly collectivized, can't even produce enough seeds for replanting. Most of them are rotting away in your concentration camps."

Rakosi turned pale.

Khrushchev, who hadn't yet spoken, pointed a finger at Rakosi and said, "You're decimating your people; you're covered in crimes. If this continues, your people will grab their pitchforks and pitch you out of the country."

Beria, who two days later would be arrested in the middle of a Politburo meeting, leaned forward and made the unkindest cut of all: "What did you want?" he asked Rakosi. "To be king of the Jews?"

Malenkov continued, in a calmer tone: "Comrade Rakosi, you're an old warrior in the movement, surely you understand the situation. You must share power with other comrades, who are also expert in government. What do you think?"

White as a sheet, Rakosi replied almost inaudibly that he had nothing against sharing power.

"That's perfect," said Khrushchev. "Propose someone to take over the affairs of state."

A long and painful silence ensued. Rakosi was sweating. He didn't open his mouth.

"What do you think," said Malenkov helpfully, "of Imre Nagy, who is present here?"

Rakosi looked at Imre Nagy as if seeing him for the first time. "Imre Nagy is a very good comrade, but — "

He gave up. The Soviets smiled under their moustaches.

"In other words, you don't see anyone with whom you can share your responsibilities. As for us, we've known Imre Nagy since the days of the Revolution. He joined the Bolshevik Party before there was a Hungarian party. He's a recognized expert in the Communist direction of public affairs. He's a member as well of your Politburo, a farmer and the son of a farmer, and has become a professor. We have confidence in Comrade Imre Nagy. With your help, he will be able to straighten out Hungary's problems."

Nagy spoke. He thanked the comrades of the Soviet Politburo for their confidence. Briefly, he outlined the tasks awaiting the new collective leadership in Budapest, which wasn't difficult since the Soviets had just enumerated Rakosi's mistakes. Nagy said he would put an end to police terror and rehabilitate the innocent. There would be a more rational investment policy: more food for the people and less gigantism in the blast furnaces and subways. And finally, more liberty for the farmers.

Malenkov interrupted. "Not only more liberty but total liberty. Those who don't want to stay on a collective farm should be able to leave. There's nothing wrong with that."

As a matter of form, the Politburo asked the advice of the President of the Republic.

"Of course, I agree, I agree completely with everything," Dobi cried in Hungarian when the question was translated. (All the members of the delegation except Dobi spoke perfect Russian. This was the first time during the meeting that the Soviets had to use their interpreter.)

It was a cry from the heart. This former partisan, a non-Communist worn down by alcohol and humiliation, felt a sudden burst of hope at seeing his country delivered from the tyrant Rakosi.

To the Hungarians, the Soviet Politburo had seemed unified. But few of those present that day lasted long in power. After the execution of Beria, Khrushchev was in control. He used Bulganin a while longer and Mikoyan longer still, but Malenkov, Kaganovich, Vorochilov, and Molotov were successively declared "antiparty" and relegated to the "Stalin Museum".

■ *"Your Uniform Doesn't Become You"*

In July of 1953, about a month after that decisive meeting in Moscow, I became Member of Parliament for the tenth district of Budapest. I can't say that I was elected, because I had no competition. The voters merely confirmed my nomination by the party.

My first visit to Parliament — which sat three or four times a year for two days at a time — coincided with Imre Nagy's first day as prime minister. As I gazed around the sumptuous chamber, with its paintings portraying the march of Hungarian history, I spotted the stocky frame of Imre Nagy, with his drooping moustache that recalled days gone by. Then I listened as Nagy rose from his seat and delivered, in his colourful country accent, a speech whose like we had not heard before.

As he announced the reforms agreed upon in Moscow, we members of Parliament, usually just automatic voting machines, listened with rapt attention. We studied the open face of the speaker and, near him, the impassive features of Rakosi. A miracle was happening. Instead of repeating the stock verses of the Marxist liturgy, a Communist statesman was treating his parliamentary colleagues as a thinking being treats his peers.

I had known that change was in the air but not what form it would take. I poked F, a model worker in the construction industry who, like me, was a new deputy: "Am I dreaming?"

"I don't think so. If you are, we're both having the same dream."

Nagy was speaking about public education. Suddenly, he used an expression that made us sit up. "We must upgrade the schooling of young Hungarians."

"Young Hungarians." Since the liberation, the noun Hungarian had been eliminated from the official vocabulary. We no longer belonged to an ethnic group, or at least we didn't acknowledge it. We were "Hungarian workers" or "the working people of the country" or "the Hungarian bastion on the wall of peace" or anything else, but never simply "Hungarians".

It's difficult to explain, but Nagy's use of the word stunned us and filled us with joy all at the same time. Then Nagy came to the subject of collective farms and private land.

"We have made serious errors in this area as well," he said. "Because of forced collectivization, our agriculture is on the brink of ruin. We are going to do away with the taxes and arrears owed by farmers. In addition, from now on the Hungarian farmer is free to choose between individual and collective labour. If he wants to leave the collective, then he is free to leave."

Nagy hadn't finished this last sentence before his audience leapt to its feet, applauding wildly. It wasn't just the rhythmic clapping inherited from fascism and mandatory under the Communist regime. This was genuine enthusiasm, straight from the heart.

Rakosi applauded too, without enthusiasm, but diligently. He was under surveillance. On the balconies, in the midst of the foreign diplomatic corps, the personnel of the Soviet Embassy looked on, among them Kiseliov, Andropov's predecessor as ambassador.

Amazed, the model worker and I made our way to the buffet that had been laid on for the opening of Parliament. The tables were well-stocked with expensive drinks and fancy appetizers unavailable in the shops of Budapest. Automatically, we ordered two *frocs,* white wine spritzers, the drink of the suburban bars. We drank one spritzer after another, raving like a couple of drunken peasants. We forgot completely that we were members of Parliament, of the Budapest party committee, of the executive committee of the Budapest municipal council, that I was a colonel and police chief, that he was director of one of the largest firms in the country, that we were both honorary presidents of I don't know how many associations for peace, for sports, for former partisans, and for culture.

Among the positions I had accumulated were several that brought home to me the unsatisfactory state of affairs to which Imre Nagy referred in his address. As a municipal councillor, I was on hand at City Hall once every two or three months to hear the problems of the residents of Budapest. Ninety-five per cent of these were requests for housing.

At that time, the government was devoting its resources to building housing, training camps, and airports for the armed forces rather than homes for civilians. The few buildings erected for model workers or other privileged types barely served to replace buildings that had been requisitioned for offices.

I was scared to death of these meetings. One case especially has lodged permanently in my memory. It was winter. The door opened to admit a woman of seventy-five dressed for summer right down to the sandals on her feet.

"Good day, sir. I have come to ask your advice. I'm Catholic and my religion prohibits suicide. But if you recommend it, I will follow your advice."

She presented her case calmly, without fuss or tears, in an even tone. She was a war widow from the First World War. Between the wars, she had made her living from one of the small tobacco shops war widows had been allowed to operate. But this type of petty commerce had now been nationalized, and her income consisted of a pension of 100 forints a month, a pathetic sum equal to a tenth of a worker's salary. Some friends allowed her to live in a coal cellar. She pushed a piece of paper toward me.

"What's that?"

"My bread calendar."

She kept a record of the days of the month and how much bread she could buy each day. Apparently, she hadn't bought any for three days.

I called the porter and gave him money to buy a meal in the restaurant across the street. While the old lady ate, a policeman went to her home to verify the situation. It was as she had said. We collected 500 forints which we gave to the old lady. At the end of my day of meeting the people, I sent her to police headquarters.

"But why?" she insisted. "Why?"

"Don't be afraid, you're going to join the police."

She was outfitted from head to toe — she even put on a policeman's cape — and was given some wool blankets. My deputy phoned everywhere to get her pension raised. The old lady returned to her cellar with my promise that she could always count on the police.

The epilogue to this story is instructive. The supply chief of the Ministry of the Interior, a certain Major-General Bela Berecz, instituted disciplinary proceedings against me for having delivered police property to a civilian. But Berecz's superior put a stop to this laughable procedure on the grounds that what I gave away was only surplus.

It was a perfect example of the mentality of the Communist bureaucrat and it was not the last time I would run into Major-General Berecz. During the insurrection, the minister sent him to me under guard to be detained at police headquarters. Knowing he was not an AVO member, although he wore their uniform, I gave him civilian clothes and showed him the open door. He refused to go, so afraid was he of being identified as an AVO officer and attacked.

He passed the crucial days in an office in headquarters and, on November 4, returned home, thanking me profusely. But at the time of my trial, he charged me before the investigator with having held him captive. When he was reproached by his own colleagues for ingratitude, he went to the post office and sent 300 forints to my wife.

A chance encounter during the same period (toward the end of 1953) illustrated for me the contradictions with which we all struggled, subject as we were to the hazards of a management that no one could control.

It was morning and I was leaving home in top form, freshly shaven and, because of an official meeting scheduled for that day, in uniform. In the car, I chatted happily with my chauffeur, George, when, on one of the main boulevards, I saw a face that made my heart stop.

"George, follow that tram."

On the tram's rear platform stood a man whose powerful build I would recognize anywhere. His black hair was streaked with white, but otherwise he was the image of the Paul Popradi I had known as a child, my father's lifelong friend, the social democrat director of the well-known workers' choir in our factory, which sometimes performed on the radio. He had been sentenced to fifteen years in prison shortly after the liberation.

"George, pass the tram and let me off at the next stop."

I got out of the car. The crowd at the tram stop stared in surprise at my uniform with all its stripes. Colonels don't often wait for trams.

"*Pali bacsi!* Hey, Uncle Paul!"

It was him all right, but he pretended not to see me, this man who had known me since childhood. I motioned to George to go back to headquarters and I climbed onto the tram platform.

"Uncle Paul. It's you?"

"It's me."

"And you don't recognize me? I'm little Kopacsi."

"Your uniform doesn't become you, son."

I insisted on his getting off the tram and having a drink with me. He accepted. We went into an espresso bar. This man had been in the Red Army of the Commune of 1919 with my father. His father and my grandfather had worked in the same factory. And I had watched powerless, eight years previously, as he was unjustly sentenced and imprisoned.

"What I want to tell you, Uncle Paul, is that *I knew*."

He ordered coffee and said calmly, "Tell me about it."

"It was because you insisted on staying in the Social Democratic Party."

"I knew that."

"That petty tyrant Captain Fogarasi of the AVO falsified a document according to which you had been in the service of the old regime. Maybe you know that not long afterward Fogarasi was lynched by the mob?"

Popradi looked at me indifferently. "That didn't do me any good; I was still in jail."

"Uncle Paul, I want to tell you everything I know. After Fogarasi's death, we opened his safe and found a confidential note to the effect that your affair had been invented by Comrade Nogradi, first secretary of the Communist Party in the district, and approved by Major Denisov of the Soviet secret service who was the Russian kommandantur's delegate in our town." (At the time there were still kommandanturs of the liberation army all over the country.)

Popradi calmly sipped his coffee without looking at me. His only question was, "This Comrade Nogradi who invented the whole thing, what's he up to these days?"

I had to admit that Nogradi had been promoted to major-general and under-secretary of Defence. Perplexed, I looked at the military stripes on my sleeve.

"I'm sorry, Uncle Paul. I'm sorry for what you've suffered."

"I've got nothing against you, my little Kopacsi. I know very well that you did what you could."

He put down his cup. "Give my regards to your father. Tell him that I'll come to see him one day."

(Popradi was with my father the day before he died. By that time I had been in prison for almost seven years. After his fifth heart attack, my father was about ready to call it quits. Two days earlier, a general amnesty had been announced and he knew that on the next day, if he were still alive, he would see me.

"I've held on this long, but I won't be able to hold on until tomorrow," he told his childhood friend.

Uncle Paul told me later that under the dying man's pillow he had found a pile of petitions for my pardon, all returned by Kadar's secretariat with the notation, "To Be Addressed to the Magistracy". Marosan and Ronai, who had been my father's comrades in the Social Democratic Party for forty years and who now occupied important posts in the Kadar regime, had refused to see him.

Popradi, the old champion of social democracy at the great steel works, ended up by committing suicide, triggered not by the loss of his ideals — those were gone the moment of his imprisonment — but by the death of his only daughter in a car accident.)

After that meeting on the tram, my wife and I spent night after sleepless night in discussion. The subject: faith in the movement, in the leadership, in the Soviet Union. It had required this meeting with Paul, martyr of modern Hungary, for me to ask myself whether this faith of mine wasn't really blindness.

Little by little, my eyes started to open to reality. I made a pilgrimage to my home town. I wanted to see old friends and see the mountains again. I arrived at the factory, as I had so many times in the past, before 6:00 a.m. and stood in front of the main entrance. I was intoxicated by the familiar smell of sulphur. The small café across the street was doing a roaring business as always. I wanted a drink so I joined the crowd. All of a sudden, as when the teacher shows up in the midst of a bunch of chattering pupils or when the sparrowhawk appears above the trees in the forest, there was a total silence. It was because I was in uniform.

I ordered a brandy. Everybody else ordered the same thing. A strained conversation began, the sole topic being soccer news. After five minutes, I was up to date on all the details of the local championship.

I found the intellectual guide of my youth, Bela Banhegyi, bent over his lathe as I had always found him in the past.

"Bela."

He straightened up; I saw that he was white at the temples.

"Bela, how are you?"

He mumbled something. Around us, everybody was silent. The only sound was the droning of the machines.

"Let's go outside."

We went out. In the yard, locomotives hissed as they passed. The same locomotives, the same hissing, as when I earned my living here. I had tears in my eyes. We walked along the rails, arm in arm.

"Sandor, we've really screwed up. Everybody hates us. The right-wingers, the ones who wanted Germany to win the war, are laughing their heads off to see the leftists scratching each other's eyes out."

"Everybody isn't on the right."

"The others, what do you expect them to admire? You remember everything we promised ourselves: we would destroy capitalism and boot the supervisors' asses outside and do away with the whole wage system. Terrific. Before, we had one supervisor for a thousand turners; now we've got one for ten. Before, you knew them, you could talk to them; now, he's standing behind you, watch in his hand, party directives in his pocket, no discussion allowed, march or die. If you open your mouth, you'll be carted off to jail the next day. That's why the guys shut up when they see your uniform."

"But really, Bela, you know very well that the working class has the power and that all these complaints against that power are little things that will pass, like childhood illnesses."

"Sandor, I know all about brainwashing. I taught Marxism for fifteen years. Here, the class struggle is meaningless. We have no barons and princes here. It's genuine proletarians who are sent away, simply because they're sick of being hungry. Or because they dare to get in a dig against the Russians who, in every corner of the factory, swipe what we produce the same as they swipe food from the agricultural depots."

He looked at me. "I can see by the scowl on your face that Colonel Kopacsi is saying to himself, 'This Comrade Banhegyi has turned into a right-winger.' God Almighty, do you really think that a worker, a Marxist all his life, with two Nazi bullets in his lungs, all of a sudden turns into a right-winger?"

"I didn't say anything."

"That doesn't mean you weren't thinking it. We've known each other a long time. Listen to me, Sandor. You and I have done some incredibly dangerous things together. I'm the one who's here. I'm the one who sees. If things continue like this, cops or no cops,

Russian Army or no Russian Army, it's going to degenerate into a massacre. Our fellow-workers are going to pound us into pulp."

His words recalled Khrushchev's warning to Rakosi: "If this continues, your people will grab their pitchforks and pitch you out of the country."

It's not always easy to be a police chief, a dignitary of the Communist Party; it's not easy to give a valid answer to old friends like Bela and Uncle Paul.

Imre Nagy and Janos Kadar

Comrade Rakosi was not eager to see the dungeons opened. By virtue of his position as first secretary of the Communist Party, he was still the most powerful man in Hungary. Surrounded by his longtime staff at party headquarters on Akademia Street, Rakosi did what he could to temper Imre Nagy's reformist zeal, principally in the matter of rehabilitating those who had been condemned under his regime. He appointed Prosecutor General Alapi, the man responsible for having condemned Rajk, Kadar, and hundreds of other innocent people, to ensure that the new liberalization proceeded as slowly as possible. The watchword was: "Every prisoner isn't innocent. Hungary was Hitler's last satellite. We have to take it easy and look at each case one by one."

Meanwhile, in Parliament, Nagy hadn't managed to surround himself with a good team. He knew full well that too many political prisoners remained behind bars. But he had to push a thousand things at once, from industrial reorganization to a new system for paying farmers. During this time, he received telegram after telegram from the British Labour Party demanding news of imprisoned social democrats and listened to the rebukes of the families of the disappeared.

On his own authority, he had some of them released, including Anna Kethly, the *grande dame* of the Hungarian social democratic movement. She had been thrown in prison four years earlier, in 1948, when the Communist and Social Democratic parties were unified, a step she had opposed.

Rakosi complained bitterly to anyone who wanted to listen. "Imre Nagy is playing with fire. The Kremlin didn't make him prime minister so that he would throw himself at the feet of the Labour Party, the valet of imperialism. It's fine with me if this bitch of an English spy gets out, but she'll never be rehabilitated. Let Nagy sign her pardon if it makes him happy."

In May 1954, the two Hungarian leaders travelled to Moscow for a meeting requested by Rakosi. He wanted an end to the disputes with Nagy and the Kremlin's blessing for him to take back his monopoly on the leadership of the party.

According to my informant, who was present as a translator, things went very badly for Rakosi. Khrushchev gave him a violent dressing down.

"Innocent people are still rotting in your jails and it's your fault, Rakosi. You're not taking affairs in hand. It's as if you were afraid to face your victims outside of prison."

"I'm doing the best I can, Comrade Khrushchev. My nerves are shot."

"Your nerves? You think this is a question of nerves? That's not what it's about, Comrade Rakosi. A person is always responsible for his acts, that's what it's about."

Khrushchev turned to his Soviet peers to explain what was going on in Hungary. "Rakosi is personally responsible for the unjust trials in Budapest. Now he's keeping his victims in prison. He should have thought about what he was doing before he did it. It's not acceptable to suspect people without grounds and to heap disgrace on innocent people."

Rakosi could have responded, if he had dared, that he was only following the example of the Moscow trials and that Comrade Stalin had sent him General Bielkin to ensure the success of prosecutions aimed at compromising Stalin's enemy, Tito. But that would have been a wasted effort. The Kremlin's new masters had already closed the matter.

Khrushchev turned to Nagy: "You are right to speed up the rehabilitations. But you have to be careful not to destroy the people's respect for the party and for Comrade Rakosi. We'll stand up for you, Rakosi, but on one condition: that you stop trying to sabotage change and that you end your silence on past errors and crimes."

At the end of May, the Hungarian Communist Party held its third congress. I was there as a delegate along with Laszlo Piros, the new Minister of the Interior. The congress ratified Imre Nagy's policies, but Rakosi's speech, an interminable panegyric on his own past reign, contained not a trace of self-criticism.

Then a strange thing took place. The president of the tribunal that had condemned Rajk committed suicide. As police chief, I saw pictures of the corpse slumped on the stove, the gas pipe near his mouth. The AVO put out the story — which fooled no one — that "by mistake, the magistrate took an overdose of medicine". At the same time a renowned and honest jurist named Kalman Czako was appointed public prosecutor. Czako and I had gotten to know each other at political meetings and had become friends.

I thought to myself that things were going to change, although when and how still remained in doubt. I greatly admired Nagy and his policies, though I still felt some loyalty to Rakosi. I hoped that these two statesmen would be able to work together for the good of Hungary. But it wasn't to be.

On a foggy morning in November 1954, Janos Kadar, Hungary's leader today, walked out of prison. All of his front teeth had been broken, he was covered in bruises and lacerations, and, it was said, his sanity had suffered while in prison.

A few weeks later, I was attending a routine meeting of neighbourhood inspectors at police headquarters. As at all such meetings, the speaker had to repeat, to the boredom of his audience, the usual denunciations of Kadar, Rajk, and the other party leaders who had spent the war in Hungary instead of Moscow. The official line was that these men had been stooges of the former regime. We had been repeating the same litany for five years and we knew each turn of phrase by heart.

I noticed my deputy gesticulating wildly at the other end of the room. I went over and we spoke in whispers.

"What's come over you?"

"Comrade Colonel, have you read this?" He handed me the party newspaper, *Szabad Nep (Free People)*.

"Of course. The moment I got up this morning."

"And you didn't notice anything?"

I began to lose my self-confidence. Had I missed a headline on page one announcing a nuclear war between the United States and the Soviet Union? My deputy opened the newspaper to the second-last page and showed me an item in the sports section: "Last night, the members of the Chess Society warmly greeted their guest,

Comrade Janos Kadar, a member of the party organization for the thirteenth district, who attended the meeting to engage in an exchange of views with the chess enthusiasts."

This was the regime's way of announcing Kadar's release from prison. It was big news in a small article. The lieutenant-general who was speaking was still going on about the misdeeds of the traitor. My deputy advised me to warn or interrupt him.

"Interrupt a lieutenant-general? Are you kidding?"

Fortunately, nobody in the room seemed to have read the item. At the end of the speech, everybody applauded enthusiastically as usual.

When I showed him the newspaper item, the lieutenant-general's reaction was simple: "Well, which is it? Janos the Shit or Comrade Janos Kadar?"

We dove into our cars and sped, not to the Ministry of the Interior where Piros, a former AVO chief, would undoubtedly tell us nothing, but to the office of the party's executive committee for Budapest. The place was boiling over with excitement.

"Kopacsi, have you heard that Colonel Oszko [a police official locked up for Titoism] has been released?"

"And they say Colonel Matyas [a former police officer] is also back in the land of the living."

Many other names of long-lost friends circulated in the offices and corridors. A series of "Spaniards" (former combatants in the Spanish Civil War, associated with Rajk), including several policemen, had been liberated. So had Major Gyenes-Dienes, a historian and the most respected professor at the police academy. Certain so-called right-wing social democrats were also released.

"Anna Kethly is out but not rehabilitated, only pardoned."

A subtle distinction.

As for Szakasits and Marosan, the two "left-wing" social democrat leaders and promoters of the unification of the Social Democratic and Communist parties, they would continue to languish in jail for two more years, as Rakosi wished.

I was particularly moved to learn that several of my comrades from the northern Resistance had been cleared. I met them shortly afterwards, at a reunion of Resistance fighters. Emaciated and in tatters, they shyly hugged the walls. But gradually, the embarrassment disappeared. Seeing so many old comrades, the martyrs opened up and forgot the agreement they had been required to sign before being released, an agreement in which they promised not to speak of what had happened in prison on pain of new charges. They talked, and it is hard to describe the atmosphere in which we listened to their revelations.

Admiral Horthy's henchmen had nothing on the methods used by our comrades of the AVO against these innocents. B, a Resistance organizer in the north and then a police supervisor in his native village, had been arrested with his wife. For weeks, they had been savagely beaten, the one in the presence of the other. Half crippled, they finally "admitted belonging to a West German spy network" (neither had ever met a West German). They were sentenced to life in prison. Their children were renamed and concealed in state children's homes; after they were freed it took them months to track the children down.

R, a photographer, whose book of photographs of Soviet Russia was the first to appear in the West, was declared a "French spy". All his teeth were broken during the investigation. (He had to pass up our modest banquet because he was able to eat nothing but pap.) He opened his heart to us: "The worst of it was the daily humiliation. Once a day, the guard took us to the latrine. Naturally, there was no paper or water to clean oneself. The examining judge knew about this state of affairs but, instead of correcting it, during the interrogations, he sniffed at us with disgust. 'You stink like an animal.' Being compared to an animal doesn't increase a prisoner's resistance."

Comrade S's wife had been parachuted with her husband (then her fiancé) into the Carpathian Mountains by the Soviets and after the war had become a top official in an important ministry. She was a charming and beautiful woman and we were proud to have her with us in the Resistance. We thought that she had died during the purges. Her story made us shudder.

"They beat my husband to death in front of me. I was accused of being the mistress of Tito's Minister of Foreign Affairs. After my husband's death, I didn't care about anything. They had sentenced me to death. Every morning for three months I expected to be executed. All the while, I was fed nothing but porridge and bread."

This woman, who had been so beautiful, had developed terrible stomach ulcers. She had lost forty pounds and when she bent close to me I could smell her poisonous breath.

How could I forget such stories? How could I stomach the fact that as a colonel and police chief I had been kept in ignorance?

In addition to the once-prominent individuals who won their freedom, tens of thousands of other innocents, mostly simple people whose crime had been to swipe a tool or a few pounds of grain "from the community", spilled out of the AVO's prisons and camps. Under Rakosi's terror, a bar glass slipped into a pocket had been good for one or two years of detention. For a farmer, just being on the list of kulaks (former owners of animals, agricultural machines, or more than five hectares of land) was sufficient cause for indefinite detention in a labour camp.

Several AVO officers known for their cruelty were expelled from the corps and placed in the army or in some anonymous part of the administration. The AVO chief, General Gabor Peter, was already in prison, Rakosi having sacrificed him several months earlier as a "Zionist".

Because the police force belonged to the Ministry of the Interior, our top officers were also summoned before the Politburo. Rakosi, together with the magistrates (whose verdicts were always decided in advance by the Politburo) informed us that everything had been our fault.

"Why didn't you inform us in time that the secular arm was abusing the labouring classes?"

Comrade Rakosi used the phrase "the secular arm" several times. I didn't even know what it meant. What I knew very well, in contrast, was how many times we had trembled in fear before the same body for "non-accomplishment of planning as regards repression".

The AVO treated us, the "ordinary police", with contempt. The truth was as Zoltan Dohany, "my" little AVO commander at police headquarters, had said: an AVO non-commissioned officer carried more weight than any police officer, no matter how high-ranking. In the early fifties, I had to consult General Gabor Peter about a request for information from the Chicago police who were looking for background on a criminal of Hungarian origin. His reaction was brutal.

"Colonel Kopacsi, you're not going to do any research for the imperialists or respond to any requests. Send us the telegram now. You're not even competent to read it."

We got the same treatment for a simple administrative step — the transfer, also during the early fifties, of part of the Kistarcsa internment camp to the authority of the AVO. Nobody in the police was informed in advance of the decision. One fine morning, the AVO troops surrounded the camp. With their submachine guns, they signalled to the police officers perched on the watchtowers to clear out on the double. Our men were literally thrown out of the camp.

The camp buildings were taken under the threat of arms as in a commando operation. Our protests to the minister were rebuffed in no uncertain terms.

"You complain about the AVO, the iron fist of the working class? Without them, this country would be a shambles."

Better than any analysis, two brief portraits will reveal the spirit that reigned at the AVO. We've already met "my" AVO officer, Zoltan Dohany. Now let's meet two others, Colonel Bela Balazsi and Lieutenant-Colonel Lombos. Balazsi was part of the brigade that arrested and tortured Laszlo Rajk and Janos Kadar. He also was on the team that got rid of Rajk's corpse.

Nicknamed "Reki", which is Hungarian for "hoarse", Balazsi was a worker from Budapest with the thickset physique of a butcher. In the Resistance, he had proved himself a courageous patriot. At the time of the German invasion, he slit his own throat because he feared that the Gestapo might capture him and that under torture he would give away his comrades. He recovered, but his vocal cords were permanently damaged, resulting in the voice that earned him his nickname.

Reki was a true fanatic. He believed totally in his victims' guilt and viewed the rehabilitations as a political farce. When a plan was announced to hold a state funeral for Rajk, he destroyed all the documents pertaining to the site where Rajk was buried. The corpse was finally recovered twenty kilometres from Budapest, thanks to the help of another member of the burial team. In 1956, Reki was temporarily shunted out of the AVO, but thanks to his close relations with the Soviet counsellors, he returned a year later with the idea of dragging Kadar (at that time already in power) into a fatal trial with Imre Nagy.

When I was arrested, he told my wife he would beat me up in my cell before my trial. Toward the end of the sixties, Kadar finally succeeded in putting him on the sidelines, this time completely, without, as in so many similar cases, bestowing on him a well-paid administrative job. Reki, still a true fanatic, again tried to kill himself with a knife and again failed. During the seventies, I ran into him in Budapest's central market. He still had a knife in his hand, but this time it was for cutting the watermelons he was selling with his new wife, a fat stallholder, the daughter of rich peasants. The watermelon juice trickled down the killer's powerful forearms.

Lieutenant-Colonel Lajos Lombos, in contrast, was a crafty character. A small, swarthy man, he had feigned madness to avoid the camps where able-bodied Jewish males had had to do forced labour for the Axis war effort. (In Hungary, large-scale deportations of Jews to concentration camps did not take place until 1944.) Because he had been one of the chief torturers in the Rajk affair, he was transferred out of the AVO after 1953, first to the fire department, then to the police as assistant director of criminal affairs.

One day, toward the end of the insurrection of 1956, my office door opened. Lombos entered, a mad look in his eyes.

"What's wrong?" I asked.

"I can't tell you. I only know that you must arrest me, and quick."

He burst into tears. I sat him down and gave him a glass of water.

"Has someone threatened you? Has someone attacked you?"

"Not at all. But a voice inside me tells me I must go to prison."

He claimed that an old man with a long moustache was within him and never stopped talking. Knowing his history, I figured that fear of the insurrection had prompted him to do his madness number again.

"My man, you're not going to prison, you're not going anywhere. Stay in your office or choose another one with a couch to lie on and you can wait out the insurrection there. You've got to get rid of these macabre ideas. No matter what happens, there'll always be a job for you."

Several months later, this job was found. I was walking down a corridor — a prisoner, between two guards — at AVO headquarters, and Lombos was coming in the other direction, his arms full of dossiers.

A glimmer of sadness appeared in his eyes. He said nothing, but as he passed it seemed to me that he tried to make a small sign of encouragement with his head.

Most of the other AVO officers to whom I had given asylum when they were in danger during the insurrection spoke at great length against me during the investigation and subsequent trial of my case. But Lombos was true to himself. He told the investigating magistrate that a nervous breakdown had prevented him from forming a judgement about my attitude, but that he thought I had been kind to him.

About 1970, Lombos was dismissed from the AVO and appointed director of the secretariat of the medical faculty at the university. When we met one day on a tram, he threw his arms tearfully around my neck, as overwrought as ever.

■ Tito's Revenge

In January 1955, the new Hungarian police force that had been created after the war was preparing to celebrate its tenth anniversary. As police chief of Budapest, it was my job to organize the banquet. I had invitations sent to the Minister of the Interior, the under-secretaries, the Soviet counsellors, and the top leaders of the armed forces and the AVO. One day on impulse I called in my private secretary, a young police officer who was a product of the party school.

"Are you sure you sent invitations to all our dignitaries?"

"Yes, I think so, Comrade Kopacsi."

"Including all the former ministers of the interior?"

He showed me a protocol list.

"Are you sure we haven't had any other ministers? Could you list them all?"

"There was Rajk. And Zold. But they're dead."

"Well, you've forgotten one. Someone who was on the list of traitors but who wasn't a traitor. Comrade Janos Kadar, Minister of the Interior in 1949, and currently first secretary of the executive committee of the thirteenth district."

The young secretary's jaw dropped. "You really want to invite him?"

"Not only invite him but seat him at the head table next to the other ministers. Comrade Kadar has been rehabilitated and reintegrated into the party leadership and he must be given his due."

My secretary swallowed hard. "At your service, Comrade Colonel."

At the time, Kadar was forty years old. Despite his suffering in prison, he radiated strength. If Imre Nagy was "a pure product of the peasantry", Janos Kadar was visibly a product of the working class. Obviously, Kadar wasn't a worker any more than Nagy was a peasant; both had spent most of their adult lives in the top ranks of the Communist Party, Nagy in the Soviet Union, Kadar in Budapest, at the head of the then illegal party organization. But both still bore the marks of their origin.

I received Kadar at the entrance to the banquet hall and led him to his place on the dais, next to Piros, the current Minister of the Interior. The two men shook hands.

"How are you, Comrade Kadar?"

"Better, thank you, Comrade Piros, much better."

They exchanged smiles. Those were the only words and the only smiles they exchanged all evening long. But Kadar didn't spend the ceremony in silence. My former minister, Arpad Hazi, despite his reputation as a hard-line Stalinist, never stopped talking to Kadar, whom he knew well from the days when the Communist Party was illegal.

What did they say to each other? The next day, Hazi phoned me. "You know, Kopacsi, it's truly horrible what we did to that man. His so-called crime was no worse than yours or mine. The people in charge of security were truly monsters or idiots to go after comrades like him."

That wasn't Piros's viewpoint. He called me to his office where he received me in the company of his staff of senior AVO officers.

"What got into you to invite Kadar? Who suggested that you do that?"

"No one, Comrade Minister. Comrade Kadar has been rehabilitated, so his name is once more on our protocol list."

One of the AVO officers laughed bitterly. "Janos the Shit on the protocol list. He was the most miserable prisoner we had."

The minister called him to order and turned to me: "Comrade Kopacsi, you must understand one thing. Yes, Janos Kadar has been rehabilitated. Yes, the party wanted to give him a post. That doesn't mean that he becomes what he was in the past. The rehabilitations now underway don't mean that the comrades who were imprisoned were all knights in shining armour. They mean that we want to let bygones be bygones and start with a clean slate as Comrade Rakosi has said. I propose to give a verbal reprimand to the chief for his, let us say... ill-considered... initiative."

On my arrival one morning at my office about six months after the anniversary dinner, I found the following message: "Urgent: Call Kobanya brewery."

With beer I had nothing to do. I was a wine drinker. But as Kobanya was in the tenth district, my fiefdom as deputy, I called the manager.

"This is Kopacsi. You need me?"

At the other end of the line, a familiar voice responded, "Yes, Comrade Deputy, urgently. We would like to know if you have decided to change your mind on the subject of your preferred beverage?"

It was Czako, the public prosecutor.

"Czako, what are you doing at a brewery?"

"I'm the new manager. Hurry up if you want to sample some of our best products."

I knew perfectly well that it wasn't an invitation to down a few beers but to hear some news. I hurried over to the brewery.

"What does this mean?" I asked Czako.

"The day before yesterday, I was called to Central Committee headquarters. Lajos Acs, who is on the Politburo, asked me to sit down and said: 'Comrade Czako, do you know the percentage of alcohol in Giraffe beer?' I said I wasn't prepared for the question but that it must be between fifteen and eighteen. Why? Because, Comrade Czako, the manager of the Kobanya brewery must be able to answer such a question without hesitation. Here is your dismissal as public prosecutor and your appointment as manager."

"Congratulations, old pal. This job means a lot less hassle for you."

"Yes, but that's not all. I was given to understand that things are going to go backwards in the courts. Everything is going to be the way it was."

"Are you kidding?"

"And not only in our field, but everywhere. The emphasis on consumption is over, heavy industry is top priority again. The collective farm is mandatory again."

"Imre Nagy?"

"In a few days, he will be kicked out as prime minister and maybe even out of the party."

Czako told me that Rakosi had just returned from a long "sick leave" in the Soviet Union, happy and full of news. Were we about to witness yet another radical change of direction by the Supreme Soviet? Everything pointed to it.

In response to the decisions of the Western powers in favour of rearming West Germany, the Kremlin had decided to create the military alliance known as the Warsaw Pact. The Soviet Army was said to be readying its Plan X, a surprise attack on West Germany followed by the occupation of Europe all the way to the Atlantic Ocean. It was the height of the cold war and many people thought a third world war inevitable.

"You understand, in such a situation, there's no more fooling around with liberalism, they're not about to install reform regimes behind the front."

I couldn't believe in these rumours of war. But my friend was right in what he said about internal affairs in Hungary.

Rakosi was on the way up again. He announced that the party was in danger because of "right deviationism", which meant the policies of Imre Nagy. He wanted the Prime Minister out, but Nagy put up a fight and asked the Kremlin to arbitrate. On January 7, 1955, Nagy travelled to Moscow with Rakosi once more, only to return repudiated by the same Soviet leaders who had directed him eighteen months earlier to undertake reforms.

Rakosi excluded him from the Politburo and the Central Committee and fired him as prime minister. He also took away his right to teach at the university where he had a post lecturing in agrarian science, thus depriving him of his livelihood. The dignity with which Nagy bore this treatment only served to enhance his reputation and increase his popularity.

Laid low by a heart attack, deprived of any income, Nagy was confined to the second floor of his house. Suslov, a member of the Soviet Politburo, came to see him at his bedside.

"Comrade Nagy — note that I still call you 'comrade' — you need only admit your errors and you will be quickly reinstated."

"Comrade Suslov, thank you for calling me 'comrade', but after forty years of struggle in the workers' movement I can't renounce the last eighteen months. I have let innocent people out of prison, authorized farmers to work individually, and worked to increase consumer goods — a series of reforms that you suggested I make, that I agreed with, and that were all ratified by the Central Committee. It's unthinkable for me to disown them now."

"That's a shame. For you."

A few months later, Nagy was expelled from the Communist Party. But it wasn't long before the pendulum would once again swing back in his direction.

Between the night of February 24, 1956, and the dawn of February 25, something happened in the meeting chamber of the Grand Palace of the Kremlin that would turn the Communist world topsy-turvy. It was the pronouncement of Khrushchev's famous "secret report".

Only about 1,600 delegates were present and they were sworn to secrecy, but it took only a few days before we found out what Khrushchev had said. He had denounced Stalin as an "ignorant and bloody monarch" responsible for the gulags, the massacres of innocent people, and the liquidation of millions of peasants.

The Stalinist leaders of eastern Europe tottered under the shock of these revelations. Bierut, the Polish chief of state, gave up the ghost on the spot. The Cominform, the body that had pronounced the expulsion of Tito from the Communist International, was dissolved. Tito was rehabilitated. In Hungary, Rajk's widow, Julia, emerged from hiding and demanded the rehabilitation of her husband. In newly founded clubs, especially the Petofi Circle, thousands of comrades demanded Rakosi's resignation, the rehabilitation of martyrs, and the return of Imre Nagy to power.

I asked Iemelianov his opinion of the situation.

"Old man not dead," he responded in typical lapidary fashion.

"You mean Rakosi?"

The Soviet officer smiled. He explained that, in the language of Comrade Mao, the "old man" meant the past; it lived still and had to be killed.

"But it's not up to us officers to do it," he added seriously. "We have taken an oath of loyalty to our leaders; politics is the politicians' affair."

I found his reasoning a bit strange. We were officers, yes, but weren't we also Communists? We had sworn allegiance to our leaders, but hadn't we also promised in our youth to be Communists and to work in every circumstance for the good of all the people?

It was clear that Rakosi, the Hungarian Stalin, no longer belonged at the head of the nation. Worse, he himself didn't realize it.

On March 27 of the same year, at the request of the Minister of the Interior and the Budapest party committee, I organized a meeting of the Communist Party members on the Budapest police force. Some 1,200 people crowded into the police school on Boszormeny Avenue. Like all the speakers, I went to the podium clutching speech notes prepared for me by my superiors. But this time, I forgot to read them.

"Comrades, do you know what the French word 'renaissance' means? It means 'rebirth'. And a renaissance is what our party needs. It must renew itself because that is the only way it can regain the people's confidence — which we have lost. Yes, comrades, lost."

The audience was listening intently. For once, they weren't being fed the never-ending litanies to the glory of the party. What I was about to say would astonish them even more.

"Now, comrades, it's necessary to discuss the problem of our first secretary, Comrade Rakosi."

I sensed movement in the room. The ministry representative cast a worried look in my direction. Rakosi's name was never mentioned except to praise it. Imre Mezo, the party committee delegate for the capital, stifled a smile. I understood that he supported me in what he sensed I was going to say.

"My friends, Comrade Rakosi has made mistakes. And we know that when a Communist makes mistakes, he must recognize his mistakes. Yet this Comrade Rakosi has refused to do. We say to him: Comrade Rakosi, admit your errors, it may be your last chance to do so. Self-criticism will not diminish you; instead it will make you greater. It is the only way to regain the confidence of the party and of the people."

A thunder of applause greeted these words. It seemed every cop in the room wanted to have his say. These people, their party manuals in their pockets, were the sons of peasants from whom the regime had taken the last handful of seeds, and the sons of workers or former workingmen themselves, who had known the hardships of being part of a wage-earning class that had borne the brunt of the regime's mismanagement of the economy. There was no doubt that these comrades hungered for a national rebirth.

At the annual state reception to celebrate the liberation, Rakosi greeted the guests at the entrance to the banquet hall. I was with my wife. When it was our turn to enter, Rakosi did not extend his hand and looked away from us. I wasn't particularly concerned but Ibolya was offended.

"What have you done now?"

"I said out loud what everybody else was thinking."

That same morning, the newspapers had published the Soviet government's telegram of good wishes to "the great veteran of the workers' movement, our highly respected Hungarian comrade,

Matthias Rakosi". The telegram was signed by Vorochilov, the president of the Soviet Union.

This was undoubtedly a last-minute salvage attempt by Rakosi, his team, and the few friends they still had at the Kremlin. But it was too late. The old leader was already condemned by the majority of his party, not to mention the public at large.

His principal and most dangerous enemy was Josep Broz Tito. The Yugoslav leader wanted the head of the Hungarian dictator who had mounted the false trials of Rajk and Kadar in which everybody had been "agent and spy for Tito's clique". In May 1956, this former "running dog of imperialism" was invited to the Soviet Union as one of many unorthodox Communists and social democrats with whom Khrushchev was seeking a *modus vivendi*. Chance had it that a holiday trip to Russia that Ibolya and I had planned and paid for a year earlier coincided with the arrival of Tito, dozens of European Communist and social democratic delegations, and the hundreds of journalists covering the event.

It was the first time that social democrats had been invited to the Soviet Union. The first words spoken by Guy Mollet, the French socialist leader, were later noted with interest in the embassies: "Ladies and gentlemen, or if you wish, comrades...." Could one now be so flip before a Soviet audience?

Our group was following the same itinerary as a group of English trade unionists on a tour of Georgia. Their plane took off before ours, but when it arrived at the airport in Tbilisi, the capital of Georgia, it was ordered to turn back. Despite the perfect weather, our plane received the same order. I asked our interpreter what was going on.

"It's nothing," he replied, embarrassed. "A slight irregularity in traffic."

But one of the journalists from Budapest, a young man attached to police headquarters, gave me a poke with his elbow. "Look below," he said.

In the bright sunshine, the streets of Tbilisi were totally empty, except for some objects that looked from above like little toy tanks but that were actually real tanks. The tanks were giving off flashes of light that made me think of flakes of cotton wool.

"Tell me, Comrade interpreter. What's happening down below?"

"Uh... manoeuvres, Comrade. Those are probably manoeuvres."

They weren't manoeuvres. The next day, reporters from the Hungarian party daily told us that we had witnessed the last phases of the suppression of an armed uprising in the Georgian capital. Several days earlier, some Russian officers had been murdered by a crowd. Army and KGB troops had moved in swiftly to crush the rebellion.

The uprising had nothing to do with the visits by Tito and the Western delegations. We were told that it had been sparked by a new austerity policy in Georgia, which, under the regime of its native son, Stalin, had once been the showcase of the Soviet Union.

Journalists are a gossipy bunch and I couldn't help joining in. We speculated that Khrushchev's change of direction was proving too abrupt in a country with so many nationalities, a country in which, Ibolya observed, it was impossible to find in the stores even a tenth of the merchandise commonly available at home.

While Tito headed south to the Crimea, we contented ourselves with a tour of Leningrad, where Ibolya stood riveted for an hour on the bank of the Neva River at the same spot where the destroyer *Aurora* fired its historic cannon shots in the direction of the Summer Palace, the first shots of the revolution. "Despite everything," she said, "the Revolution was really something, wasn't it?"

Speaking of revolution, on our return to Budapest, we found ourselves in the midst of unusual excitement. My friend and neighbour Joska Szilagyi welcomed us with open arms and a jocular reprimand: "History with a capital H is happening here and you're busy amusing yourselves abroad."

Joska lived near us, in a modest lodging. He was no longer in the armed forces or at Central Committee headquarters on Akademia Street. He had a small job in the state grain and seed enterprise and spent his free time analysing the recent works, available only in manuscript form, of that great Marxist theoretician, Imre Nagy.

"I'd very much like you to drop in tonight. We're going to receive some interesting friends," said Joska with an air of mystery. We accepted. Arriving at Joska's place, we saw other guests we knew, including a young writer, a policeman from Debrecen, and a civil servant from the Ministry of Foreign Trade. I was shocked to see two that we had never met — Imre Nagy and his wife.

"Comrade Nagy. I'm delighted to meet you. Your speech to Parliament in 1953 was truly a revelation for me. My life has changed since then."

"Mine too," replied Nagy with a smile.

"Especially yours. Rakosi destroyed you, and we all watched from the sidelines."

"During your trip, Comrade Kopacsi," said the writer, who had been listening, "the balance has shifted. Rakosi is on the way out."

We learned that at public meetings held by the Petofi Circle, the philosopher George Lukacs and the famous writer Tibor Dery had been openly dissecting the defects of the party leadership. Although the Petofi Circle was an adjunct of the official Young Communists, part of its leadership backed the Nagy reforms. The *Literary Journal,* the publication of the Hungarian Writers' Union, was publishing virulent attacks on the crimes committed by the Rakosi regime. The opposition had become powerful within the party. As a result, the dictator was losing his head and was readying some old-style repression, complete with mass arrests, newspaper and theatre closings. He had already suspended certain clubs, including the famous Petofi Circle.

Imre Nagy smiled. "Do you think we could talk of something else? I'd love to know how the beautiful Mrs. Kopacsi enjoyed the Soviet Union."

"Moscow not at all. Kiev, yes. Leningrad, a terrific city."

"That's true," said Nagy. "Leningrad is Europe."

Nagy and his wife smiled as Ibolya described a scene we had encountered in the streets of Kiev: people seated on the sidewalk in front of a store in the process of trying on and exchanging among themselves pairs of shoes they had just bought. In the face of interminable line-ups, the store required its customers to choose their shoes and take them away without trying them on.

Nagy took off his pince-nez, wiped them, and remarked to his wife, "You see, unfortunately, things haven't much changed since we lived there...and those were the hardest years of the war."

To my great surprise, Nagy said he planned to travel to the Soviet Union. Ambassador Andropov (Ibolya couldn't repress an exclamation of "Oh, that one!") had called him in for a friendly conversation. According to Andropov, Nagy's problems with Rakosi and his exclusion from power hadn't in any way changed the Kremlin's esteem for him. The Soviet leaders wanted an exchange of ideas with Nagy. At the same time, there was interest in the publication of a Russian edition of his writings during his time "in the desert".

"But, Ibolya, what did you have to say about Andropov?" someone asked.

"That he was an excellent dancer. And a real gentleman to boot." Ibolya told the story of her evening with Andropov, and of how, the day after, Colonel Petofi ("You know, these counsellors call themselves anything at all but some of them have good manners, too"), on a mission from Andropov, asked Ibolya to go home ("Can you believe it, in the middle of the day!"), where he brought her a basket of white roses, the like of which she had "never seen in my life". That wasn't surprising: the daughter of a workingman and wife of a metalworker didn't often have occasion to enjoy white roses. What refinement! What luxury!

Nagy smiled. "Russia is an immense Byzantine empire where the manners of the former great landlords are strangely mixed with revolutionary traditions. Sometimes also with barbarism. You have to have lived there to understand it and love it."

In mid-July, I received an urgent phone call from some of the members of the party organization for Budapest. I was to get down to their headquarters on Koztarsasag Square on the double. Not a word of explanation and an exceedingly abrupt tone. A sudden death? The Third World War? I asked George to step on it and to hell with the speed limit.

"What's up?" I asked, charging breathlessly into the party office.

"What's up is that the party needs your famous *underground*."

"For what?"

I was informed that several old comrades, including Imre Nagy, were "in danger", that they needed a safe house for several days or maybe weeks, "until the clouds disperse".

"What clouds?"

The comrades exchanged glances. Swearing me to secrecy, they said that Rakosi was getting ready to strike. He had called the Central Committee to ratify a list of four hundred opponents to be arrested. The first name on the list was Imre Nagy, followed by a whole series of writers, intellectuals, and senior civil servants. Included were some, such as Janos Kadar and Julia Rajk, who had only recently escaped the AVO's dungeons.

I suspected a hoax. People knew that I was sympathetic to Nagy; was someone trying to trap me into an act of disloyalty to the current regime? Nevertheless, very discreetly, I took the necessary steps. A former underground fighter, now a doctor, was running a nursing home in a forested area up north. An isolated house could be made available. My friend asked few questions. He readily agreed to my request that he accommodate a small group of undercover agents that I would send in advance. Meanwhile, Imre Mezo, a member of the Budapest party committee, warned the Kremlin of what Rakosi was planning.

The Central Committee of the Hungarian party was summoned to meet on July 17. Rakosi, a pile of documents in his hand, began to explain why he proposed to arrest four hundred opponents of his regime. At that moment, the door opened and Comrade Mikoyan of the Soviet Politburo entered in the company of his bodyguards and his interpreter.

Silence. Some members of the audience stood up.

"Continue," said Mikoyan. "Make your report, Comrade Rakosi."

Rakosi proceeded to denounce "the open opposition against the party and the popular democracy organized by Imre Nagy". He spoke of the Petofi Circle. The interpreter translated. Mikoyan raised his hand.

"Excuse me, Comrade Rakosi, you say the Petofi Circle [which had been suspended two weeks earlier] is made up of enemies of the people and counter-revolutionaries. But from what we've heard the cry 'Long live the party' was heard at every meeting and everybody sang the Internationale at the end of each meeting. If counter-revolutionaries love that song, it's the first I've heard of it."

Large drops of sweat rolled down Rakosi's face.

"Nevertheless, Comrade Mikoyan, what I am saying is true."

He asked that the meeting be adjourned and left, accompanied by the Soviets.

Several minutes later, Mikoyan gave him a message from Khrushchev: "In view of the measures being planned by Comrade Rakosi, he is advised to resign from all his positions in the Hungarian party and leave the country."

In a state of shock, Rakosi picked up the red telephone that connected him to the Kremlin.

"Comrade Khrushchev, I have difficulty believing my ears. . . ."

"It would be in your interest to believe them."

The next day, Rakosi left for Moscow, taking all his belongings with him. For the newspapers, he left a communiqué saying that his departure was necessitated by high blood pressure. For the country, he left a replacement who was hardly any better than he was: Erno Gero, his longtime right arm, the former political commissar of the Soviet secret police in Spain and the champion of bizarre industrial plans that in ten years had ruined the Hungarian people.

After the dictator had slunk out of the country, the opposition within the party obtained the full rehabilitation of the most notable of Rakosi's victims, principally Laszlo Rajk. After long and difficult research, his remains were found, miraculously intact, in a wood alongside the national highway leading from Budapest to Lake Balaton. The quicklime that was supposed to have destroyed the body had preserved it instead. The burial was scheduled for October 6, 1956. The party opposition and Rajk's widow insisted on a solemn public ceremony. Attendance would be large.

This was dangerous. The general public didn't care much about the settling of accounts within the party, but poor management of the economy and shortages of goods had pushed them to the end of their tether. This was the first time the criminal incompetence of the regime was to be exposed publicly and it was feared that Rajk's funeral would degenerate into a riot. As police chief of Budapest and as a Communist, I wanted to ensure that the ceremony unfolded without incident. The leaders of the opposition assured me of their co-operation. There would be no inflammatory language, nothing that might arouse the passions of the crowd.

The morning of the ceremony, the first secretary of the Budapest party organization, a notorious Stalinist, phoned me in a panic.

"Kopacsi, what's to become of us?"

He was in a pitiful state, his voice trembling.

"What are you afraid of, Comrade?"

"A riot."

"It's going to be okay, Comrade. You've nothing to fear."

Over the phone, I heard a sigh of relief. "May God hear you, Kopacsi."

This time, God heard me. A throng of two hundred thousand people paraded in front of the funeral chapel, but there was no riot. The guard of honour changed every five minutes. I took part myself as a representative of the Partisans' Union.

When it was the turn of the members of Rakosi's Politburo, a fierce wind started to howl. Everyone noticed the phenomenon. A supernatural production for a Shakespearean drama full of spilled blood and treachery.

From Demonstration to Riot

Autumn comes early in central Europe. In Budapest, children are in pullovers for the start of school, and by October the rainy season is usually well under way.

But the weather in 1956 was as abnormal as everything else. Tuesday, October 23, dawned hot, yet another radiant day in what had been a memorable Indian summer. My wife, who started work at the Ministry of the Interior at Roosevelt Square at 7:00 a.m., had already left the house. Our nine-year-old daughter, Judith, was getting ready for school, eagerly awaited by Tango the dog and Fifi the cat. These two loyal friends followed her to class every morning and were at the school entrance to greet her every afternoon, to the delight of the other pupils and the great displeasure of her nanny, whom we called "Mammy".

"Sandor, you should forbid Judith to make a spectacle of herself in the street with her troop of animals."

Mammy, who had known me since my adolescence, was very authoritarian. Judith smiled at me imploringly. I adopted a commanding tone.

"Tango! Fifi! Stand at attention."

The two animals looked at me in such a comical way, with an almost human astonishment, that Judith burst out laughing. The wolfhound was a gift from a police station to which he had been turned in as a stray. The cat, imported from my northern homeland, was a descendant of a breed of mousers and the only cat we'd had with the nerve to go after the rats that liked to roam our garden and take shelter in the tool shed.

"Papa, what time will you be home tonight?" asked Judith who for some reason was lingering at home later than usual that morning. "I don't know, six or seven as usual. Why?"

She looked at me with her large black eyes, the same as her mother's, then turned and ran off, followed by Tango and Fifi.

From the neighbouring garden, I could hear children laughing and running. The two children of my neighbour and friend, Joska Szilagyi, had chosen the same moment to depart for school.

Joska was the diminutive by which I called my friend, as he called me Sanyi. Formally, he was Dr. Joseph Szilagyi, the son of a poor farmer from eastern Hungary who had earned his doctorate in law. He had been a Communist since his adolescence and had attained the rank of colonel. After having been my mentor at Central Committee headquarters on Akademia Street and after having written his fatal letter to Rakosi ("Rajk can't possibly be guilty"), he had dropped out of sight, banished to the country. "For me, politics is finished," he had told me in 1949 before quitting Budapest.

On his return to the city, he found a modest job and spent his evenings studying engineering, which he chose because it had no political overtones. (By 1956, when I met up with him again, he was close to completing his engineering degree.) Meanwhile, the old political wounds were reopened. Szilagyi watched his old friends reappear — phantoms emerging from torture chambers, sick, constrained to silence, viewed from all sides with suspicion and doubt. He shouted his indignation to all who would listen.

One night, a man came to visit him. It was Laszlo Foldes, a former partisan, a member of the Central Committee, and one of those in charge of rehabilitation.

"Joska, you were right," he said.

Foldes went on to explain that the party was going to offer reparations to its victims. He asked Szilagyi to be patient. He opened a briefcase full of large banknotes.

"Please accept this in partial compensation for the injustice you have suffered."

Szilagyi's wife, Ella, and their three children stared at the briefcase bulging with money. My God! After three years of bread, lard, and frost-damaged potatoes — the cheapest in the market — their poverty was suddenly at an end. But only momentarily. Before Ella could touch a single banknote, Szilagyi had sent the briefcase flying out the window and Foldes out the door.

Szilagyi lost his little job. It was about then that we struck up our friendship again. He wasn't bitter; he proclaimed himself more of a Communist than ever. For him, now was the time to begin the liberation of Hungary, with a purified party dedicated to democracy. He had seen Kadar several times. He knew that the country needed Kadar at Nagy's side and begged him to take the helm of the reform movement. But Kadar rebuffed him, saying Szilagyi was too much "under the influence of the writers". Kadar was a prudent man.

We'll read later of Szilagyi's fate, of how he would die a hero, executed in secret, heaping scorn on the court. After his execution, Colonel Mihaly Korom brought Ella his clothes. "We'll ensure that you are well provided for," he told her.

"I don't want to be provided for by assassins," she shot back. "I'll raise my three children with my sewing."

"Then let us send you a sewing machine."

"No. From you, nothing!"

Joska's son died of leukemia, shortly after learning what had happened to his father. Ella is half blind after twenty years of sewing, misery, and pain. None of this is borrowed from a novel by Dickens, none of it comes from the nineteenth century. It happened in our time in an industrialized country in Europe.

But to return to October 23, 1956. My second in command was waiting for me impatiently that morning. "The phones are ringing off the hooks. Everyone is looking for you. Comrade Horvath wants you to call the minute you get in."

Horvath was director of the party newspaper and a substitute member of the Politburo. Normally he had nothing to do with the police. When I called him back he was annoyed.

"I've been trying to get you on the ministerial phone since dawn. Why, in the face of so grave a situation, are the police getting their kicks by provoking the crowd?"

I was completely taken aback. What grave situation? What provocations? I knew, as everybody did, that the young people were stirring. The university students had a series of demands that mainly concerned student issues but also touched on wider political ones. In the last few days, they had plastered the streets with tracts advertising a demonstration that afternoon in solidarity with Poland and Gomulka, the reform leader whom the Soviets opposed. That morning, the Minister of the Interior had issued a radio announcement banning the demonstration.

Clearly, a demonstration not organized by the official party leadership was an event. But did it justify calling me "since dawn" and speaking of "police provocation"? I asked Horvath for an explanation. In an offensive tone, he said that members of his staff had reported the presence in the streets of "large mounted police units". For me, the problem with these reports was that I had no mounted police units, large or small.

"Comrade Horvath, I've just returned from holidays. I'll find out what's going on and call you back."

Pocze, deputy minister of Interior, had the same reaction. "Mounted police in the streets? What's this all about?" Suddenly, he laughed. "Shit! The National School of Mounted Police."

There were plans to add mounted constables to my municipal police force, but none of these had yet completed his training. To accustom both students and horses to traffic, the teachers took them on a little excursion every Tuesday morning through the streets of Budapest. Despite the planned demonstration, they were on the streets today as usual. Pocze said he would order them back to the school at a gallop.

"On the same subject, Kopacsi, the minister wants to speak with you urgently. Get over here right away — but not in civilian clothes like last time. They hate that here."

The minister, Piros, was in a nasty mood. This former butcher's assistant, still in his mid-thirties, had for several years been commander-in-chief of the AVO forces guarding the borders before being promoted to minister. He didn't much like me; nor did he share my sympathy for Kadar, my friendship with Joska, or my admiration for Imre Nagy.

"Kopacsi, this is a nice damn mess your friends have arranged for me," he said bluntly.

"Are you speaking of the demo, Comrade Minister? I'm just back from holidays, but from my reports, these are Communist students who are planning to demonstrate."

"You'll tell that to some other comrades."

He opened the door to the conference room. I greeted five undersecretaries and noticed that Iemelianov's habitual seat, on the minister's right, was empty. When I asked Pocze why the Soviet counsellor was absent, he responded in a whisper: "Dismissed, left for Moscow."

At that moment, the minister entered, accompanied by a Russian in civilian dress whom none of us had seen before. He was a crafty-looking little man with blue eyes, blond hair, and an air of self-importance. He reminded me of the German officers who, during the war, had supervised the workshop where we turned out guns for their war effort. The minister introduced us: "Comrades, please meet the new comrade counsellor who has just arrived from Moscow."

We greeted him. He returned the greetings with a cold blink of his eyes. Everybody sat down and the minister began the meeting.

"I invited Comrade Kopacsi, our police chief, to explain his plans for this afternoon. As you all know, early this morning, I forbade the demonstration."

All eyes turned to me. I rose.

"I would like to begin with a question, Comrades. What should we do if, despite the ban, this demonstration goes ahead? According to my information, the students may carry on regardless."

There was silence around the table. The minister gestured impatiently. "You are here, Comrade, precisely to respond to that question."

"Fine. To prevent a demonstration, it's necessary to be properly equipped. Before the war, Horthy's police had billy sticks. We don't. Horthy's police had sabres that you could strike a flat blow with; they were effective, but they rarely killed anybody. We don't have those either. Their mounted police could dominate a crowd without killing people except occasionally by accident. We don't have any mounted police except for those still in training. Our firemen aren't trained, as theirs were, to use their hoses to control a mob. The only weapons at our disposal are dangerous ones: submachine guns and rifles."

"A rifle has a butt, doesn't it?" asked the minister.

"Suppose that rifle-butt blows don't persuade the students to move on? Suppose they resist or even counterattack? That's when the shooting starts. Comrade Minister, *who will take the responsibility for having shot at the crowd and possibly caused dozens of deaths?*"

The "new comrade counsellor" frowned. So did the minister.

"And what do you conclude, Colonel?"

"What I conclude is this. The situation is as tense as it could possibly be. The people want a resolution of the political crisis." At this, the minister and the little Russian both grimaced their displeasure.

"You have been wrong to reduce a political problem to the dimensions of a police matter and I completely condemn your order banning the demonstration. I would like to know if the most senior party officers are up to date on the situation and what their opinion is."

The minister couldn't hide his annoyance. "I informed Comrade Gero. You all know that he's just back from Yugoslavia. The Politburo has been called together and it is deliberating now." (Gero had gone on orders from Khrushchev to patch things up with Tito.)

To everyone's surprise, the Soviet newcomer rose without even requesting to speak. In a characteristic gesture, he pushed back his unruly hair, signalled to his interpreter, and began speaking, gruffly spitting out each syllable.

"The fascists and imperialists send their shock troops into the streets of Budapest and there are still comrades of your armed forces who hesitate to use arms."

The interpreter translated and we listened, jaws agape. He spoke of capitalists disguised as students, of landowners' representatives preparing for battle in the streets, and of the need "to teach a lesson to the fascist underworld". All the aggressive and hackneyed terminology of *Pravda,* the Stalinist cold-war jargon dating back three years. On the sly, the vice-ministers exchanged glances. No, in Hungary in 1956 this style was no longer acceptable. These senior AVO officers were certainly not democrats; they believed in using force if need be. But old-fashioned jargon bothered them. Their signals encouraged me to respond.

"If you'll permit, Comrade Minister? Just a word. Clearly, the comrade counsellor from Moscow hasn't had time to inform himself of the situation in our country. He should know that it is not fascists and other imperialists who are planning this demonstration. These are university students, sons and daughters of peasants and workers, very carefully chosen, the pride of our intelligentsia who demand their rights and want to manifest their sympathy for the Poles."

Red as a tomato, the little civilian spoke quietly with the minister. He had my words translated and flew into a rage. Then the deputy ministers spoke and, one after another, they urged the minister to pass the responsibility for banning the demonstration on to his superiors. The minister picked up the "red phone". In a second, he had First Secretary Gero on the line and he briefly passed on my opinion. Gero asked the minister to hold.

We waited silently. The little Russian stared at me, then bent over his notebook and scribbled a few lines.

Suddenly, we could hear Gero's croaking over the phone. The minister's expression changed, tension giving way to relief and obsequiousness.

"Yes, Comrade Gero, I agree, Comrade Gero, your orders will be executed, Comrade Gero."

The Politburo had decided to lift the ban. The news was immediately announced on the radio. The deputy ministers and myself were asked to visit the various university departments to inform the students of the decision and to urge them to proceed in an orderly fashion.

The new Soviet counsellor rose, gave me a last belligerent look. and turned away. The rest of us hurriedly quit the conference room. The demonstration would begin shortly.

Accompanied by Deputy Minister Fekete, I entered the amphitheatre of the School of Engineering. Crowded into the corridors, seated on the floor, and standing on the rows of seats were several thousand students. One of them, microphone in hand, spoke of the need for change, for the democratization of the party, for leadership worthy of the name. On the rostrum, among seated students and uniformed officers from the military institute, I spotted the large peasant form of my friend Joska bent over some papers.

The speaker noticed the commotion caused by the appearance of the other officers and myself. He continued: "I will profit from the presence of police officers in the room to tell them that the students of Budapest have decided to do without your authorization. The demo will take place anyway. We will shout in the face of the leadership that we want change."

Everybody turned toward us and some of them started to boo. I pushed my way through to Joska.

"Tell them not to get worked up. The ban is lifted."

"Brilliant idea," he said sarcastically.

"We would like to announce it ourselves."

Deputy Minister Fekete climbed to the rostrum and, amid deathly silence, repeated the Politburo's orders word for word. ("The ban is lifted, but the students, mindful of the cause of socialism, are begged to expel all agitators from their ranks," etc.) He finished with these words: "The party organization of the Ministry of the Interior, of which I am secretary, declares itself entirely in agreement with the students' noble determination for renewal. It has asked me to offer its message of solidarity to you."

The ovation exploded like a bomb. While it continued, I was suddenly seized with foreboding. I saw again the belligerent face, the dirty blond hair, of the new Soviet counsellor, and heard his brutal Russian voice.

Joska squeezed my hand. "Don't worry, Sandor, everything will be fine, I'm certain."

But I knew very well that there was no guarantee everything would be fine. Only a few months earlier, at Poznan, fifty thousand Polish workers had paraded in the streets, demanding bread, free elections, and the departure of the Soviet troops. The Polish security forces had fired on them. Result: one hundred dead, three hundred wounded, three hundred arrested. Certainly, the anonymous victims had in a way wrested concessions from the Russians because, a month later, the leadership had repudiated the secret police and brought Gomulka, the reformist leader who had been imprisoned, back into the party.

In Hungary, people were starting to call Imre Nagy "the Hungarian Gomulka". They expected him to triumph as Gomulka had done recently when, in a secret ballot, he had become first secretary of the Polish party while Marshal Rokossovsky, a Soviet citizen of Polish origin and head of the Polish Army, the symbol of subjection, was removed from power.

Khrushchev and his colleagues in the Kremlin had given their blessing to all these changes in Poland. Why should we Hungarians not hope for a similar transformation in our country?

My driver, George, interrupted my thoughts.

"Where are we going, Comrade Colonel?"

"Follow the procession." The demonstration, now fully authorized, was accompanied by a police motorcycle escort. There was no good reason to expect trouble, but I couldn't help worrying. As I had explained at that morning's meeting, the civil police force was poorly equipped. Since Communism was supposed to end the social injustices that cause crime and disorder, crime did not officially exist, and the police were not supposed to need billy clubs and mounted officers to combat it. This fiction has long since been abandoned in Hungary as in other Communist countries.

The students were marching in order, pride and seriousness of purpose visible on their faces. Almost all of them wore rosettes in our national colours of red, white, and green. Some bore flags, and

others carried placards on which were written messages for Poland
and various demands:

STUDENT GRANTS STUDENTS CAN LIVE ON

NO MORE COMPULSORY RUSSIAN

DEMOCRATIZE THE PARTY! WE WANT IMRE NAGY!

RUSSIANS GO BACK TO RUSSIA!

As they marched, they sang and from time to time chanted slogans.
Some of them broke ranks and handed out leaflets containing the
principal demands of most Hungarians.

Before we could cross the bridge linking Buda to Pest, our car
had a long wait on the Danube quay as crowds of students from other
parts of the university joined the procession. Suddenly, a huge black
limousine slid to a halt near us. Its windows were masked by curtains
and its licence plate identified it as belonging to the Soviet Embassy.
A young man got out of the car and came over to ours. I lowered
the window and he spoke to me in Hungarian.

"Comrade Kopacsi? I am Comrade Andropov's interpreter. I
recognized your car. The comrade ambassador wonders if you would
be kind enough to help us get across the bridge. We are rather pressed
for time."

"Of course. With pleasure."

I motioned to George who put on his white gloves, grabbed the
disc used by traffic police and got out of the car to stop the procession. I glimpsed Andropov's head through the open door of his limo.
He signalled me to approach and said a few words.

"Comrade Kopacsi, the ambassador thanks you," translated the
interpreter.

"Not at all, it was the natural thing to do."

Andropov continued in Russian and the interpreter translated:
"Comrade Andropov asks whether, in your opinion, things aren't
going a bit far. Some of the banners are insulting to the Soviet Union."

I turned crimson under the piercing eyes of the ambassador. I
tried to explain that these students were under the supervision of
the Young Communists. Unfortunately, the procession stopped three
metres away and we overhead some unfriendly remarks about my
uniform and the Soviet pennant attached to the limousine. The

ambassador gave me a cold look and thanked me again.

A minute later, Andropov's limousine drove across the Danube bridge. I recalled that morning's incident with the new counsellor and his talk of counter-revolutionaries and "fascist bandits". And in my mind, I heard Andropov's question: "In your opinion, aren't things going a bit far?" Even if the students on the Danube quay had cast a critical eye at my colonel's uniform, even if they were a little rude to the occupant of the huge Russian car, I didn't see in them what the new counsellor or the ambassador seemed to.

Distractedly, I listened to the young people singing. Then I noticed something. We were driving along the quay past the barracks for the army's student officers. The army's future commanders were at the windows, most of them perched on the edge, legs dangling. They waved to the procession and took up the students' chants. Over the barracks flew an enormous Hungarian flag such as I'd never seen before. Normally, the Hungarian flag carried a Soviet-style emblem, conceived and designed by Rakosi himself, signifying popular democracy. But on this flag there was a hole where the emblem should have been. By cutting out Rakosi's emblem, the student officers had transformed the flag into a Hungarian tricolour with no indication of the country's political affiliation.

I couldn't believe my eyes. The demonstrators roared in triumph. I ordered George to return to my office as quickly as possible.

A pile of messages awaited me. The twenty-one precincts had all called for orders. The most pressing message was from the small police post at the edge of the municipal park. It said: "THE CROWD IS KNOCKING DOWN STALIN — REQUEST ORDERS IMMEDIATELY — LIEUTENANT KISS, No. 3."

I knew Kiss well. He was a young metalworker recently graduated from the party school and ready to sacrifice his life for the party. But would he sacrifice it for Stalin's statue?

I called him at the precinct immediately. "So, Comrade Kiss. Is it coming down?"

The young lieutenant informed me that there were at least one hundred thousand people around Stalin's statue. What scared me wasn't the destruction of the huge bronze statue. The municipal council had already decided either to get rid of it entirely or to move it to a less conspicuous place. What was frightening was the size of the crowd.

"Are you sure there are that many?"

"Comrade Kopacsi, there may be as many as two hundred thousand! All of Heroes' Square and all along the park, it's jammed with people. What do I do?"

"You are how many at the precinct?"

"Twenty-five, Comrade Colonel."

"I suppose that with twenty-five men, you're not about to break up a crowd of one hundred thousand people?"

Kiss waited a few seconds before replying. "We have forty rifles, Comrade Colonel," he said finally.

My order would have been enough and he was ready to fire on the crowd. But I particularly wanted to know who the people gathered around Stalin's statue were. Kiss suggested sending his three inspectors out to take a survey of the crowd.

"That's unnecessary. Look at what they're doing and you'll know right away."

Some of them were passing a large steel cable around the statue's neck, which was twenty-five metres off the ground. Others had blowtorches to cut Stalin's big bronze boots.

"You see, Comrade Kiss, these are specialists. They're workers from one of the large factories in Pest. They are the only ones who would have access to that equipment." I might have added, "... and the balls to undertake an operation like that."

I ordered Kiss to send in as many plainclothes policemen as he could to warn the crowd that the statue weighed hundreds of tons and that anyone nearby would be in mortal danger when it fell. "Make sure they're at least a hundred metres back while the specialists are on the job," I told him.

An hour later, Stalin came crashing down in the middle of Heroes' Square. His fall caused not the slightest injury to anyone.

Years later, in prison, I was frequently to hear the question, "Why are you here?" and the reply, "I'm a sculptor." To be a sculptor meant to be imprisoned for having participated in the destruction of Stalin's statue. The "sculptors" had merely executed a decision of the municipal council. But they had acted on their own initiative and that was forbidden.

Thanks to the telephones, which rang constantly in my office, and to our motorcycle cops, who were reporting back to police headquarters from points throughout the city, we were soon able to assess the situation. After destroying Stalin's statue, the crowd gathered in Parliament Square in hopes of hearing a speech by Imre Nagy. But as dusk fell, they learned that Nagy was reluctant to speak; he held no official post, neither in the party nor in the government.

But the immense throng wouldn't give up. "Speech! Speech! Imre Nagy!" it chanted.

Official government estimates put the crowd at three hundred thousand. But according to our own estimates, there were half a million people on Parliament Square. Their chants shook the windows of the neighbouring buildings like a squadron of supersonic jets.

Nagy was far away, probably eating dinner in his house in Buda. He had stopped answering his phone. Throughout his whole life, Nagy had submitted to the iron discipline of the Communist Party. He couldn't imagine taking any step without a direct order from the party leadership.

Meanwhile, I received a phone call that sent chills up my spine.

The police department had a child protection branch staffed by policewomen. The comrade in charge of this service asked to speak to me directly.

"Comrade Kopacsi, are you the only one who can hear me?"

"Yes...I suppose so. Speak all the same."

"Comrade Kopacsi. *There are people on the roofs.*"

It wasn't difficult to guess whom she meant by "people". Without even informing me, the Minister of the Interior had stationed armed security troops on the roofs of the buildings adjoining Parliament.

This was serious business. The AVO had heavy submachine guns. One hasty order, a single misunderstanding, and we'd have a catastrophe on Parliament Square.

I grabbed the red telephone. Impossible to reach the minister; all the lines were busy. As for Gero, his secretary would only say, "Please don't disturb Comrade Gero. He is preparing his speech for the radio."

Meanwhile, I learned that some of Nagy's close friends had gone to his house and, almost by force, dragged him to Parliament Square where, from a balcony and without aid of a microphone, he gave an impromptu speech in which he asked the people to have patience, to go home, and to trust in the party to work things out. The crowd booed, having expected something more, but finally left the square.

My Soviet counsellor, Petofi, whom I never thought to see that night, wandered into my office with his slow, hesitant, sick man's walk. "How's it going, Sandor?"

He had come to take the pulse of the city and to listen to

First Secretary Gero's speech, to which he seemed to attach great importance. An interpreter was with him.

"Your Gero is a wise man and a very old comrade."

We wished he could be proved right. Words of reassurance and wisdom from Gero could produce miracles. He was back from a visit to Tito. Following the Poles' example, he could admit past errors, announce reforms, and accede to the general demand for Nagy's return to a leadership role.

The radio announced Gero's speech. Silence filled my office followed by Gero's unpleasant voice. "Dear comrades, dear friends, working people of Hungary, it is our firm and unshakeable intention to develop, enlarge, and deepen democracy in our country."

It was a good beginning. The interpreter translated for Petofi, who nodded agreement. But then Gero's voice became harsh: "The chief goal of the enemies of the people today is to sap the power of the working class, to cut the ties between our party and the glorious party of the Soviet Union.... We condemn those who have taken advantage of our democratic liberties to organize a nationalist demonstration."

The faces around me grew darker as Gero spoke. "He's crazy!" "He doesn't know what he's saying." "He hasn't the slightest idea of what's going on in the streets." It was true. Listening to Gero was like listening to someone holed up in a tower with only a few classic works of Marxism for company. The interpreter continued translating and Petofi listened silently, his forehead resting on his hands. Was this pose an effort to concentrate or was he feeling the weight of worry that afflicted us all?

At the end of the speech, he asked, "What do you think, *Tovarishch* Kopacsi?"

"It couldn't be worse, Comrade Colonel. A stupid and belligerent speech, totally lacking in tactical sense. Let's hope that it's not the straw that breaks the camel's back."

All my phones started ringing at the same time. Comrades from the ministry, other friends, the army chief of staff, all expressed feelings of fear and disappointment. "That's all we needed." "He's poured oil on the flames." "That's it, now the dance begins." Following Gero's speech, the radio was broadcasting an ill-timed program of dance music.

One of my deputies had heard the speech at Central Committee headquarters in the company of leaders of the AVO whose detachments had occupied the entire building on Akademia Street. Even these people, accustomed as they were to mistreating the public, were appalled by the speech. One superior officer actually grabbed his pistol and threatened to go to Gero's office and shoot him. The others had to restrain him forcibly. The man threw his gun on the floor and exclaimed, "Because of that bastard Gero we're all going to die."

Old Colonel Petofi listened to us babbling in Hungarian, plunged in his own reflections. He was an experienced man who understood the seriousness of the situation. He knew that our agitation and despair stemmed from the certainty that some of us would not live through the days to come.

■ A Nasty Blow

For longer than anyone can remember, the favourite rendezvous for lovers in Budapest was under the clock in a small but much frequented square between the National Theatre and the offices of the party newspaper. The clock is gone now and the theatre has been razed, but in 1956 the square was still as it had always been. It's a little-known fact but true that the revolution of 1956 had its beginnings in this unimposing spot.

One of my police stations was just across from the square. The lieutenant was someone I knew well. At about 8:30 p.m., he called me in a panic.

"Comrade Kopacsi, it's started!"

"What's started?"

"They're shooting."

An hour earlier, our lieutenant had called to say that a detachment of AVO troops had positioned themselves on the roof of the building in which the police station was located. It was an ideal location from which to guard the headquarters of the national radio service. When I asked the deputy minister of the Interior what these troops were planning to do, he denied they were there. The AVO commonly issued such lies when a top-secret operation was underway.

I asked the lieutenant if anyone was injured.

"No. As soon as the shooting started, people ran for cover under the theatre arcades and in the side streets."

"Could the AVO have been shooting blanks?"

"You must be joking. I saw bullets ricocheting on the asphalt. We went out to see the marks and they were there."

Obviously, one of the AVO soldiers, seeing the mass of people around the building, had lost his head and let loose a burst of gunfire. Since no one had been injured, we could hope that the incident was over.

A few minutes later, I spoke on the phone with the editor-in-chief of *Magyar Nemzet,* the daily paper, which employed several of my friends who supported political reform. The paper had just received word from its Warsaw correspondent that Gomulka had emerged victorious from his test of strength with the Soviets and that Khrushchev had wired his congratulations.

"You can't imagine the feeling of jubilation down here. The Russians have adopted Gomulka and they'll do the same with Nagy. It's a question of days, even hours."

I let myself be persuaded by the optimism. Everything was going to work out. The tug of war between Gero's conservative wing of the party and the progressives was going to end. Following Poland's example, the country was going to start over again on the right foot. The demonstrations by students and the population of Budapest would be the final shove needed to get the renewal underway. Gero's speech was a gaffe that would serve only to facilitate his removal. We had won. The march of history and the liberalization in the Soviet Union had opened the way for Hungary to become a prosperous and democratic country guided by a leader who was well-liked and highly regarded by all, Imre Nagy.

"Comrade Kopacsi, it's for you." My deputy was holding the phone, a grim expression on his face. "It's the lieutenant again."

"Hello. More bad news?"

"Comrade Kopacsi, the people have weapons."

I asked for complete silence in the room. I thought he had gone mad.

"I didn't quite get you. Could you repeat that, Comrade Lieutenant?"

Sadly, he gave his report. A motorized army detachment had been passing and the soldiers had seen the AVO troops shooting at the crowd and the ensuing panic. In an instant, they were surrounded by angry passers-by who pleaded for weapons to "defend ourselves against the murderers in the AVO". The recruits — young peasants newly arrived from the countryside — didn't take long to react. They knew the cruelty of the AVO and had just witnessed a new example of it; the smoke and powder of the fusillade were still in the air.

One soldier, then two, gave guns to members of the crowd. Others followed their example.

Absolute silence reigned in my office. My associates stared at me, frozen. By the gravity of my voice and the sweat covering my face, they knew it wasn't joyful news I was getting.

I had confidence in the lieutenant's judgement. "What arms did you see being distributed and how many?"

"Twenty-five or thirty rifles and as many submachine guns. Boxes of ammunition as well. What are your orders?"

"Call all your men into the station. Barricade the doors. Put out the lights."

As the radio announcer had said after Gero's speech, "And now, dance music." The musicians had their instruments ready. Crowded into a narrow street in the centre of the city, not far from the radio building, groups of young people surrounded a car belonging to the radio service.

"What's that?" they asked, pointing to a microphone.

"We're recording the street noise."

"Neat. We want to speak in the microphone."

"What do you want to say?"

"We want to read our list of demands."

"Which are?"

"National independence, liberty. . . . Pass me the microphone, you'll see."

The leader was a young girl, probably a student or a worker. She took the microphone, perched on the radio vehicle's hood, drew a sheet of paper from her handbag and, in an emotional voice, began to read her group's demands.

The street was crammed with people. The crowd saw the young girl standing on the car, clutching a microphone. "Bring your radios to the window," the crowd yelled at the residents on the street. They wanted to hear what she was saying broadcast on the radio. The crowd became silent. But only music came out of the radio. The crowd began to shout: "They're not broadcasting our demands. We've been had."

People who had spent their lives on an assembly line or construction site didn't know that a radio broadcast consisted of several steps and that a voice speaking into an exterior microphone wouldn't necessarily pass directly to the air. (Quite apart from that, there was little chance that the radio station management would broadcast a radical speech by a young unknown.)

The crowd forced the radio employees out of the car, overturned, then burned it, and pushed toward the bolted doors of the radio headquarters.

At that moment, the red telephone on my desk rang. It was an army friend, Major-General F.

"Sandor, we've got trouble."

"I know. Your men are handing out weapons on the streets."

"That's the first problem. Listen to the rest. A pitched battle is under way in front of the radio building. The crowd is returning the AVO's fire. And that's not all. There's a third problem, even bigger than the others."

"Let's hear the worst."

"Our best units are out of control."

"Which means?"

"I sent two motorized units to stop the carnage. Instead of cleaning up the streets, they started to take shots at the AVO. They've joined up with the crowd to attack the radio building."

He didn't see any way out. He was certain that if he sent more troops, they would do the same.

"The AVO is a band of assholes and animals. They started this. But if we stay on the sidelines, we'll watch the army crumble away. At the moment, it's fighting the AVO. Before long, this could turn into a civil war."

"What do you suggest?" I asked.

"We have to confine the blaze. You send a detachment to relieve the radio building. Your men aren't compromised in the eyes of the crowd. There's a good chance they'll let them pass while they're busy burning the cars that the AVO had the asinine idea of disguising as ambulances. We've got to put a stop to it, Sandor. Otherwise...."

He was right. We had only one card left and it was up to me to play it.

I alerted the Mosonyi barracks where I had a commando of one hundred officers armed with submachine guns, grenades, and two heavy machine guns. They were specially trained for street combat. The commander, one of the bravest men I have ever met, didn't hesitate a second.

"No problem, Comrade Colonel, I'll go at the head of the commando."

"I'll tell the defenders of the radio building that you'll arrive when?"

"If everything goes well, we'll be inside in thirty minutes."

I informed the army that my commando was on its way. Next I had the difficult chore of calling the director of the radio service. This was a woman named Valeria Benke, a Resistance veteran, cantankerous and feared by all. She took the phone; her voice was distorted and unrecognizable.

"What do you want from me?"

"Comrade Benke, help is on the way. Stand firm."

Over the phone, I could hear the din of shooting. Benke was in hysterics.

"Kopacsi, come quick, or we're all done for."

In fact, the commando never got to its destination, and it wasn't the fault of the crowd but of the AVO force charged with protecting the radio building. These secret police officers had seen the army distributing guns to the people and now they trusted nobody. As the police commando tried to approach, the AVO unit increased its fire and drove them back.

The commander called me from a private apartment. "Comrade Kopacsi, it's not going very well. I've got two men seriously wounded and we can't advance a centimetre. The moment the AVO sees us, they spray us with bullets."

"But I told everybody that you were coming."

"The defenders are like maniacs. The only thing we can do is keep out of their line of fire."

I asked if the crowd was armed.

"Apparently not, although I can't guarantee there isn't a weapon or two hidden under some of their raincoats. But the people aren't threatening us at all, just the opposite."

"What do you mean?"

"They're surrounding our men, talking to them, trying to help them pass."

I didn't have to be a great strategist to give the following order: "Send your wounded to hospital, and return the unit immediately to the barracks."

A half hour more and my special unit would have been disbanded and merged, like so many other units, into the population at large in revolt.

The Mosonyi barracks were in no danger of being attacked. They contained too many well-trained officers for the crowd to try to break in for fresh supplies of weapons. But the small station near the ring road that encircles central Budapest was vulnerable. Toward midnight, a sad little troop of policemen arrived at headquarters. "We've been kicked out," explained the young commander.

The crowd had surrounded the station and demanded that the officers either join the revolt or at least give up their weapons. The men had been instructed beforehand on how to respond to such a situation: they were to render their weapons useless by removing the breeches and to abandon the station by a route worked out in advance.

This was done and the station was left in the charge of one officer, Major Lajos B. I knew Lajos very well. After the war, he had been, like me, in the provisional police. We had had neither guns nor uniforms and had been identified only by a simple armband. Tragically, when Lajos had tried to prevent some drunken Russian soldiers from raping a woman, one of them had shot him in the temple. He had always been a bit queer after that.

I called the station and he picked up the phone.

"Lajos. You're still alive?"

"Why should I be dead?"

"What's happening?"

"Not a whole lot."

"I hear shooting."

"That must be the people opposite. They are laying siege to *Free People*." He was talking about the party newspaper.

"Why would they be doing that?"

"Who knows? They were talking before about getting a notice published calling for a strike tomorrow to protest the massacres by the AVO. Maybe the paper refused to publish it."

That turned out to be the case. The editors had even refused to let a delegation into the building. So the crowd collected those who were fighting at the radio building and, together, they penetrated the party bookstore that was located in the same building. After the shop had been turned upside down, they made their way to the editorial offices of *Free People* and kicked the staff out. There was no paper the next day.

"And what did the rebels do to you, Lajos?"

"They came in and very politely asked for my revolver. Can you imagine? I said, 'Listen, guys, I can't give you this revolver because my name is on the inventory. I signed for it personally.' That surprised them so much that they just left."

At that moment, loud gunfire sounded over the phone. Someone whispered to me that the insurgents were succeeding in driving the AVO out of a position it held near the abandoned police station.

"Lajos?"

"Yes, Sandor."

"Don't you think you should come over to headquarters?"

"To do what?"

"I don't know. It's quieter here. There's too much shooting where you are."

"Shooting? Here? Wait a second. . . . No, Sandor, not at all. That's one of the rebels tramping down the corridor, that's all."

The noise was so fierce that the telephone practically shook in my hand. But his run-in with the Russians in 1945 had left Lajos more than a little hard of hearing.

It was midnight. The nation's leaders were in an emergency meeting at Politburo headquarters and none of them was reachable by phone. The crackle of gunfire could be heard across Budapest and the only order we had been given was to "keep the police strike force intact and ready".

It was the moment to open the large red envelope marked on the front: "PLAN M. Top Secret! Open only in case of ABSOLUTE NECESSITY."

Plan M had been conceived by the Ministry of the Interior at the time of the events in Poznan, Poland, with a view to dealing with a similar situation in Hungary. I called my senior officers, then broke the seals on the envelope, five large and fourteen small ones, and skimmed the text.

It started with an exhaustive list of the weapons and ammunition that were supposed to be in the arsenal at police headquarters. I was stupefied to learn that we had "20 heavy machine guns". In fact, we had only one. As for "80 machine guns", that was seventy-six more than we actually possessed.

And so on: "ammunition, hand grenades for 72 hours of combat" (we had enough for twelve hours), "fresh underwear and uniforms, tinned foods, drinks, cigarettes, etc., for 1,000 people, 6 days of combat". We had none of that except a few uniforms and a few crates of apples.

My officers smiled bitterly. Some of them had recently had a tour of AVO headquarters at Roosevelt Square. Never had they seen such a wealth of supplies. There were weapons galore, machine guns at every window, piles of brand-new police uniforms — *our* uniforms in case the AVO found it convenient to change the colour of their skins — and oceans of coffee, not to mention booze. For obvious reasons, I was happy to be deprived of the latter.

The famous Plan M was a fantasy and a fraud. Like so much else the Hungarian bureaucracy put on paper, it bore not the slightest relation to reality. It was up to us to devise our own plan.

"Come and look, Comrade Colonel."

In the large square in front of police headquarters where, in preparation for a subway construction project, workers had stored cement blocks, spools of cable, metallic air vents, and other knick-knacks, shadows were swarming mysteriously about.

By the weak light of the few street lamps spared by the rioters we saw that these silhouettes in the night were erecting a barricade. I gaped at the scene in disbelief. Didn't these people realize they were in front of police headquarters? I was both outraged and humiliated, as police chief, as a soldier, and as a Communist. I knew that my men felt the same.

I told the head of the intervention force to prepare a company and wait for me at the front entrance. I slipped into my colonel's kepi and my jacket decorated with medals, grabbed a submachine gun and met the troops in the vestibule.

"Follow me."

I was putting on a show just like the characters out in the square. Leading a detachment, revolver in hand, was not my usual style. For several years, police regulations had forbidden a commander to march at the head of a troop. This rule was derived from Soviet military practice and was intended to ensure the commander's survival.

It was over quickly. We fanned out on both sides of the barricade and, at a prearranged signal (a burst of gunfire in the air), charged the barricade builders. They got off a few wild shots, but all were taken prisoner in less than three minutes. The only casualties were the occupants of a passing taxi. The driver was killed instantly by a stray bullet, and his passenger was wounded.

We led our prisoners inside. There were fifteen of them, all youths under twenty. I passed in front of them as in a military review.

"Your papers."

They showed them willingly.

Seventeen years old. Young Communist card.

Nineteen years old. Factory worker.

"What does your father do?"

"He's a farmer. It's on the card, you only have to look at it more closely."

There were four metalworkers among them, two students, an apprentice caster, and two farmer's sons. One of them showed me a party membership card. I almost lost my head and gave him a kick in the butt — I, who was known for dragging my men into military court if they dared lay a finger on an accused person. A party card — and a gun in hand?

What was going on? He was a Communist Party member like me. How could we be on opposite sides of the same barricade? What was the meaning of this night full of mortal pranks?

"We are for a liberated Hungary," they told me.

"Give them something to eat and drink and put them in the cells."

My men were perplexed. They checked the files. They fingerprinted the prisoners. Nothing. What previous records would you expect to find for such kids? Later, when the chaos was such that the doors of the prisons swung open and dangerous criminals were freed, we would have other visits, including that of a convicted murderer sentenced to life imprisonment who came for "the head" of his investigating officer. We gave him a different reception from that accorded these young "night workers".

I went down to the cells. The prisoners were smoking and conversing in low voices. I felt like staying and looking at them through the peephole. They so resembled what I had been as an adolescent. A being with problems, sure of the truth. "We are for a free Hungary." What did they mean by that? Wasn't I also for the liberty of my country, against the Nazis, the imperialists, the warlords, and the landowners? Wasn't I also for a better life, for the workers' party? Why then did these youngsters, so like me, choose me as their target?

Someone came on the run to get me. "It's the red telephone. The minister is on the line."

Piros sounded weary, as if he had been drinking.

"Kopacsi, what do you want from me?"

"I've been trying to reach you all evening, Comrade Piros. The situation is critical and I've received no orders from anybody."

"Orders. You've got it easy. You're not being attacked with howitzers like my men." (His men were the AVO.) "Concentrate your forces at police headquarters, I'll let you know when I need them."

I then made the mistake of mentioning our lack of supplies and equipment and the hollowness of Plan M, of which he had been the author. The minister blew his stack.

"Are you crazy or what? You ask me for deliveries of supplies while all my vehicles are under attack and my drivers are being slaughtered? Just be happy you're not wearing the AVO uniform."

Piros's voice again became a weary, lifeless whisper: "Do your best. Report from time to time."

He hung up. The horse had been given its head and could gallop whichever way it wanted.

We couldn't continue to grope in the darkness. A military corps can't remain content to listen to the sound of shooting in the night. It needs orders, it needs to act. According to the latest news, Imre Nagy had been brought back into the Politburo and was going to be named prime minister. We were going to have a leader. Because we couldn't reach Akademia Street by phone, we formed a delegation to go to the seat of power for orders.

I couldn't be part of the delegation because I couldn't leave headquarters. I watched the small group set off in the night. While waiting for its return, I gathered news from friends and family. Joska Szilagy couldn't be found. I talked to Mammy, Judith's nanny. During the evening, our daughter had suffered a great fright. Mammy had had the dumb idea of telling her that "the Fascists are knocking down Stalin's statue". Judith had hidden photos of me in my uniform and her little book, *Russian Tales*. My wife had reassured her by telephone that nobody wished us harm and that she had nothing to fear. Mammy was scolded and then she too was reassured: "You'll see, Mammy, life will be better tomorrow."

But one shouldn't anticipate the future.

My wife decided to spend the night where she worked, among her colleagues. According to her, the word was out that Kadar had been chosen by the Soviets as the replacement for Gero at the head of the party.

"As for me," I said, "as soon as I can, I'm quitting."

Ibolya was silent for a moment, then replied that I should follow the dictates of my conscience. "Be careful, Sandor. Don't forget that your life belongs to us too, to me and Judith."

The police delegation returned from Akademia Street with bad news. Nagy, although brought into the Politburo, was authorized neither to take part in its deliberations nor to receive friends. Delegations had been waiting for hours to speak with the nation's leaders. Gero had passed through without stopping. Finally, when my officers managed to speak to Gero's young administrative assistant, he sent them on their way summarily, saying, "We don't need you. We know what to do to subdue the counter-revolution."

"Sandor," said the officer who had headed the delegation, "I'm afraid something very serious is about to happen."

"What? They're not about to send the air force to bombard the working-class neighbourhoods?"

"I tell you the atmosphere at Akademia Street is frigid. The building is buttoned up tight, there are senior AVO officers swarming through the corridors, the leaders are coming and going with an arrogant manner that seems quite at odds with the situation we're in. And the quasi-confinement of Nagy is worrisome. I'm telling you that we're about to get a nasty blow."

What would this nasty blow be? At around 2:00 a.m. we found out. One of my policemen took me energetically by the arm.

"Comrade Colonel, my wife would like to speak to you urgently."

A charming little voice, all excited, spoke to me over the phone: "Excuse me, I live in the southwest part of Buda and there's a terrible racket; a huge armoured division is coming into the city."

Our army had no bases in the southwest. Its reserves were concentrated entirely in the eastern provinces.

"Have you heard this noise for long?"

"For about the past ten minutes."

"Have you seen any tanks?"

"Yes. They're moving along the base of the hill. They're huge with a very long cannon. A hundred of them have passed."

"Huge with a very long cannon." That was the "Joseph Stalin" tank. Hungary had only a few of these. The tank columns the woman was describing could belong only to the Soviet Army's armoured reserves stationed near Lake Balaton, southwest of the capital. The Russians were entering Budapest.

■ *"Civil War"*

The whole world wanted an answer to one question: Who called in the Soviet tanks on the night of October 23? Was it the detested First Secretary Gero, or was it outgoing Prime Minister Hegedus, or incoming Prime Minister Imre Nagy? The recently signed Warsaw Pact solemnly stated that no member of the alliance could send its forces into another's country without first receiving an appeal for help. But, in reality, the Soviet armoured division had been stationed on our territory for years. Its officers and soldiers lived in villages built specially for them; their children played side by side with ours on the Lake Balaton beaches; their jeeps haunted the region, and their tanks criss-crossed the fields and surrounding woods. They didn't need permission from Gero or Nagy. A word from Soviet staff headquarters was enough to start them on the one-hour journey to Budapest.

Hegedus himself, in an autobiography published in Vienna in 1984, admitted that he was the one who signed the order, at Andropov's insistence. He signed the request for military intervention, however, on October 26, three days *after* the Russian tanks moved in. To give it a semblance of legality, the order was antedated October 23.

Soviet tanks were positioned quickly around the most important buildings, including the Soviet Embassy, the seat of the Hungarian Politburo, the ministries of Defence and the Interior, and AVO headquarters. But phone reports I was getting every five minutes from my police stations told me that most of the division was held in reserve in the northeastern suburb of Nepliget.

It was a hasty operation; the tanks sped into the city without the slightest infantry cover. The Soviets gambled that they could replay their success in East Berlin in 1953 when, in the midst of uprisings protesting poor economic conditions and political imprisonments, the mere appearance of Soviet armoured divisions had been enough to restore calm.

Harshness and intimidation were the orders of the day. We saw a column of T-34s speeding by at full tilt, their turrets closed, firing on anything that was lit up. It's hard to describe the horror that seized us when the lead tank's turret pivoted toward the facade of our building on Tanacs Boulevard. Everyone in the building screamed, "Lights out!" But before the lights could be cut at the central switch, a long spray of machine-gun fire had already swept the façade, leaving bullets embedded in the wall.

We were stunned. It wasn't only the fear of death that gripped us; there was also a feeling of fatal confusion, of being powerless to make the Russians in the tanks understand: "Hey, we're supposed to be friends." We were seized by the soldier's supreme fear — death by friendly fire.

Our telephones started ringing as if the shooting had set them off. The calls were from my men who were stationed as observers on the top floor of a building, today the site of a bus station, on Engels Square. The T-34s were spraying heavy fire on a block of apartments occupied by civilians who had neglected to turn off their lights. The commander of the observer team screamed in fear, "Comrade Kopacsi, do something! One of my men is wounded."

In that instant, I recalled the incredible brutality with which the Soviet war machine had swept through the north of Hungary at the end of the war. At that time it had had a monster to contend with: the debris of Hitler's army. But today? In the middle of our beautiful Budapest, the Soviets were pitting their military might against the civil police, men of peasant and working-class backgrounds, all devoted to socialism.

"Comrade Kopacsi, do something!" But Comrade Kopacsi was pale, crushed, useless, powerless, and wondering who he was.

We could make out strange goings-on across the square in Anker Passage, an alley squeezed between two attractive buildings. Shadows crept along, hugging the walls and then disappearing into the entrances. Who were these people?

As the third or fourth armoured column passed beneath our windows, the last tank in the convoy stopped. It was towing a mortar and was having trouble. The turret opened and a soldier got out, dropping heavily to the ground, apparently with the intention of adjusting the towrope.

A window in Anker Passage opened, a shot was fired, and the Russian soldier fell. A second later, we heard two or three explosions. They came from bottles of gas thrown at the isolated tank from the higher floors of the buildings on Anker Passage. As the primitive "grenades" exploded they illuminated the early morning with bursts of light. One of the bottles fell right into the open turret and ignited inside the tank.

There were five or six soldiers in the tank; only two of them survived the explosion. They leapt out of the burning turret, and one hid under an entranceway while the second ran across the square as if trying to reach our building. He ran twenty metres and had just reached a bank of flowers in the centre of the square when a hail of bullets cut him down.

We saw a silhouette leaning out of a window on Anker Passage, machine gun in hand. It was a young man sporting a Basque beret. He let off a long salvo, then a second and a third. The Russian's body wriggled about by the flower bank to the rhythm of the impact of the bullets.

"Saaan-dooor. Saaan-dooor."

Behind me, in the darkness of the office, someone was repeating my name in a Russian drawl. For a split second I thought, "The dead Russian soldier, he's there behind you, calling your name."

But it was only Petofi. Unshaven, his civilian suit pulled on over his pyjamas, he stared over my shoulder at the horrible spectacle.

"*Grazhdanskaya voyna....*"

Civil war. He muttered the words over and over like a broken record. Awakened by an urgent phone call from his bosses, he had hopped in his car and made his way through a series of detours to police headquarters. Behind him stood his companion, Magyar-Miska, a dumbfounded Charlie Chaplin, his hair all dishevelled.

I looked at them, begging them silently to say something. Something comforting. A word of explanation, of instruction. You are our Soviet counsellors. So counsel us. We looked at each other, wondering what was to become of us tomorrow. Or in an hour.

Petofi, with Magyar-Miska trailing behind him, watched the Soviet tank burn, looked at the corpses of the Russian soldiers on the pavement, and listened to the explosions, which continued to erupt as the fire consumed the stores of ammunition inside the tank.

Civil war? Actually, it was a war of Russians against Hungarians. The tank burned. From the building next door, our wounded officers telephoned their pleas for help. In the grey early October morning, in the police chief's office, Russian and Hungarian officers stood side by side, smoking, distraught, not daring to look at each other.

"Let's go, comrades, time is short."

The Russians' chauffeur had come up to my office. He wasn't confident of his ability to transport the counsellors safely to the Ministry of the Interior where their bosses had summoned them to an emergency meeting. Across the square, the young man in the Basque beret still crouched behind a window. Was he a murderer? Or were the murderers the ones burning to death inside the tank?

Petofi and Magyar-Miska cast a troubled glance my way and walked out without a word. I pitied them. I could only hope they weren't intercepted by a group of rebels. Or that a Soviet tank didn't make their jalopy one of its targets. I wondered if we would ever meet again in this office, chatting calmly in front of the open windows about the siege of Leningrad and about the ladies of easy virtue who, at the stroke of midnight, showed up on the Nevski Prospect, Leningrad's main boulevard.

At 4:00 a.m., the voice of authority finally made itself heard. Although there were no broadcasts in the middle of the night, the radios had been left on in all our offices in the expectation that some announcement would be made. We couldn't contact the government by phone; maybe it would contact us over the air. Suddenly, the radios emitted a peculiar barking sound — it was the voice of a half-literate announcer stumbling over each word.

"Good morning. Please listen to our morning broadcast. Here is a communiqué. . . ."

Within a quarter of a second, everybody had crowded around my radio. It was obvious that the radio station was no longer functioning. This untrained voice was coming directly from Politburo headquarters.

"Reactionary fascist elements have launched an armed attack against our public buildings. They have also attacked our police detachments. In the interest of public order, it is forbidden to hold any assemblies, meetings, or parades. The police have been ordered to apply the full force of the law against any persons who disobey this decree."

Then he repeated the communiqué, which contained not a word

about the presence of Soviet tanks.

So we had been ordered to bring the "reactionary fascist elements" into line as well as those who would "hold meetings and parades"? My officers, normally so discreet and disciplined, burst out laughing. We had received no order concerning the application of "the full force of the law" in the streets, and for good reason. A policeman who showed his face in the streets was a policeman disarmed by the people. His uniform, unlike that of the AVO, hadn't been dishonoured by cruelty, but as for "the force of the law", it was being applied by the insurgents.

Their law was simple: "Keep your nose out of our affairs."

We didn't much like the Politburo's first public reaction to the uprising. It had been written by people who knew nothing about the state of public opinion or the capabilities of the so-called forces of order.

In the early hours of the morning, reports on the military situation began to flow into police headquarters. Contrary to the government's predictions, the arrival of the Soviet tanks had angered the people instead of intimidating them. Our policemen were in less danger of being disarmed by members of the public because many residents of workers' neighbourhoods had already been armed by the workers in the Lampart factory, the largest armaments manufacturing plant in the country. The arsenal of the officers' school had been emptied, and certain army barracks had also co-operated to help arm the civilian population. The arms were transported to the suburbs where they were distributed among the people.

Early in the morning, police headquarters came under attack by rebels who wanted to get their hands on our weapons. The buildings across the square had been infiltrated by armed groups of young people. I saw them running bent over and hiding in entranceways. They occupied the apartments in the upper storeys, took positions at the windows and started to fire on our building.

At the beginning, I didn't attach much importance to this harassment. I ordered the offices overlooking the square emptied and stationed my sharpshooters on the upper stories. We started to fight back as well as we could. We controlled the square and, for the moment, I was satisfied with that. Unfortunately, the rear of the buildings on Anker Passage gave onto little streets that we didn't control. A sortie to seal off the perimeter was out of the question because we would have come under fire from the insurgents.

At 9:00 a.m., my deputy entered my office, armed, like everyone else, with a sight-equipped rifle.

"Comrade Kopacsi, I think we ought to consider the consequences of what we're doing."

I'm ashamed to admit that I was so engrossed in battle that I barely understood what he was trying to tell me.

He rested his hand on my rifle.

"Stop firing. There are several hundred of them now. There's a submachine gun in each window of the building facing us. We've only got ammunition left for an hour or two. They're going to wear us down. After that, they can take us by storm."

I woke up, as one awakes from a dream.

"And the trucks we sent for ammunition?"

"Captured."

"And my Mosonyi commando that's on its way here?"

"Intercepted."

Now the automatic weapons across the way were spattering bullets against the façade of our building. It was clear that they were preparing for an assault. I phoned the Minister of the Interior.

"If you don't want police headquarters to fall, send us a delivery of ammunition, send it with a tank escort, and send it now."

"We're in a battle with the insurgents ourselves. As for tanks, stop dreaming, Kopacsi. You'll have to look after yourself."

I phoned the army minister. I knew a man named Foldes, an influential member of the war council that had been formed during the night. He was an ex-Resistant like me.

"Can you deliver me at least a minimum of munitions?"

"Would twenty boxes do? Come get the form and you can pick them up at Depot Number Seven."

"Two of my trucks were intercepted a hundred metres from that depot. There's no way of getting it here without an armoured escort."

"Our tanks aren't available. Old friend, I'm sorry, but I can't do any more."

My deputy looked at me. The bullets were crashing against the walls like hailstones. I told him to order our people to save as much of their ammunition as possible. Then I played my final card — my old friend, Major-General F of army general headquarters. He wasn't easy to reach by phone.

"I'm asking a personal favour. I'm encircled, in shit right up to the neck. I hear you've just been reinforced with the thirty-third

Piliscsaba armoured regiment. Loan me two tanks, just long enough to escort my delivery of ammunition."

His reply was heartwarming. "Sandor, I'm going to do the impossible to get you your two tanks. In the meantime, stand firm."

Stand firm is only a saying. One has to live that saying, several hours at a stretch, to understand what it means. I gave the order that no one was to fire except on precise targets such as an armed individual visible through a window or in the square. The sharp-shooters positioned themselves on the roof. Armed detachments guarded the rear and sides of the building. Ammunition and provisions were severely rationed, and we prepared a retreat route to the rear.

During this time, the radio came on. (We found out later that these broadcasts were coming from the basement of the Parliament building, which was surrounded by Soviet tanks. The radio building, almost completely destroyed, was occupied by the insurgents.) The entire population was listening, including our attackers. One could imagine what they made of this announcement:

"Attention! Attention! Disgraceful armed attacks by counter-revolutionary bands have created an extremely serious situation. The gangsters have invaded factories and public buildings, murdering civilians, soldiers, and members of the security police...."

It's painful to listen to such crude lies even when one is being attacked by the selfsame "armed bands", who, in fact, were nothing but young people in revolt.

Toward the end of the morning, our attackers' fire slowed down, then stopped entirely for several minutes. We soon understood the reason. Imre Nagy, who had been appointed to head the govern-ment, was speaking for the first time on the radio. The whole country was listening. Present and future depended on what we were about to hear.

"People of Budapest, be informed that all who have laid down their arms and ceased combat as of two o'clock this afternoon will not be prosecuted under martial law...."

What a poor start. "Prosecuted under martial law...." For the moment, it was us, the armed forces, who were subject to that law. To give time limits, to play at being magnanimous when the entire population of the city was in armed revolt and expecting a radical change, was to continue to ignore reality, to chase after pipe dreams.

Almost as soon as he had spoken those words, the firing started up again, twice as intense as before, drowning out the rest of Nagy's speech. Our attackers weren't listening, but Nagy promised some good things. He indicated that he intended to renew his program of three years ago. "I have already tabled a law in Parliament to democratize our government, our party, and our political and economic life," he said. But he avoided any mention of Gero's crimes against the people, of the AVO's murders, and especially of the Russian tanks that at that very moment were patrolling the streets of Budapest. Who had called in the Russian might? And to ward off what "outside aggression"?

In the middle of an afternoon interspersed with sporadic but persistent gunfire, Ibolya paid me a visit. She arrived on her bicycle, a scarf knotted over her head. She handed me two packs of cigarettes.

"It's a present from the people across the way, in case you've nothing left to smoke."

She sat down on a chair in my office. Quickly, I found her another place to sit; the chair was right in the attackers' line of fire.

"You must be crazy to come down here."

"I wanted to see you."

"What's this story about cigarettes from the people across the way?"

She untied her scarf and crossed her legs.

"It's true. I went to see them."

"Are you out of your skull or what?"

"Of course not. I was very nicely received. You know, they're just kids, high-school students. I explained that I was your wife and that I was sure you didn't wish them any harm."

I was used to Ibolya's impulsiveness, but this was too much.

"What do you think you're getting mixed up in? You could have been killed."

She stroked my cheek.

"You look scary with your two days' growth. You should clean yourself up, your uniform is all crumpled," she said with a smile. Then, more seriously, "Those kids listened to me, Sandor. Their leader, an apprentice caster — as handsome a boy as you'll ever see — told me, 'We don't have anything against your husband either. If he's for liberty, let him put the flag in his window.'" She stopped, then asked me softly, "I suppose you've got a few flags around here?"

"Ibolya, I've got news for you. If they don't stop firing right now, in fifteen minutes I myself am going to lead an assault across the square."

"They'll stop, they'll stop," she said patiently.

Somebody knocked on the door. I opened it. It was my deputy, carrying the Hungarian flag.

"What do you want?"

"Mrs. Kopacsi said you would be needing this."

"Yes, that's good," said Ibolya. "Thank you."

She took the flag. I noticed that the Communist emblem in the centre had been cut out with scissors.

"Are you crazy? What is this nonsense?"

"Mrs. Kopacsi said we had to cut it," my deputy replied. "Today everybody is showing the flag with the emblem cut out like that."

Before I could say boo, Ibolya opened the window, stuck the flag out, secured it with a chair, and closed the window again. Shouts of triumph erupted on the other side of the square and the shooting stopped.

Ibolya came to me.

"There. You see."

She kissed me and left to cycle back to her office. Ten minutes later, boys and girls poured out of the buildings opposite, bent over and running. I ordered my men to stop shooting. We waited until the last one had disappeared, then sent some warning shots into the windows. Nobody fired back. The battle was over.

But calm didn't prevail for long. Soon two huge Hungarian assault tanks arrived to take up position in front of our buiding.

At the same moment, my friend F was on the line. "Sandor, I sent you two tanks."

"Thanks, they just arrived."

I ran down the stairs. The turret of the first tank opened and a military head emerged.

"I'm Major X, commander of this unit. Sorry we're late, but you know, we don't know our way around Budapest, we're from the country. Where are the enemy's positions?"

"Oh. The enemy...they've been firing all day; their last shots came from the turreted building across the square, but now they've all left. On the other hand, I need to talk to you about resupplying our ammunition. If you'd like to come up to my office...?"

"Thank you, Colonel. I'll be with you in a moment. Please wait for me upstairs."

His head disappeared and the turret of the tank closed over it. Then the two tanks started shelling the building across the street.

First, they destroyed the pharmacy on the main floor. They adjusted their firing position and proceeded to shoot the turrets off the building, then took aim at the building itself. Of course, as we hadn't been forewarned of the shelling and had left all our windows closed, not a single pane of glass was left unbroken on the façade of police headquarters.

Desperately, I beat my fists against the tank. In vain. Major X and his men unleashed another volley of shots. You'd have thought it was the battle of Stalingrad. I got out of there as fast as I could. These guys had never even been in manoeuvres before. This was the first chance they'd had to let loose to their heart's content.

With the grace of two elephants, the tanks pivoted in unison and, with their heavy machine guns, systematically destroyed all the windows of the building opposite. From behind the broken windows of my office we watched, powerless to stop the destruction.

Then, the turrets swung around 180 degrees and the heavy machine guns began to spew gunfire on. . .the British Embassy, its Union Jack flapping proudly from the balcony.

"Shit! Let's hope at least they haven't mowed down the ambassador."

At that moment, the phone rang. It was a secretary at the British Embassy, speaking Hungarian.

"Sir, I am speaking to you lying down on the floor beneath a table in the salon. For the love of God, what's going on? Why are you firing on us?"

I didn't know what to say or what to do, whether to laugh or cry.

"Listen, tell the ambassador that the men in those tanks are bumpkins from the boondocks who don't know what they are doing. Please relay our apologies and tell the ambassador that we do not wish to provoke the British Empire. We are trying to communicate with the leader of the tank unit and as soon as he sees our signals, he'll understand."

I ran downstairs, followed by my top officers. Dancing in front of the turrets, we finally got the attention of the maniacs inside. The commander came out, his handsome face blackened with smoke, and planted himself in front of me with the air of an opera tenor.

"So, Comrade Colonel, how did you like that?"

"That was just superb. All my windows are broken, the British Embassy is half wrecked, the square is splendidly decorated. Not a building is intact and the pavement is covered with rubble.

Come up and have some coffee with us."

The major was a thirty-year-old peasant from the area around Eger, famous for its red wine, Bull's Blood. While his men were sharing a snack with mine, he sipped his coffee, all the while glancing worriedly at his watch.

"I have to get back to our base, and it's difficult for us in this big city. If you've nothing else for us to shoot at, I'd like to go."

I sent him out through the maze that was Budapest with one of our supply trucks. They were back in record time, the truck filled with ammunition and the tank bulging with two hundred thousand cigarettes of the kind packaged specially for the army, police, and AVO.

"You understand, Colonel, I can't give this merchandise to just anybody," said the man of Bull's Blood.

As dusk fell, the fourteenth precinct called me with an urgent request for permission to evacuate. The insurgents had already encircled them on three sides and were threatening to surround them completely.

"How much longer can you hold out?"

"A half hour at most."

"I'm going to try something."

I called army headquarters again and got my friend on the phone.

"This time, it's simply to assure the retreat of one of my precincts. Loan me Bull's Blood again. He's exactly the kind of ogre I need."

I heard my friend's laugh. "He's on a mission. But I'll send two other tanks."

Half an hour later, someone ran up to me in a corridor. There was an urgent call from the fourteenth. It was the superintendent and the news, it appeared, was catastrophic.

"What, the two tanks didn't show up?"

"Yes, they showed up. The insurgents surrounded them and it took them less than two minutes to convince the soldiers to join them. Now the turrets are pointed towards us and the guns are aimed at my office."

I lit a cigarette.

"Okay, Comrade, this is no time to get excited. I know your station like the palm of my hand. Make an opening in the fence behind. Go through the garden in the house next door. It's night. You can hide your men in the house or bring them here."

I called my friend at army headquarters. "Thanks for the helping hand. But you know, your tanks are like weather vanes. They shift direction depending on which way the wind is blowing."

It was the second or third time I'd had an anonymous call from a certain "Captain Nemo". Each time, he gave five minutes of propaganda on the subject of my duty towards the "patriots" of Budapest in revolt. He claimed to be the commander of a regular army unit who had seen the light and joined the "revolutionaries". I had tried many tricks to get him to tell his real name but without success. Curiously, his voice reminded me of our military instructor at the party school.

This time, Captain Nemo had something new for me.

"Colonel Kopacsi, next to me I've got the Pongratz brothers and Steven Angyal. They want to talk to you."

Yesterday they were totally unknown, but today these were the most prestigious names in Budapest. The Pongratz brothers, young workers from the Budapest suburbs, and Steven Angyal, a young worker from Csepel Island, were the commanders of the two most important groups of insurgents.

The brothers held the Corvin movie theatre while Angyal had his headquarters several streets away in Ferencvaros, an old proletarian neighbourhood. They had obtained anti-tank weapons and the remains of ten Soviet tanks were testimony to the effectiveness of their work. To know that these men were at the other end of the line impressed me. The armed forces, and especially the high command of the Soviet Army, were itching to get their hands on them.

"Let me speak to them."

There was a brief conference. Then I heard the soft voice of a young man, a voice tinged with irony.

"The police chief of Budapest, I suppose? This is Steven Angyal, commander of the guys of Tuzolto Street. How do you do, Comrade Colonel?"

"How do you do, Angyal? But why do you call me 'Comrade'? We're adversaries, as far as I know."

I sensed that he was smiling at the other end of the line.

"Adversaries today, perhaps, but yesterday we were in the same party. I've been a member of the Communist Party since I was eighteen."

That floored me.

"What do you want?"

"To see you. I respect you and I'd like you to fight on our side."

"Fight, fight. The fighting has to stop. There is no more reason to fight. Comrade Imre Nagy has become prime minister and we're going to get everything we wanted."

Angyal relayed that to his comrades and they all burst out laughing. "I'm sure you're sincere in saying that, Comrade, but you don't see what's happening in the streets."

"Okay, what's happening in the streets?"

"What's happening is that we are in the middle of a war between Hungary and the Soviet Union. Not a friendly match. A war. And we're not going to lay down our arms until the Russian Army has gotten the hell out of the country. Having said that, we'd like to meet with you. We want you to understand our point of view."

"Give me a phone number where I can reach you. I'll have to get instructions from my superiors and call you back."

Without hesitating a second, he gave me a number.

I called the war council immediately and told Laszlo Foldes of my conversation with the rebel leaders. The council reacted swiftly.

"Comrade Kopacsi, we order you to open negotiations immediately with the insurgent groups in the name of the government. The objective is to find out their intentions and persuade them, if possible, to surrender, by assuring them of a total amnesty."

"The site of the negotiations?"

"Whatever place you judge best for your personal security. We would prefer that it be one or the other of our general headquarters. If it's at police headquarters, we'll send our representatives."

I dialled the number and Angyal picked up the phone. The meeting was quickly arranged. For the preliminary negotiations, we proposed the conference room at police headquarters. The meeting would take place the next day at 9:00 a.m. My word of honour was offered and accepted as their guarantee of safety.

The war council's delegates arrived on foot at about 8:45. There were two of them: General Varadi and an old friend of mine, Major-General Kovacs. The atmosphere was strained; it would be the first time we would find ourselves face to face with the leaders of those who had been shooting at us. For a soldier, that is always a crucial moment.

Their arrival was remarkable. A few minutes after nine, the guards informed us that a half-track taken from the Russian Army was looking for a parking spot on our lot. The vehicle was decorated with the Kossuth emblem, which had been adopted one hundred years earlier for the flags of the Hungarian War of Independence and which had appeared on all our public buildings from the end of the Second World War until the Communists took power in 1949. The tank was full of young civilians armed with machine guns.

"Do we let them all in?"

"Absolutely not. Only a small delegation. They have to leave their automatic weapons at the entrance, but they can keep their revolvers."

A few minutes later, three young men entered the conference room. The two eldest resembled each other; these were the Pongratz brothers, both tall and slim. The eldest was about thirty-five. The third man was much younger, small and stocky and wearing a turtle-neck sweater that he kept on throughout the insurrection: this was Steven Angyal, leader of the forces of Tuzolto Street. We shook hands and sat down around a long table modestly laid with sandwiches, apples, black coffee, and packs of cigarettes.

The conversation began immediately, with Major-General Kovacs wanting to know what political arrangement would satisfy the insurgents. The eldest Pongratz brother replied:

"The only viable arrangement would be for the Soviets to get their army out of our country. We don't have any illusions. The people aren't strong enough to get rid of the Soviet Army themselves. But the government must realize that there will be no ceasefire as long as the Russians are here."

To my great surprise, Major-General Kovacs replied that two important Soviet representatives, Suslov and Mikoyan, both members of the Politburo, were in Budapest at that moment, having arrived from Moscow in the middle of the night.

"Without having exact information, I wouldn't be surprised if the object of their talks was precisely that — how to arrange an honourable retreat by their army."

The government delegation wanted to know how the rebel leaders foresaw life after the departure of the foreign army. Each gave his opinion. A Nagy government could satisfy public opinion, but only on condition that the Stalinists in it be replaced by representatives of the non-Communist segment of the population, and that democratic reforms, including free elections and a declaration at the United Nations of Hungary's neutrality, be quickly enacted. The government representatives were receptive to these ideas. Neutrality for

Hungary eventually became part of Nagy's reform program.

The conversation continued on a variety of topics. The rebel leaders told us of their combat experiences in the streets.

"The government takes us for gangsters and monsters. That's what the radio says. Kopacsi, the scenes you've witnessed, Russian tank soldiers cut down with machine guns, weren't the work of our people. You know very well that there are many factions. We've got dozens of Russian tank soldiers as prisoners in our place. The wounded are being cared for and they eat the same as us. The Geneva Convention is perfectly respected. You can pass that on to the Soviet high command."

Most of their groups were made up of young workers and university and high-school students. The Pongratz brothers' forces contained many soldiers, including all the student officers from the Ferencz-Rakoczi School. These were boys chosen uniquely from among the children of civil servants and officers. Fighting in their school uniforms, they had suffered their share of losses but had also added some military successes to their record of achievements.

"When you talk to their parents, tell them they can be proud of their sons."

Our friend Kovacs gave the young warriors some encouraging news.

"The old Rakosi emblem will no longer be on our flag. The Minister of Defence has ordered it replaced by the Kossuth emblem, the same one you have on your half-track. Something else. At the Ministry of Defence, as in the police, there is a spontaneous movement in favour of electing revolutionary committees by secret vote. This might be the best way to achieve the democratization that we want as much as you do."

The meeting lasted two hours. When it was over, everyone agreed that it had been useful and that both sides now saw matters more clearly. After agreeing to keep in touch, we separated. The rebels reclaimed their machine guns, climbed into the half-track, and roared off in the direction of the working-class neighbourhoods.

One of the two officers exclaimed, "Sandor, when all this is finished, your Partisans' Union will have to welcome some new members."

I saw the rebel leaders later on several occasions. Two days later, when I was on a nocturnal mission with a commando, Angyal's men took aim at us but let us pass. The next time, on October 30,

I had the honour to command a detachment of the Pongratz brothers' forces in defense of the Ministry of the Interior, which had been deserted by its employees. The military men who negotiated with the rebels were punished later. Major-General Kovacs, who became head of the military staff during the insurrection, was sentenced to six years in prison for "collusion with the gangsters". General Varadi was sentenced to ten years on the same charge. I was to see this exceptional Communist officer again one afternoon in prison where we listened in wonder together to a violin concert given by another officer who had got the instrument from a gipsy just as the latter was being released from prison. The concert hall was the prison morgue and Varadi and I sat side by side on coffins.

■ *On a Plywood Chair*

It was almost noon, on that memorable day of October 25, and our Soviet counsellors, Petofi and Magyar-Miska, were in my office discussing the situation when we heard the grating and clanking of a huge Joseph Stalin tank just below our windows. The monster stopped and a Soviet major got out and rushed into our building. Two minutes later, someone knocked on my door: it was one of my men, accompanied by the Soviet officer who, dirty, unshaven, and weary, collapsed on the sofa.

The counsellors' interpreter explained that the Russian was asking for help. Two of his men had just been killed. I sent my men to pull the two bodies from the tank and add them to the heap of corpses already being stored in the parking lot behind the building. We offered the major some coffee and rum as well as something to eat. He drank the rum and slumped crying on the table.

"It's horrible," he said. "Since yesterday morning I've lost most of my men. We are fighting without food or sleep, and without the least infantry cover. We're a sitting duck for Molotov cocktails and anti-tank weapons."

The two men he had just lost were on leave. Two days earlier, they had received their papers and train tickets.

The Soviet major was dazed. "What am I going to tell their parents? What am I going to tell their parents?" he repeated.

He collected the dead soldiers' papers and left without finishing his meal.

The large Joseph Stalin had just departed when we watched five T-34 tanks of the Hungarian Army pass. Pennants flapping in the wind, officers standing up in the open turrets, the detachment was headed toward the workers' neighbourhoods in the Ulloi Street area.

"It's Colonel Maleter."

We had all recognized the slender man standing up in the first tank as Paul Maleter, the leader of the detachment. This legendary figure had been an officer in Horthy's army during the war. Wounded and captured by the Soviet Army, he eventually threw in his lot with his captors, was parachuted into Transylvania to lead the partisans fighting there, and fought so magnificently that he lost not a single man.

"Hello, Maleter!"

We yelled and waved in unison. He looked up, saw us, and gestured happily in return. We wondered what would happen if his detachment encountered Angyal and the Pongratz brothers' half-track, which had gone to the same area.

If we weren't having much influence on the course of events, at least we had front-row seats. For quite a while we had been hearing a noise, like that of a storm, punctuated by ringing cries. Suddenly, from the upper windows, we saw an immense crowd arrive on the adjacent street. They had come from the municipal park, and were carrying flags and banners and chanting "Russians go home" and "Down with Gero". (Despite the appointment of Nagy as prime minister, Gero was still party chief.)

Men, women, young people — there must have been at least ten thousand of them. From where we were, we saw, as the crowd could not, three large Soviet Joseph Stalin tanks coming from the opposite direction, straight toward the crowd.

It was like a nightmare. How would the crowd react? Would the Russians panic? We were petrified, powerless to do anything but pray. The tanks arrived on the street. The tank soldiers saw the crowd and the crowd saw the tanks. They were nose to nose.

The tanks stopped and stayed in place, motors idling. The crowd couldn't stop; it kept coming, swarming around the tanks.

Unshaven and haggard, Petofi and Magyar-Miska clutched my arms, their Adam's apples rising and falling faster and faster. Any second, the automatic weapons in the tanks could trigger a bloody slaughter. Instead of that, something else happened.

A boy, undoubtedly a student — the scene took place just below us — pushed his way through the crowd to the first tank and passed something through the loophole.

It wasn't a grenade but a sheet of paper. It was followed by others.

These sheets, many of which my men would later collect, were tracts in Russian composed by students in the faculty of oriental languages. They reminded the Soviet soldiers of the wishes of the Hungarian nation and of the unfortunate role of policemen in which they had been cast. The tracts started with a citation from Marx: "A people that oppresses another cannot itself be free."

We counted the minutes. Nothing happened.

Then the top of the turret of the lead tank opened a little, and the commander, with his leather cap and gold epaulettes, emerged slowly into the view of the apparently unarmed crowd. Then he flung the turret open and perched himself upon the top of his tank.

Immediately, hands reached out to him. Young people leapt up on the tank. A young girl climbed up and kissed him. Someone handed the commander the Hungarian tricolour, and instantly the flag was affixed to the tank. The crowd erupted in a frantic ovation. In this jubilant atmosphere, the commander's cap was thrown into the middle of the crowd. In exchange, someone plunked a Hungarian Army kepi on his head. The crowd sang "Kossuth's Song" and then the Hungarian national anthem. And, at the top of their voices, they cried: "Long live the Soviet Army!"

Yet these were the same people who, fifteen minutes earlier, had determinedly chanted, "Russians go home."

Petofi and Magyar-Miska stared breathlessly at the scene. I'm sure they felt the same relief that we felt, but they let nothing show. Turning toward me, Petofi said, through his interpreter: "The population has not shown itself hostile toward the Soviet military."

Then he went into his office to report to his superiors by telephone.

For me, it was like the climactic scene of a great film, the dissolving of barriers between two hostile worlds through a simple quotation from Marx. My deputy and I exchanged glances. Although we were soldiers, the theory of our movement bypassed caste, nationality, personal interest, and prejudice. A word from Marx, passed through a loophole, was stronger than a tank directed against a crowd.

My phones started ringing. Comrades and friends called from offices and homes to share their astonishment. "Did you see it? You know what has happened? An armoured Soviet unit is passing showing the Hungarian flag and surrounded by a jubilant crowd."

The crowd, chanting, "Down with Gero," and "Long live the Soviet Army," assembled on the esplanade in front of Parliament.

Half an hour later, I received a frantic call from Julia, the female police captain who directed our social service bureau. It was she who had called the previous day with the news that an AVO platoon armed with heavy machine guns had positioned itself on the roof of the Parliament building. Since then, this unit had been reinforced by another heavily armed platoon taken from the parliamentary guard. I couldn't find fault with this — not that anyone had asked my opinion. Tactically speaking, it was normal for the defenders of a target to position groups of scouts in advanced positions.

"Comrade Kopacsi, a big crowd is demonstrating on the esplanade and they're all crying, 'Down with Gero!' There's going to be trouble."

"But no, Julia. The crowd isn't armed. I saw it half an hour ago, it's full of women and children. It's a peaceful demonstration."

"That's not the opinion of the lieutenant commanding the platoons on the roof. A little while ago, he came down to get water for his men. When he saw the crowd, he hurried back up yelling, 'This can't happen. We've got our orders.'"

I passed this news along to my senior officers. No one could believe that the AVO would fire on an unarmed crowd accompanied by Soviet tanks. Just to make sure, I called the Ministry of the Interior and explained the nature of the crowd. I was listened to distractedly and assured that the ministry knew what was going on.

Three minutes later, I had a heartrending call from Julia.

"Comrade Kopacsi, the machine gunners are firing on the crowd."

"Impossible!"

But now I could hear the crackling of gunfire myself over the phone. Julia was crying.

"Comrade Kopacsi, this is unbelievable. The AVO is firing from every roof. Now the Soviet tanks are firing on the AVO! They're defending the crowd...."

We heard the roar of the battle. Julia had dropped the phone; she couldn't speak any more. Another woman from the social service bureau picked up the phone, her voice drowned by sobs.

"Comrade Colonel, it's a disaster, it's dreadful. People are screaming, they're dropping like flies. There are hundreds of victims, women, children, listen to the wounded crying, it's horrible... monstrous...."

The butchery ended only because of the intervention of twenty Soviet tanks that surrounded Parliament. Fortunately, their captain, deciding that enough was enough, fired his guns at the security forces on the roof, forcing them to abandon their position.

In the meantime, I was able, with enormous difficulty, to get through to Imre Nagy. He was busy and in a poor humour.

"What do you want, Kopacsi?"

"There's a crowd in front of Parliament demanding Gero's dismissal. They're being slaughtered."

"The comrades from the Soviet Politburo have just left. Gero has been dismissed and replaced by Kadar at the head of the party. I am prime minister. What else does the crowd want?"

"Comrade Nagy, perhaps you haven't been informed of what is happening. The AVO is slaughtering unarmed people. There are three hundred dead in front of Parliament. Your new government is drenched in the blood of innocent people. I can't find the words to tell you. . . ."

Nagy understood. In a voice suddenly changed, he said, "I'll do what's necessary right away. This is horrifying, it's a disgrace."

The Minister of the Interior was relieved within the hour, but that was no help to the victims. I sent my men to help in picking up the wounded. Students from the medical faculty rushed to help with two large moving trucks to supplement the regular ambulances. The first truck was completely filled with corpses and the second with the severely injured, most of whom were young people, women, and children. A few seconds later, they roared past police head-quarters at a hundred kilometres an hour, leaving a long trail of blood on the pavement.

The radio announced the fall of Gero. But not a word was whispered about the butchery in front of Parliament. (The official explanation, issued much later, had it that the perpetrators were not AVO at all, but provocateurs.) Nevertheless, the horrible news spread quickly through the city and the hunt was on for those responsible. Toward 3:00 p.m., ten thousand people surrounded the national police headquarters — the centre from which the law enforcement in Hungary's nineteen counties was directed, which they mistook for the headquarters of the AVO. (It had ceased to be AVO head-quarters two years earlier when Imre Nagy reduced the status of the secret police from independent agency to a division of the Ministry of the Interior.)

Half an hour later, ten thousand more gathered around my own police headquarters. This time, they weren't women and children.

They were young people, a good many of whom sported a big lump
— the butts of their machine guns — on their left shoulders under
their raincoats.

In unison, the crowd shouted, "Take down the star."

The roof of our building, like that of every public building, bore
a large, five-pronged star in red metal, studded with a hundred red
electric bulbs. Ours was at least five or six metres high. I listened
to the crowd and watched it, surrounded by my officers and the two
Soviet counsellors. Everybody was pale. My officers were watching
me, waiting for their orders. This was a delicate situation: the red
star was the symbol that had always guided my path. It was my identity, the distinctive symbol of the "great family". The crowd was
getting impatient: "Down with the star, down with the star."

"Better go up and take it down, guys."

The secretary of the party organization at police headquarters,
a former Resistance fighter who had fought in Tito's underground,
looked at me unhappily.

"We...take it down? You don't think it's a dumb move?"

My deputy sent a commando up to the roof, equipped with tools.
When the crowd saw the policemen taking down the star, they shouted
with glee. The hostility they had demonstrated since the massacre
to everything and everyone associated with the red star dissipated
a bit.

"Bravo!"

"Way to go, cops."

Suddenly, they started chanting in chorus again. This time, they
wanted the release of our prisoners. "Release the fighters for liberty!"
The crowd's mood was once again demanding and hostile.

"Let us in, bastards!"

"We want to see your cells, torturers."

"Open or we'll smash the place down."

Thanks to the friendly activities of "Bull's Blood", we had plenty
of ammunition. Tear-gas grenades were lined up on the window-
sills and everybody was casting furtive glances at them. But we might
as well sprinkle the crowd with holy water for all the good tear gas
would do; after the massacre at Parliament, the people were no longer
susceptible to mosquito bites. We would have to resort to the heavy
stuff, machine guns and fragmentation grenades. A replay of what
happened at Parliament? Three hundred dead, followed by certain
lynching for us, the perpetrators?

"Open! Open!"

"Come on. Let's break the door down!"

"You've got three minutes to open."

I took off my gun belt and put my revolver, wallet, and ring on my desk.

"Two volunteers, please, to help me get through the crowd. I'm going to talk to these guys. I want to look them in the eyes."

Petofi jumped to his feet and grabbed my arm.

"*Nyet*, Kopacsi, *nyet, nyet!*"

He had his interpreter tell me that a commander has no right to risk his life, that, wearing my uniform, I might be lynched by the crowd. It would be better if I picked one of my officers to deal with the insurgents; that way we could stall for time until reinforcements arrived.

My deputy and several officers echoed his advice.

Poor Petofi. He understood nothing about anything. If I was successful in establishing a dialogue with the people outside, so much the better. If they shot me or lynched me, that would be fine. This Thursday, October 25, 1956, I had seen so many horrors, endured so many disappointments, and accumulated so many unsolvable problems, that if I hadn't been surrounded, if I had been alone in my office, I probably would have put a gun to my head anyway.

The two volunteers were waiting for me at the door. One was George, my chauffeur. The other was a hefty sergeant I didn't know.

"Comrade Colonel, I'm from the Fourteenth."

His handsome young face was scarred.

"A souvenir?"

"A piece of metal."

He had been a metal turner, like me.

I grabbed a chair — an ordinary plywood office chair — and, with my two policemen on either side, walked out into the midst of the rebels.

At first, the crowd wasn't aware of my presence. It was too busy chanting its threats. "Bastards, open up!" "We're going to break the doors down." It was like a dream, moving through this ocean of hostility roaring with anger. We walked through the crowd without incident. It was totally unreal. The people — most of them young — glanced incredulously at our uniforms, without realizing that it was me, the "chief torturer".

The scarred sergeant seized my arm.

"It's here, Comrade Colonel."

I shook myself, as if waking from a dream. We had arrived at the centre of the square. If the sergeant hadn't stopped me, I think I would have walked right through the crowd without being noticed.

"Some room, please."

I placed my little chair on the pavement and climbed up.

Gradually, silence prevailed. A deathly silence. I understood that the silence of ten thousand people could be as frightening as its cries of rage.

At the top of my lungs, I began to speak my mind.

"My name is Sandor Kopacsi. I am police chief of Budapest. I am going to give you what you ask. I assume that we all want revolutionary order and not anarchy. You are going to choose a delegation of five persons to enter the building. They will inspect the conditions under which I hold prisoners and choose among them those who qualify as 'fighters for liberty' or political prisoners. I assume that your sense of revolutionary democracy tells you, as mine tells me, that common criminals should not be liberated. Who is and who isn't, your delegation will decide with the help of my officials. That is what I have to say to you."

The ovation caused the few windows left on the square to tremble. These people were ahead of me because it took them only seconds to name their delegation. They came to find us and entered the building accompanied by my two men.

I remained on my chair. Silence fell again. I still had something to say.

"As soon as the question of prisoners is settled, I ask you to return to your homes. The state of siege is still in force and I wouldn't want any of you to have a nasty run-in with one of our patrols."

That only made them laugh. It was the police, not the general population, who risked having nasty run-ins.

"Kopacsi," someone yelled out, "give us your arms and ammunition and come with us."

"My friends, we would prefer to stay here and to keep our weapons and ammunition. I see that I am in the presence of the population of Budapest and the Budapest police are not the enemy of the population of Budapest. We are here to ensure public order and to protect the public from lawbreakers. Surely you don't expect the police to confront criminals empty-handed?"

"Let them keep their guns," someone cried out, and the majority shouted assent. I cast a glance at my senior officers and Soviet counsellors leaning out the window and could almost hear their sighs of relief.

The sorting of prisoners didn't take long. Fifty men and women appeared at the entrance and the crowd surrounded them, shouting questions.

"Did they beat you?"

"No."

"You, did anyone touch you, did they give you anything to eat?"

The questions rained down on the liberated prisoners and they replied to all of them. Nobody had been beaten, the injured had been taken care of in the infirmary, and everybody had had enough to eat. The liberated prisoners began to tell of their experiences. They were applauded and carried away on the demonstrators' shoulders. Hands were extended to me. "Kopacsi, you're okay, you're not like the others."

"Down with Piros, long live Kopacsi."

With this new slogan on their lips, the crowd left the square and headed toward the centre of the city. I still had my little plywood chair. I grabbed it in one hand and returned to my office.

Although officially relieved of his functions and replaced by Kadar at the insistence of Mikoyan and Suslov, Gero was still exerting influence as the head of the Stalinists in the government. He reacted to the episode at police headquarters by having all our direct lines, including the "red phone", disconnected. Having negotiated with the crowd made me an outlaw.

The sergeant with the scar knocked at my door.

"Comrade Colonel, there is an insurgent here who wants to talk to you."

It was my friend and neighbour, Joska Szilagyi. I had trouble recognizing him. His face was filthy, his clothes torn.

"Where have you come from?"

During the two days of insurrection, he had been everywhere. Without firing a shot, he had followed the rebels, from the Csepel factories to the massacre at Parliament to the siege of police headquarters. He wanted to see all and to know all.

"Sandor, there have been tragic events and blood has been spilt, but this is a revolution, a wonderful revolution. These people are honourable and ethical, enough to put the greatest heroes of history to shame."

He had seen jewellery shops, their windows smashed by bullets, where the insurgents had posted guards so that nobody would steal the contents. He had himself added his contribution to the open boxes, flanked by the national flag, where passersby were leaving stacks of banknotes without anyone laying a finger on them; the money was for the widows and orphans of the uprising.

"But Sandor, the most important thing is the future that is in the making. I don't know if you realize it, but in the factories, the business enterprises, the municipalities, the army, people are electing revolutionary committees by secret ballot. From now on, the committees will be running the affairs of all these organizations."

Joska had visited several provincial cities where Soviet garrisons had stood by while revolutionary committees had been created within the army and the general population.

"These are soviets in the making, Sandor, real soviets, the kind that could not survive in Russia in 1917. Our nation is bleeding and maybe will bleed again, but everything leads me to believe that out of this bloodbath will emerge the first and only socialist democratic state in the world!"

He wasn't interested in food, even less in clothes.

"But where are you running off to in that condition? Stay with us awhile."

"I'm going to try to tell the old man everything I've seen."

He phoned Parliament, got Imre Nagy on the line, and the new prime minister agreed to see him immediately. Before leaving, he told me, his face shining with happiness, "I inspected the revolution for him."

As he left my office, my head was filled with dreams and my heart bursting with pride. The revolutionary utopia existed after all and it was my country that was going to realize it for the first time in history!

Joska stayed with Nagy as director of the prime minister's office. He followed him in his precarious exile in the Yugoslav Embassy and then preceded him to death, still dreaming the same dreams he had offered me that morning.

Perhaps, one day, those dreams will come true.

When the new Minister of the Interior, Major-General Ferenc Munnich, re-established the red telephone link between his ministry and police headquarters, he used it immediately to summon me to his office. This worried my senior staff.

"Don't go," said the secretary of the party organization. "It's a trap."

In fact, I had committed no infraction of the regulations that could justify any measures against me by the minister. Munnich, Kadar's friend, wasn't a Nagy supporter, but he had always fought against Rakosi. I wouldn't have gone to see Piros, certainly, for he was a fanatical Stalinist. But to Munnich I could always present my reasons for "connivance with the crowd". A reasonable man would understand me.

Finally, my staff transformed itself into a party committee and passed the following resolution: I would go to the ministry, but an hour later my deputy would phone the minister's secretary to see if things were going well. If I hadn't returned after an hour and a half, my deputy would declare the independence of the police department and, if necessary, its alliance with the rebels.

I left on foot, accompanied by George and the sergeant with the scar, all of us with submachine guns slung across our shoulders. A colonel and two non-commissioned officers armed with submachine guns crossing the esplanade...I wondered what the people in the British Embassy would say if they were watching. These days, senior Hungarian officers weren't in the habit of circulating in the streets.

The ministry was surrounded by Soviet tanks. We presented ourselves. The guard asked me to hang my submachine gun on a peg before entering the building. I pretended not to hear him and entered carrying the gun in my hand.

"Comrade Minister, Colonel Sandor Kopacsi, at your service."

Munnich made no comment on my submachine gun. He asked me to sit down across from him. I asked permission to smoke, as the regulations required, and he gave it. The submachine gun clasped between my knees, I started smoking and answering his questions.

It didn't take long for me to realize that his predecessors and his current staff hadn't painted a favourable picture of me. In Munnich's eyes, I was a man who was sympathetic to the rebels, who might already secretly be allied with them. He asked me, point blank: "Can you be counted on to execute the orders of Imre Nagy's government?"

I couldn't give a straight yes or no. I told Munnich that, like many others, I had expected the government to stop the AVO's cruelty and slaughter.

"From here on, that can be guaranteed," the minister replied.

"The AVO will shortly be dissolved. Are you satisfied?"

"Yes, Comrade Minister. You can be certain that the government's orders, and yours, will be carried out."

He rang and had coffee and cognac brought in. Everybody knew Munnich was a heavy drinker. He gave me some information about how the security force would be dissolved. They were to be given two months' pay in cash as a humanitarian measure to ensure their reintegration into society. I was to provide the severance pay to the small contingent who had been such a nuisance at police headquarters.

We were deep in discussion when his secretary entered.

"Police headquarters would like to speak with Colonel Kopacsi."

The minister, annoyed, replied, "Tell them he's in a meeting with me."

The secretary hesitated.

"It would better if the colonel took the call."

"Why is that?"

I coughed, a little embarrassed. The secretary did likewise. Munnich understood. He exploded, "Thank you for your confidence! And that of your colleagues. No, no, take the telephone, please. Otherwise, I suppose, your friends will bring round their heavy artillery!"

This incident wasn't the determining factor in the souring of our relationship. That had a different origin. I learned from the indiscretion of a friend that a higher authority had spoken unfavourably of me.

Yet again it was the little blond Russian who looked like a German — the mysterious "new Soviet counsellor". He had warned the minister against me.

Nobody seemed to know the man's name. It was only later that we found out he was Ivan Serov, head of the KGB. They called him "the new one" or "the one from Moscow". He never came to the ministry. If he wanted to intervene, he always did it on the "red line". Sometimes Munnich dropped everything, put on his hat, and climbed into a Soviet tank that took him to an unknown destination to meet Serov.

Coming out of his office that day, I ran into under-secretary Bartos, the AVO's quartermaster. We had been at the party school together for two years and for this reason were on familiar terms.

"Kopacsi! Good to see you."

It was quickly apparent that this encounter was not accidental.

Bartos led me to his office and admitted he had been on the lookout for a chance to speak to me.

"Listen, Sandor, there are several of us who don't feel at home in this dump."

Submachine guns were installed on every windowledge in the "dump", and boxes of ammunition and grenades were jammed into every corner, not to mention expensive cigarettes, cognac, and food.

The door opened and Major-General Fekete, the other AVO undersecretary, entered.

"Listen, Kopacsi, come with me, your comrades from the Partisans' Union are waiting for you."

I saw several officers, former Resistance fighters, all ex-workingmen like me, now members of the AVO.

"Sandor," said one of them, "things are going from bad to worse."

I asked what was the matter. From what I knew, none of them had been involved in unjust trials or in commanding the troops that had committed atrocities during the uprising.

"It's not the anger of the public we're afraid of," one of them told me. "It's the savagery of the AVO troops."

I learned that two days earlier they had been ordered to help provide an armed guard for the Ministry of the Interior. They witnessed a horrible scene. Some students from the AVO school arrived, also to help guard the ministry. The AVO guard that they had come to relieve opened fire on them, killing and wounding many.

"They are so panic-stricken that now they're slaughtering their own comrades. You can understand why we're trying to get out of this nightmare. By any chance, would you be able to give us refuge in the police department?"

"The answer is yes. But why the police department?"

"Because we've heard how you know how to talk to the crowd. If things get bad, here we wouldn't have a Kopacsi to defend us. Here it's a general panic, every man for himself."

More than one hundred AVO officers spent the critical days of the uprising at police headquarters. Some sought and found refuge with us, like my friends from the Partisans' Union or like Bartos, who I knew had never been involved in anything but the supply corps. I let them have several offices where they played cards or used the phone to look for a more private hideout. Several dozen officers and men gave themselves up as prisoners, while others were hauled in by the new National Guard. They were fed as we were and lived in open cells until the day of the second attack by the Soviet Army.

■ *Operation Sunday*

On Sunday, October 30, at about 7:00 p.m., my friend Joska Szilagyi summoned me by phone to Imre Nagy's parliamentary office.

"Sandor, Hungary needs the forces of order that you've kept intact."

Since the famous scene in front of police headquarters, many things had happened. The AVO had been dissolved and its members fired. Revolutionary committees had been elected in most of the businesses and government agencies in the country, including the police department. The Russians themselves seemed to have changed their allegiance. Talk of negotiations between the Soviet and Hungarian governments on the retreat of the Soviet troops was on everyone's lips.

Filled with excitement, I arrived at Parliament where, since 1953, I had taken part in sessions as a deputy and which had now become the seat of the new power in the country, Imre Nagy's government. On this day, the immense "Westminster-on-the-Danube" resembled Smolny Palace at Petrograd, the Bolsheviks' centre in 1917, more than it did the Houses of Parliament in London. The corridors and anterooms were crowded with delegations of workers, peasants, artists, writers, and politicians of different parties who had rarely shown their faces since 1947. There were soldiers also, of course.

In Nagy's anteroom, I met an old Hungarian Communist who had been one of Lenin's personal guards soon after the Bolshevik Revolution. He said to me: "Kopacsi, I've read ten different histories of the party, each one as packed with lies as the last, and this is the first time I've experienced the true atmosphere of the 'ten days that shook the world'."

Szilagyi hadn't left Nagy's side for ten days. Officially, he was director of the prime minister's secretariat; in reality, he had all the

nation's affairs on his hands, just like a real prime minister. He held
out his arms to me: "Sandor, you'll have to pass your turn to see
the old man. You'll see him later. He is...*very busy.*"

I didn't understand what he meant by "pass my turn" and "the
old man is very busy". While waiting, Joska introduced me to a
tall civilian whose stiff posture revealed him immediately as a military
officer.

"Colonel Kopacsi...Major-General Bela Kiraly. You'll probably
be seeing a lot of each other."

I knew that during the war Bela Kiraly and his units had joined
forces with the Soviet Army. After the liberation, Kiraly had been
a senior staff member in the new Hungarian Army. Then he had
fallen out of favour with Rakosi. Sentenced to life in prison in a
phoney trial, he had just been freed and named by the Nagy government to one of the top posts in the army. Kiraly was totally devoted
to Nagy and his ideas. He believed we had to solve the crisis in
a socialist context, in friendship with the Soviet Union, all the while
ensuring a maximum of democratic guarantees.

He took my arm and whispered in my ear, "I know who is with
Nagy...it's Mikoyan. I saw him go in a little while ago. A lot depends
on what is said right at this moment."

We slipped out into the corridor to be able to talk more freely.
The population was now armed from one end of the country to the
other. The creation of revolutionary committees had given a sense
of direction to fighting that until that point had been anarchic. But
the army had to be taken in hand before it fell apart completely.
It urgently needed new leadership. Nagy had proposed three candidates: Kiraly as commander, myself as his deputy, and Paul Maleter
as Minister of Defence.

Szilagyi came to get us. "It's about to be your turn."

We went back to Nagy's anteroom, which was crammed with
delegations. After several minutes, the office door opened and the
Kremlin's special envoy, Anastas Mikoyan, appeared. He was a small
Armenian with dark skin, a pencil-thin moustache, and salt and
pepper hair. He wore a blue suit and carried an overcoat. At the
threshold, he turned and said several words in Russian to the man
walking out behind him.

This was Nagy, whose demeanour revealed no sign that he was
feeling the strain of the past few days. While talking to Mikoyan,
he noticed Kiraly and me.

"*Tovarishch* Mikoyan, here are two of the future leaders of the Hungarian Armed Forces."

Mikoyan shook hands with us and said, "Now we have to leave your country. Do all you can to help Comrade Nagy."

The delegations of peasants, of workers from Transdanubia, of ragged rebels from Csepel, and of soldiers from units that had rebelled listened silently to Mikoyan as he extended his hand to Nagy and said: "Comrade Nagy, save what can be saved."

The two men embraced each other. When they withdrew from the embrace, Mikoyan's eyes were filled with tears.

"*Dosvidaniya, tovarishchi,* goodbye, comrades," he said.

He turned and left, accompanied by his two athletic bodyguards who had been standing quietly next to the entrance.

Nagy was in an excellent humour. "We may be at the turning point," he said.

Suslov and Mikoyan had accepted the main Hungarian demands: the retreat of the Soviet troops and the democratization of power.

"The leaders of the two armies will soon meet," Nagy said. "The tanks will leave Budapest, and within three months all of the Russian Army will be out of the country. We will proceed to general elections in which all democratic parties will present candidates. Land, banks, factories, and business enterprises will remain in the hands of the state." (On this latter point, Nagy had already obtained an agreement from the other parties.)

It was time to transmit this good news to the public. Joska Szilagyi had already prepared a communiqué for the radio. Nagy excused himself, saying he had to go over the text one last time. His famous pince-nez firmly adjusted, he was reading the communiqué when the door was abruptly pushed open and Kadar swept into the room.

"Imre, have we done it?"

"We've done it, Janos!"

Kadar had just accompanied Mikoyan and Suslov to the tank that was awaiting them at the foot of the front staircase of the Parliament building. The Soviet statesmen flew back to Moscow immediately. Kadar turned to me.

"We are overhauling the Communist Party, Kopacsi. It's going to be called the Hungarian Socialist Workers' Party. Right now, we're forming a provisional Politburo. There are Comrade Nagy, myself, Losonczy, George Lukacs, Donath, and Szanto, all comrades who suffered under Rakosi. We'd like you to be part of the leadership. Do you accept?"

"I didn't really suffer under Rakosi, as you know. Why did you pick me?"

"Because public opinion has adopted you, as you are. You'll do a major service to our new party by accepting. Do you accept?"

"I accept with pleasure, Comrade Kadar. With pleasure and pride."

"Thank you, Comrade Kopacsi."

He turned toward Nagy. "Do you know that the writer Tibor Dery refused?"

Nagy smiled indulgently. Tibor Dery was one of the *bêtes noires* of the Rakosi regime; three months earlier, the dictator had had him expelled from the Communist Party.

"I'll have a word with him," Nagy replied.

After Kadar left, we had a discussion with Nagy about a plan to create a new National Guard, combining regular police and armed rebel forces, to cleanse Budapest of adventurers and other doubtful elements. Nagy hoped I would be one of the commanders of this new force. When we were finished, Nagy held us back for a moment.

"I can't just name you to this post. You have to win support from the revolutionary committees and have yourself elected." By this time, there were revolutionary committees within the Ministry of Defence, the army, and the police. "The bayonet can't make itself respected without the support of the people," Nagy continued. "You have the opportunity to be among the revolutionary captains who, unfortunately, have been so rare in history."

To become a "revolutionary captain", I first had to deal with members of the government who didn't think like Imre Nagy. I'd just returned to police headquarters when I had a call from Munnich.

"Comrade Kopacsi, I have a very urgent mission that I want you to handle personally. Take a detachment of officers and go to arrest two journalists, Miklos Gimes and Paul Locsei, who are in the process of putting out a rag at the print shop of *Free People (Szabad Nep)*."

One of these journalists had been on the editorial committee of *Free People*, the party newspaper, and the other was an editorial writer on the same paper, but both had been dismissed from their posts some months earlier at Rakosi's insistence. Before replying, I sent everyone, including my wife who had come to visit me, out of my office.

"Comrade Munnich, I know both those journalists very well. They are good Communists. Since October 23, hundreds of publications have been put out and I'm astonished that it's precisely two

Communist comrades that you want to arrest."

Munnich replied curtly that an order was to be followed, not discussed.

"And you insist that I head the detachment?"

"The order is in your name and you are personally responsible for its proper execution."

"Thank you, Comrade Minister."

I smelled a trap. Since the day before, the office of the party paper had been serving as headquarters of an armed group directed by one of the older insurgent leaders, Joseph Dudas, a man in his forties. A former Communist, he had been expelled from the party in 1946 for being a member of the minority Demeny faction and had spent eight years imprisoned in a forced labour camp. He was now said to have anarchist leanings. Dudas had more than three hundred followers, armed to the teeth. They were printing a new paper at the newspaper office and were using the six-storey building as a fortress. Dudas hadn't recognized the Nagy government as having more authority than any other insurrectionist group. For the moment, he was uncommitted.

If Munnich had ordered me to attack Dudas, that would have been different. We would have rounded up our forces. But he had merely said to "take two journalists" who just happened to be working in Dudas's fortress. It was night. I took twenty-five men with me. My deputy demanded to accompany us but I refused permission.

"Tell my wife that I've left on a routine patrol."

The secretary of the party organization at police headquarters ran after me. "Sandor, let me wear your uniform. I'll command the detachment in your place."

I was embarrassed in front of my men and declined his offer. We climbed into an open truck and headed for the newspaper building. On the way, I briefed the men. I said we were not going to use a combat formation. As soon as the truck stopped, we would get out and stroll toward the fortress. They were not to open fire.

The truck stopped and took cover against the St. Roch Hospital. In the darkness, we walked off, myself in the lead, with my sub-machine gun slung over my shoulder. Near the National Theatre, my heart skipped a beat. On the roof of the building, I could make out the silhouette of a heavy machine gun. Evidently, Dudas, as a former military officer, knew that a fortress needs weapons as backup. The machine gun's barrel pivoted as we approached. Around us, the lampposts were all knocked down, the overhead wires for the streetcars were on the ground, and the picture windows of the editorial office were on the asphalt in a thousand pieces.

We reached the newspaper office without being fired on. At that moment, we heard a loud whistling. A second later, we were surrounded by at least fifty people, civilians and soldiers, all armed with submachine guns or rifles. An army lieutenant, a revolver in his fist, came up.

"Who are you? AVO?"

"You crazy? Look at this shit we're wearing." The AVO, when they disguised themselves as "simple police", wore brand-new uniforms.

I gave my identity and position and lied that we were on a routine patrol.

"Besides, Lieutenant, we don't often find guys like you who smoke real European cigarettes; since the night of the insurrection we've only had 'wooden-bench'." (Wooden bench was slang for the foul-smelling cigarettes issued to the police and armed forces, the cigarettes that the man from Bull's Blood had brought us.)

The officer looked at me in astonishment; he slipped his revolver into its holster and pulled a package of cigarettes out of his pocket. "Help yourself."

He gave me a light. But the heavy machine gun on the roof of the theatre remained pointed in our direction. My men began chatting with his while I asked him, "You haven't seen any journalists in the building, have you?"

"Which journalists?"

"I've got two close friends, two journalists who are Communists like me. I'd really like to talk to them."

Their names meant nothing to him. Then I described them: a short, fat one with glasses and a tall, skinny one with long hair.

"Oh yeah. They were inside putting out their rag. They both left earlier tonight."

I breathed a sigh of relief. To arrest Gimes and Locsei would have been worse than painful for me. The lieutenant looked me squarely in the eyes.

"Do you work for Imre Nagy?"

"Of course. There is a legal revolutionary government and Nagy is the prime minister."

"Thanks for the information, but we don't recognize it."

"That's your business."

"We don't want Communists running the country or the army any longer."

"That's your right."

"And we don't want Imre Nagy's people sniffing around here at night."

"Then all you have to do is order your man behind the gun on the roof over there to let us go quietly and we'll clear out."

He looked at me.

"Tell Imre Nagy that instead of sending patrols of cops, he should be negotiating with Dudas."

At a scarcely perceptible signal from the lieutenant, a man left the group and entered the building. Almost at the same time, the barrel of the machine gun on the roof pivoted. The way was clear and we left as we had come.

We had barely arrived back at the St. Roch Hospital where our truck awaited when we were ambushed by gunmen hidden in a cross street. My men threw themselves on the ground and awaited my order to return the fire. I was so surprised I remained standing, shouting epithets at our attackers.

"Shit! Fucking assholes, who are you? What in hell are you shooting like lunatics for?"

From the shadows, a voice shouted, "You're not the AVO?"

"You stupid runt, why don't you ask who we are before you shoot? We're from the ordinary police."

In the silence that followed, we saw a crowd of black silhouettes crouched under the entrances to the buildings on the street. One of them approached me, a small, young man in a turtleneck sweater with a revolver in his fist.

"Good evening, Kopacsi."

He pocketed his revolver. It was Steven Angyal, commander of the young workers of Tuzolto Street, our negotiating partner of the other day. He offered me a cigarette and took one himself.

"What are you looking for here?"

I gave him a light.

"And you?"

Angyal smiled.

"Patrol."

"The same for us."

We didn't speak of Dudas or the AVO. We smoked without saying anything.

"Angyal...."

"Yes, Kopacsi?"

"We've got an appointment tomorrow."

"It's possible."

I knew that he and the Pongratz brothers had been invited to the inaugural meeting of the revolutionary committee of the armed forces. His people stayed hidden in the cross street. Mine remained standing, submachine guns slung across their shoulders. The nocturnal interlude was over. I shook hands with Angyal and climbed into the truck with my men.

Half an hour later, I reported by telephone to Munnich. If he was disappointed to discover me still among the living, he didn't show it. He didn't ask any questions about my nocturnal meetings, but he undoubtedly made a mental note to the effect that it was true what they said about Kopacsi: he was a lad who consorted with the insurgents.

After this episode, I remained suspicious of Munnich as did others in Nagy's closest circle. He was excluded from playing any part in the formation of the National Guard.

"Daddy, I broke Stalin's bust."

The lack of sleep had me in such a state that at first I didn't understand what my daughter, Judith, was saying over the telephone. She explained: together with Joska Szilagyi's children, she had spent part of the morning making a clean sweep of the house. They had found some little porcelain busts of Stalin and Rakosi that were sold to every office and factory worker in the country. They had started with Rakosi's. With the help of a hammer, they had smashed in Rakosi's head and thrown the debris in the garbage. Judith had hesitated a bit before assigning the same fate to Stalin. She had been heavily exposed to the Stalin personality cult during her early school years. But the children gave each other mutual encouragement and this idol too finished in the garbage can.

"Daddy, then I saw the roasted Russian."

"What!"

I almost fell out of my chair. It turned out that during the morning, the children had gone off by themselves into the centre of Budapest. Judith went into Old Comedy Street where people were surrounding a Russian tank that was burnt to a cinder with the remains of one of its occupants visible in the turret.

"Judith, are you crazy? Who let you wander around like that in a city where there is still fighting going on?"

"There's no more fighting, I saw the Russians leaving in their tanks. Everybody was shouting, 'Goodbye, *bon voyage*,' at them. People passed Hungarian flags to the soldiers and I gave my doll to a soldier in a tank."

With that eyewitness report, I learned for the first time of the general retreat of the Russian armoured divisions from the capital. My men furnished other details: the so-called Russian area around the Soviet Embassy was moving out *en masse*. The large modern buildings built for the foreign guests were emptying out floor by floor: mattresses and sofas were strapped onto the roof racks of cars along with fat suitcases made of real leather (available only in special cadre stores in Budapest) and silk-covered duvets. As the floors emptied, squatters of all ages and in all conditions, from the poorest sections of Budapest, occupied the apartments, with their children, their old, and their sick. There were no incidents; the new occupants waited patiently for the Russians to leave before moving in. We didn't have to intervene until the Home for the Deaf and Dumb called for help. Some people were trying to occupy their building, which was near the former Soviet residences.

I was able to bid farewell to Petofi. He came to see me, dressed in a dark suit, with flowing pants and silvery tie, very much in the style of old Russia. He seemed perplexed.

"Sandor, I'm leaving with my compatriots. I don't know what's going to happen; I don't even know if we'll ever see each other again."

He seemed preoccupied with his fate and mine. Rumour had it that their political police were particularly severe toward all the Soviets returning from Budapest. Just like the tank soldiers of the brief and disastrous invasion, Petofi in their eyes was nothing but a contaminated man who had seen too many things that are not written about in the party manual. I thanked him for the good times we had spent together and we embraced. He told his interpreter to go down and warn the chauffeur that he was ready. As soon as we were alone, he bent close to my ear.

"Sandor. . .you. . .be careful."

I looked at him without understanding. In broken Hungarian, he whispered, "New Russian counsellor. You understand? Him stay Budapest."

The "new Russian counsellor". . . .Petofi was undoubtedly referring to the little blond man I had met at Minister Piros's office on the day of the insurrection.

Petofi looked at me and put a finger in front of his mouth, indicating that this warning had been given in strict confidence. Then he turned on his heel and went out. Through the window, I saw him bending down to get into his car. I never even knew his real name.

That night, the senior officers of the Ministry of Defence came to see me. Major-General Istvan Kovacs, chief of the general staff, and major-generals Varadi, Uszta, and Toth arrived, each with his half-track and his own little personal guard. These were all friends, all sincere democrats and patriots. But they hadn't yet gotten into the habit of revolutionary austerity.

We were all to attend the first meeting of the revolutionary committee of the armed forces. The generals left their guards behind and together we piled into a jalopy. And that's how we took over the leadership of the Kilian Barracks, a recognized centre of armed insurrection, a legendary place that the Russians had assaulted ten times and from which they had ten times been repulsed with bloody losses. We approached Ulloi Street, the main artery of the workers' neighbourhood on the banks of the Danube, the cradle of the insurrection. Two hundred metres before the Kilian Barracks, we were stopped by a barricade of ropes jointly guarded by insurgents in civilian dress and ordinary soldiers.

"Stop. Where are you going like that?"

"To see Major-General Maleter."

"Major-General Maleter is busy, you can't disturb him."

"We're invited to attend the meeting of the revolutionary committee of the armed forces."

"You? At the revolutionary committee?"

The little insurgent looked at us incredulously, staring at the generals' kepis and their jackets decorated with medals. But he finally let us call Maleter, who gave the word to let us pass.

Before we arrived at the gate of the barracks, we passed through a veritable museum of the insurrection. I saw four very large Russian 150mm guns; they had been unlimbered without any infantry cover and taken before they had fired a shot. The coffins of Russians and Hungarians killed in the same battle were side by side in the street, bearing chalk marks identifying them as either "Russian" or "Hungarian".

Everywhere, we saw burnt-out tanks, the remains of half-tracks.

On one of the guns, a Budapest humourist had carved in large letters the slogan, "Scrap metal strengthens peace." Amidst the debris I spotted the three large police buses that I had lent to the army on the first day of the insurrection. Riddled with bullets, and with windows smashed, sides dented, and tires burnt to cinders, their days of usefulness were over.

In front of the entrance to the barracks was parked Paul Maleter's legendary T-34, with the Hungarian flag attached to its turret. The tank was too big to get through the gate of the barracks, which dated from the reign of the Empress Maria-Teresa. Since we'd last seen him from our windows at the police station heading his detachment of five tanks, Maleter had joined the revolutionary forces he'd been sent to crush. Maleter's prestige was such that when he changed sides, it inspired many others to do the same. People came to touch the T-34 as they would a good luck talisman.

Guards led us to Maleter's office, which had been converted into a meeting room for this occasion.

Although this was the first time we had spoken, we embraced like old friends. We had seen each other before at the Partisans' Union, where Maleter had always seemed to be busy finding accommodation or work for the family of a friend recently liberated from prison.

The room was an amazing sight, right out of an Eisenstein movie about the October Revolution. At the back were some sailors from the Danube fleet, decked out in striped jerseys. In one corner of the room was an old man with a bushy moustache and string of cartridges slung over his shoulder, the representative of an insurrectionists' group. A short, young man had pistols sticking out of every pocket and even out of his boots, as though he had got himself up as a revolutionary for a costume ball. But this was no masquerade; the bandages covering the foreheads and hands of various delegates were soaked in real blood.

Maleter, who had asked each revolutionary group to send delegates to the meeting, spoke first:

"We have fought and some of us have died in the cause of an independent, socialist Hungary. Right now, everything seems to be coming together. The Russians are leaving. The purpose of this meeting is to lay the foundations for a new armed force in our country. This force is born of the insurrection, but we must ensure that reactionary elements, wanting to re-establish the old prewar regime, don't worm their way into it. That regime, fortunately, is dead, and there will never be capitalists and landowners in Hungary again. Am I understood? Does everybody agree?"

The response wasn't overwhelmingly positive; the days when unanimity was *de rigueur* seemed to be over. But everybody murmured a clearly audible yes.

Maleter continued: "Our new armed force will be there to prevent foreign elements from penetrating into our country, from the western borders as well as from the east. Our country will be neutral, without foreign influence."

This time, the applause was unreserved.

Bela Kiraly and I, Nagy's candidates to lead this new force, introduced ourselves. Then the debate began. Programs of "thirteen points" and "sixteen points" rained down on the audience. There were all sorts of political programs, each representing a different shade of opinion, with many eccentric variations. Finally, Maleter interrupted.

"My friends, an independent Hungary will proceed to free elections in three months. Let the parties fight out the political issues among themselves. Our task is different. It is to re-establish public order and avoid at any price providing the slightest pretext for another intervention by the Soviet troops who, as you know, are still surrounding Budapest. So let's proceed to the election of a unified command. Let's vote."

An old insurgent with a decidedly martial air raised his hand.

"I'm the commander of the combat group of South Railway Station in Buda. We've just heard the list of dignitaries of the new Communist Party read on the radio. In second place, just after Janos Kadar, was the name of Sandor Kopacsi. I would really like to know why this man is among us and why he wants to be elected deputy commander of our armed forces."

Another insurgent, a younger man, went further.

"Exactly! Kopacsi's got no business here. My group fought on October 24 against the police. We had men wounded. How can you propose such a man to a high post in our revolutionary militia?"

Maleter asked me to respond and I did.

"Okay, I've not hidden the fact that I'm a Communist. That is my past, present, and future. But I was among the first in the party to oppose Rakosi's tyranny. As far as the fighting is concerned, you know well that when someone shoots at you, there aren't thirty-six different ways to respond — you shoot back.

"When the people call me, without shooting first, I come out unarmed among them as I did on October 25. To the question, 'How can you propose me as a candidate to a high post in the revolutionary militia?' my reply is that I haven't asked for anything. I'm a good soldier, loyal to Imre Nagy. Each of you has a vote and each can exercise it as he wishes."

I sat down, in a very poor humour, just as the telephone on Maleter's desk rang. He picked it up and said he didn't want to be disturbed, but the expression on his face quickly changed.

"Yes, Comrade Nagy, I'll do what's necessary."

He turned toward me.

"Kopacsi, Imre Nagy tells me that the abandoned Ministry of the Interior building is being sacked by passersby. It's your jurisdiction. Alert your men and go. You can use my phone. This meeting will reconvene later."

Almost immediately, however, I learned that I no longer had any available forces. After eight consecutive days of uninterrupted service, my men had gone home to have a meal and change their clothes. Only fifty officers remained on duty, not enough for a mission like this.

I looked at the elder of the Pongratz brothers.

"Will you lend your men?"

"You can try asking for volunteers."

Pongratz's headquarters was just across the street, at the Corvin movie theatre. I rushed down the stairs and ran across the street, which was covered with debris and dead bodies. At the theatre door — now nothing more than a gaping hole — two young civilians seized me by the arms.

"Who are you? An AVO colonel?"

"Don't be stupid, I'm the chief of police of Budapest. I've just been informed that a crowd is sacking the Ministry of the Interior and I need volunteers to go there with me."

Two minutes later, a large truck jammed with one hundred maniacs armed to the teeth left the theatre's courtyard under my command. We stopped in front of police headquarters to pick up a commando of uniformed policemen. At the windows, I saw a stunned Ibolya and my senior staff, who were doubled up in laughter at the sight of me at the head of such an unlikely force.

The operation was a success. The curious intruders wandering about the ministry were asked to leave. We had arrived just in time.

Safes had been broken open. Informers' files and tape-recordings, the results of wire-taps, were scattered about the floors. An angry population in possession of these documents might well have organized a massacre.

I left a guard, asked the university militia to send reinforcements, and went back to the Kilian Barracks to report to the insurgent leaders. I was then elected second in command of the Patriotic Revolutionary Militia.

Among the results of the election were frequent visits by members of this militia to my office at police headquarters. On November 2, there was a knock on my door.

"You'd better come down, Comrade Colonel; the militia has landed a big one."

I found a group of militiamen, trembling with indignation. They had detained a couple who were also trembling — from fear and anger. The woman was Elizabeth Andics, the director of the party school during my two years there. The man was her husband, the famous (or rather infamous) economist Andor Berei, president of the planning office. The commander of the detachment, a student, was boiling with rage.

"Comrade Colonel, when we asked this bastard here [pointing to Berei] for his papers', he couldn't think of anything better to do than to fire on us with his hunting rifle."

The militiamen, reinforced by other insurgents, had made a raid on the chic neighbourhoods of Buda inhabited by privileged members of the regime. They went from house to house, purportedly "to check identities", but really to try to flush out persons tainted by involvement in Rakosi's government. Berei, a small, bald man who looked like a shopkeeper, had always been part of Rakosi's entourage. He had grabbed his rifle and emptied it in the militia's direction. He was quickly subdued and, though he wasn't mistreated in any way, was brought to police headquarters, along with his wife.

In these revolutionary times, a prominent Rakosi supporter who fired on the militia risked being lynched. As I looked at this chubby little man I couldn't help but admire his guts. I had the couple taken into an adjoining room.

"Fine, comrades, I've taken possession of the prisoners."

The militiamen protested.

"Absolutely not. We're not leaving until we know what you're going to do."

I had an idea. During my time at the party school, I had learned that Elizabeth Andics had dual citizenship, Hungarian and Soviet. I had them brought back.

"Tell me, you two who were so happy to take potshots at these patriots, what is your nationality?" I asked sternly.

The man and woman replied in unison: "We are Soviet citizens."

The militiamen shouted in indignation: "You're Russians and you amuse yourselves shooting at Hungarians in their own country? Comrade Colonel, we'll hang them from a lamppost!"

They were pushing up their sleeves, ready for action. Berei gave me a look of contempt, while his astute wife, aware of what I was up to, gave me a grateful look.

"Wait a minute, comrades," I said. "Listen to me before you do something stupid. You know the orders: do nothing that might give the Russians a pretext to invade Budapest again. No one was hurt. These are foreign citizens. Reasons of state require that they get the same treatment as any other foreigner: they will be handed over to their own authorities, to their embassy. Duty officer, quickly, please, a car and two policemen. The rest of you can accompany them as far as the Soviet Embassy."

The insurgents weren't eager to visit the embassy, which was guarded by tanks. But they patiently awaited the return of my officer who confirmed that the couple had been turned over to the Soviets.

Elizabeth Andics and her husband would spend almost three years in the Soviet Union, along with Gero, Piros, and other high-ranking members of the Rakosi regime. They would take the trouble to testify in my favour at the Hungarian Embassy in Moscow. In the investigating officer's office, I read their testimony, which accorded exactly with what had happened. But this evidence was never presented in court. It disappeared, along with other items favourable to my defence.

▌ Continue as if Nothing Were Wrong

After the Soviet forces had withdrawn from Budapest, certain elements of the population felt a strong urge to have an inside look at a tyrannical power that had worked in the most absolute secrecy for the past dozen years. That was what prompted the invasion of the Ministry of the Interior as well as the breaking into and virtual sacking of the luxurious homes of Rakosi and Gero, vacant since their occupants had fled to the Soviet Union, and of the Farkases, senior and junior, the famous torturers now in a Budapest prison.

It occurred to no one to enter Kadar's fiefdom, the party head-quarters on Akademia Street, although it too had been abandoned by the Soviet tanks. Nor did anyone attempt an invasion of Parliament, the centre of power and residence of Imre Nagy, although the small guard left there would have been no match for the armed population of the city. However, one building whose secret life sparked the interest of its neighbours was the office of the Communist organization of Budapest, on Koztarsasag Square. For several days, the residents of the square had noticed an unusual commotion, as trucks arrived carrying AVO troops or large quantities of supplies (new police uniforms taken from the central depot, ammunition, and arms).

In reality, certain second- and third-ranking party leaders, conservative elements, and other persons petrified with fear, were organizing a sort of "parallel police" in the building, paramilitary shock troops who could provide protection for them if necessary.

These preparations would lead to their ruin. At about 9:00 a.m.

on October 30, a neighbourhood delegation asked to enter the house for purposes of "inspection". The neighbours were detained and thrown into cells. From the upper windows, troops fired on anyone who approached the building. People on the square pulled out their own guns and fired back. At about 10:00 a.m., we saw students and young workers running in the street, yelling, "The rats are slaughtering people on Koztarsasag Square."

The "rats" – the hated AVO – legally no longer existed. I called my friend Imre Mezo, first secretary of the Budapest party organization, to find out more about what was happening and to offer him police help to organize a retreat. I couldn't understand how Mezo, who had fought in Spain in the International Brigade, could have become involved in this. He was too busy to talk and passed me over to the third secretary, a certain Mrs. Csikesz, a worker with a harsh personality who had made a spectacular ascent in Rakosi's regime.

"Comrade Kopacsi! Don't worry, the last thing we need is a police commando of the Kopacsi persuasion."

I understood that in addition to ex-AVO officers, there were several army officers in the building, including some former Resistance fighters who were personal friends of mine. I asked to speak to one of them, Lieutenant-Colonel Lajos Szabo, but he was busy. Finally, I was connected to Lieutenant-Colonel Asztalos of the Ministry of Defence.

"What are you military people doing in there?" I wanted to know.

They had gone there that morning to try to set up a parallel police force that they planned to call the "Workers' Militia" in opposition to the National Guard. This was totally unrealistic.

I wanted to tell him, "Wake up, the workers are outside on the square with their guns pointed at you. The workers and you are shooting at each other." But I didn't.

"Asztalos, what is the situation?"

"Lousy. There are wounded and dead."

"Did you prepare something in case things turned out badly? Do you have a retreat route?"

"The AVO guys think we'll get out of it. We've been promised reinforcements, some tanks."

I was deeply puzzled by the credulity of my military friends. For several days now, the Hungarian armoured units had systematically refused to intervene against the population.

As it turned out, three tanks were sent to the scene, but it didn't take the crowd in the square long to convince the soldiers that the villains of the piece were the AVO officers inside. The turrets pivoted and pointed against the front of the party building. At the third shot, a breach was opened, large enough to persuade the building's defenders to surrender.

Rather than find a way out the back, they walked out into the square holding a white flag, into the middle of the crowd they had just peppered with bullets. At each step, they stumbled over the wounded and the dead. They didn't get far. Mezo, my friend, who was walking bravely at their head, was cut down by a bullet from the gun of "Wooden Leg", an elderly insurgent who, throughout the uprising, had been on the spot wherever and whenever things got hot. (Mezo was taken to hospital by the insurgents, but died the next day.) The officers from the Ministry of Defence, including my old friend from the Resistance, Lajos Szabo, suffered the same fate. They were taken for AVO officers and killed. Some fifteen AVO troops wearing police uniforms had hardly left the building before they too were shot. The bodies of some were horribly mutilated by the angry mob.

But the thirst for vengeance disappeared as fast as it had come. The crowd freed the delegation of neighbours imprisoned inside and took the rest of the defenders prisoner. When our newly formed patrols arrived, the leader of one of them called to me.

"Comrade Kopacsi, we're holding the woman Csikesz, one of the worst of the ones that were shooting on the crowd. What do we do with her?"

"Let her go home."

The militiamen put her on a half-track, delivered her to her home, and gave oranges and chocolate to her children.

Another survivor was Laszlo Molnar, one of my comrades from the anti-German Resistance in the north. An official of the Budapest party organization, he wore civilian clothes, but sported the partisan emblem on his jacket lapel. One of the insurgents grabbed him by the lapel, calling attention to the emblem. His arm was already raised to hit Molnar when another insurgent stopped him. "Don't touch that guy. *He's one of ours, a partisan.*"

When Molnar was released, he asked me to find him a job where he could be useful. I called Nagy's office and asked Joska if he could use a reliable person and Molnar was given a job in the prime minister's secretariat.

Nagy was pressing us to get the new National Guard functioning as quickly as possible. Bela Kiraly was doing his best and I could only admire his energy and organizing talent. Our goal was to put a strike force capable of ensuring the return to normal life at the government's disposal as soon as possible. I know that the word "normalization" has unfortunate overtones today after what happened in Czechoslovakia in 1968; but our normalization meant only an end to the fighting and a return to daily life, a resumption of production, and, especially, a rebirth of confidence among the people that their government had matters under control.

By Sunday, November 4, we expected to be able to mount two divisions of the National Guard, enough to get life going again in Budapest. Our adversaries were neither numerous nor strong enough to constitute a menace to public order. The insurgents themselves were quick to stop any acts of cruelty and disarm the perpetrators, most of whom were criminals who had taken advantage of the turmoil to escape from jail.

On November 1, Kiraly, myself, and our senior staff were hard at work when the orderly entered and announced, "Comrade, an armed group is in the building and they want to speak to Captain N."

I wasn't thrilled to have unknown armed groups wandering at will into police headquarters. As we dashed down the stairs five armed men confronted us. Their spokesman, a fat butcher, planted himself in front of me. "Do you recognize me?" he demanded.

I said I didn't know him from Adam and added that if he and his friends wanted to enter the building, they could leave their guns at the entrance.

"Not until I see Inspector N. I've got a couple of things to tell him."

"And what would those be?"

"A load of machine-gun fire in his belly."

I made a sign to the guards. A minute later, the butcher and his band were disarmed.

"Now let's talk. What have you got against Inspector N?"

The fat butcher had lost none of his gall. He explained that the inspector had headed an investigation that revealed that the butcher had killed his wife. As a result he had been sentenced to fifteen years, hard labour.

"Inspector N is a son of a bitch and whether you like it or not I'm going to get him."

"I doubt that."

I had all of them arrested. The four others were released soon after; they had tagged along with the butcher without knowing exactly what it was all about. The killer stayed in prison to serve out his sentence, which was extended on the charges of armed attack on police headquarters and murder threats against a member of the police.

Bela Kiraly was put through a much more serious test. Dudas's group, which still occupied the offices of the party newspaper, decided it was time for action. Dudas gave the order to occupy the Ministry of Foreign Affairs, which he believed was infested with Russians. (In fact, the only Soviets present at that time were those negotiating the withdrawal of Soviet troops and they were in the Parliament building.) Nagy responded by ordering Kiraly to dislodge Dudas's forces immediately. Kiraly arrived with a detachment of the new National Guard and was able to recapture the building without any loss of life. Dudas then declared he was "ready to talk to Imre Nagy". Dudas declared himself loyal to the new government and was allowed to leave on his word of honour that he would stop fighting. He was received by Nagy and from then on was considered a "benevolent observer of the political experiment in progress".

My deputy told me that I was wanted at Nagy's office. As I walked to the Parliament building, I found the atmosphere in the streets encouraging. Of course, a week of murderous fighting had left its traces. I saw overturned trams and the remains of burnt-out cars and tanks. But the fighting was visibly over. At a street corner, I came across a group of peasants distributing plucked ducks and sacks of potatoes from a truck — free of charge. The farmers were expressing their gratitude to the working class of Budapest for ending a regime that had imposed forced collectivization of agriculture.

In front of the old stock exchange building, employees of the Ministry of Finance were discussing the elections to their revolutionary committee — to their soviet as they called it. Along with Imre Keszi, a writer friend of mine who was hanging about there, I went in for a minute to see what was going on. My police colonel's uniform didn't upset anyone. We sat down on a row of seats reserved for the public. Complete free speech reigned, including a fierce attack on the government by an embittered old financial expert who was a holdover from the Horthy regime. But he was booed by the audience. The favourite of the assembly was a younger employee, a former social democrat and ex-jailbird under Rakosi, who had led the ministry's armed detachment during the uprising. Elected by secret ballot as president of the ministry's soviet, he was to represent all the personnel in its dealings with the government until the end of his mandate. The minister had to take his opinion into account or resign.

Back on the street, Keszi, a former Stalinist who had repented, drew my attention to the newspapers that young people were selling (yes, they were selling and no longer "distributing" them) on the street. The papers included publications no one had seen for ten years. The small farmers were once more publishing their old paper. The Catholics had founded a new one. The army was putting out a paper aimed at the public. The social democrats had split their former publication in two: those who had joined the Communists eight years earlier when the two parties amalgamated were publishing a small paper aimed at workers. Those who had refused to join the Communists were now once again members of a legal party and, under the direction of veteran militant Anna Kethly, had resumed publication of their party organ, the *People's Word (Nepszava)*, which had been founded a hundred years previously.

Meanwhile, the Communists had changed the name of *Free People*, the paper that until recently had followed the Rakosi line. It now carried the title *Freedom of the People (Nepszabadsag)* and displayed a Kossuth emblem on the front page next to an article by Kadar that ended with these words: "Our people have proven with their blood their intention to support without flinching the government's efforts to obtain a complete removal of the Soviet forces."

The newly employed journalists on all these fledgling newspapers were working without pay, as were the printers. And the money collected from selling the papers was going to collection boxes for the uprising's victims.

While the occupation of the Suez Canal zone by British, French, and Israeli forces was a major story that day, the news-hungry citizens of Budapest were more interested in another page one item — the official statement of the Soviet government on the subject of Hungary. The story went like this:

> The Soviet government has ordered its military command to remove its formations out of the cities as soon as the Hungarian government deems it necessary. [Troops were still stationed in Pecs, Miskolc, and other large centres.]

It declares itself ready to engage in negotiations with the government of the Hungarian Popular Republic and other signatories to the Warsaw Treaty concerning the presence of Soviet troops on Hungarian territory.

People were favourably impressed by this declaration. I bought several newspapers to show Joska, who received me in a mood I didn't like at all. I found him extremely talkative, which wasn't like him. He spoke quickly, giving me news of our children, who were all being cared for together by his wife, Ella. He then offered a vague description of the paradise on earth that would be "Hungary after Sunday". (Sunday, November 4, was when Kiraly and I had scheduled the definitive clean-up of Budapest.)

"Joska, what's got into you?"

"Nothing. I only wanted to see you to...to get details of your operation on Sunday."

"The plan is sound. Kiraly is a terrific guy. By Monday, there won't be anyone carrying arms in the streets of Budapest except members of the army and the National Guard. The workers' councils know what's happening. They've given the green light for a resumption of production. What else do you want us to do?"

"And so a new Hungary, democratic and neutral, takes wing," said Joska, his eyes full of tears.

I grabbed him by the shoulders. "Now you're going to tell me what's worrying you."

He looked at me, his black eyes so sad that my heart went out to him.

"Sandor, promise me that you'll continue with Kiraly as if nothing were wrong. The old man insists on that above all else."

Naturally, I promised him. Then he opened up.

"I'm afraid."

"Of who, of what?"

"The Russians. I've got the impression that they're setting a trap."

"Which means?"

"That they're coming back in force."

"That's impossible! The declaration of the Soviet government...."

Joska looked at me and spoke in a solemn voice. "Here are the most recent reports. Since October 29, the chief of our post on the Soviet border has reported the entry of new troops and materiel into Hungarian territory. Since yesterday, all the provincial army headquarters have reported heavily equipped troops on the roads, *en route* to Budapest. Russian troops and equipment are also flowing in from Romania. We no longer have any aerial reconnaissance because planes can't take off. All the military airports are surrounded. The stations at Kisvarda and Nyiregyhaza are in the hands of the Russian Army, which is exchanging fire with our railwaymen. According to the reports, the Soviets have 200,000 men massed in eastern Hungary, twelve divisions, of which eight are armoured. It's enough to flatten us like a pancake."

My first reaction was to sputter, "Does Imre Nagy know about this?"

He did, of course.

"Ambassador Andropov has just left his office. He was summoned to hear the Prime Minister protest against the massing of troops in Hungary. The old man added that this was a violation of the Warsaw Pact and if the troops weren't withdrawn to their previous positions, the Hungarian government would renounce the treaty."

"How did Andropov respond?"

"I think he's lying in his teeth. He said that the Soviet government was adhering entirely to its declaration of October 30 concerning the retreat of its troops and that the movements we observed were only a kind of 'relief'. In fact, the Russians are invading us in force."

I asked him what we were going to do.

"Continue! Continue as if nothing were wrong. We will arrange life as if there were life to live. We will organize Hungary as if it had a thousand years of liberty ahead of it."

He made me promise to keep absolutely secret what I had just learned. In return, he promised to keep me up to date. We managed to part with a smile.

The reader might ask why we did not make plans to resist the invasion we now knew was a certainty, why Nagy never ordered his followers to fight back. First, we lived in hope that perhaps the Western powers who had hitherto refused assistance might come to our rescue after all. Second, what commander would take the responsibility for the death of perhaps 200,000 men, women, and children to prolong the life of a government by perhaps only days or weeks? It would be national suicide. I've never admired Masada.

Two hours later, Nagy phoned Andropov. He informed him that his military experts had formally established that new units had crossed the border and that, in violation of its own declaration, the

Soviet Union was reoccupying Hungary. As a result, Hungary renounced the Warsaw Pact, effective immediately. At 4:00 p.m., the cabinet, with Kadar present, declared the neutrality of Hungary. At 5:00 p.m., Andropov was again summoned to Parliament, where the declaration of neutrality was handed to him in the presence of the ministers. Good at dancing the polka, but a diplomat without ethics, Andropov assured Nagy that the Soviet troops would leave the country and asked the Hungarian government to withdraw its complaint to the United Nations. Nagy agreed on condition that the troops be withdrawn.

During this meeting, Kadar was particularly enraged. (This was ironic in light of future events.) He declared in front of Andropov that if Soviet troops re-entered Budapest, he, Kadar, would "go down into the streets and fight them with my bare hands". Andropov adopted an air of innocence. "But really, Comrade! This is all a misunderstanding. Let's continue the military negotiations." (While there was agreement in principle, the details of the withdrawal remained to be negotiated.)

Hungary had been invaded again. All that remained was the order to march on Budapest. But the Russians insisted on acting out to the end their horrible drama of intrigue, taken from the Asiatic repertoire of past centuries, just as they had done in 1939 before the conclusion of the German-Soviet pact and as they would do again in 1968 in Czechoslovakia. The "negotiations" continued.

Farewell to Our Dreams

I was up to my neck in work in connection with the new National Guard. In making the final arrangements for what we were calling "Operation Sunday", Kiraly and I had to deal with fifteen different local headquarters of this new force as well as eighty committees in the large factories and ten in the universities.

When I was in the midst of these labours, Ibolya suddenly appeared. It was just a short walk from the Ministry of the Interior in Roosevelt Square, where she worked clipping the foreign press, to the police station. All the employees there had been told to stay in the building, day and night. No one could leave without a pass; but she had managed to slip away.

"I've told George and he'll drive us to the house," she said innocently.

"What's this?"

Ibolya explained calmly that we hadn't seen our daughter for eight days and it was time to go and give her a kiss. An hour or two of relaxation would do us a world of good and Kiraly should come along too.

"Ibolya, please, there's no time. This is a revolution."

She frowned.

"For Sandor, it's always the revolution. I've heard it since I was a child that you have to know when to end a strike, and I say you also have to know when to finish a revolution. You've made your revolution. Now it's time for an hour of rest."

Kiraly, courteous man that he was, took Ibolya's side. Our

Operation Sunday was ready. Forty-eight hours later, there wouldn't be a single gun in the streets that wasn't in the hands of the new forces of order, not a factory that wasn't back at work, not an office or store that hadn't opened its doors. The teachers would resume their courses and the children would pick up their pencils and books. After the convulsion of rebirth, the country would begin again to live — in liberty.

"Of course," said Kiraly. "I'll stay here. You go and relax for an hour or two."

George drove us home. For the next hour, I spent most of my time fixing the heating. Then, with my daughter and Joska's children, we played with the animals, who were mad with joy. Judith said they had been like that since the fighting stopped.

"They hated the shooting. They were hiding under the table during the whole revolution. Now they're happy because there's peace."

They weren't the only ones. During the ride back to police headquarters, we looked out silently at Budapest, whose citizens had fought so hard for liberty. Seen from the hills of Buda, the great city seemed serene; the Danube flowed along, immense and calm, as if nothing were amiss. It wasn't the blue Danube, that's true, but the grey Danube of autumn.

"Sandor," said Ibolya softly, "what if we went back to the north?"

I had been thinking of the same thing. Our years in Budapest, Rakosi, the trials and tribulations as well as the good times, Andropov, "Petofi", the smell of fresh wax on the floors of the police station — all that seemed to me now like a dream. Suddenly, I burst out laughing.

"What are you laughing about all by yourself?" Ibolya asked.

"I was thinking of the little red-headed police inspector who told me, 'If you start too soon you'll finish too high.'"

"We'll begin again at Diosgyor."

"Of course. I can't wait to see Banhegyi [my old teacher] again, and my pals. I can't wait to find out if I can still turn a piece on the lathe."

Ibolya threw her arms around my neck and George turned around with a little smile on his lips.

"So, Comrade Colonel, are we going to headquarters or to Diosgyor?"

Diosgyor would have to be for another time because Kiraly and I were due shortly at Parliament. Once there, we found the corridors filled with military men, summoned by Maleter, the recently named Minister of Defence. Maleter wanted to assess the morale of our forces before beginning the final phase of negotiations with the Russians. There were also civil delegations of workers and peasants who had come from the four corners of Hungary to see Imre Nagy. I was surprised to find, among some people from Diosgyor, Andras K, one of the old foremen in my former workshop.

"Andras, what brings you here?"

"I represent Engineering Number Two [a workshop of about 300 people] where you were brought up, son. I'm here to decide whether we should go along with Nagy or continue on strike."

"But, Andras, the whole country is going back to work on Monday. The Russians are leaving. We have to start over again. It's clear."

The old foreman looked at me, an ironic smile on his lips.

"For you and your father, everything was always 'clear'. But for us, you know, it's different. We want to be shown."

The remark about my father saddened me. He had never been a yes-man. On the contrary, he had always been filled with doubts. As worker social democrats, father and son had gravitated naturally to Communism. The example of the Soviet Army in fighting German fascism had played a big part in that.

But we felt deeply the injustices committed by the Communists against our social democratic comrades. It needed years of cold war and all the Communist Party's anti-imperialist propaganda to lead us to the conclusion that, all in all, it was the Soviet Union that most effectively defended the rights of ordinary people, and that during a period of cold war it was the Communist Party in our country that could best look after the workers' interests.

Doubt doesn't easily find its way into the conscience of those who for generations have thought of nothing but how to improve conditions for workers. We had been sincere social democrats, but we felt fear and panic at the idea that our country could again fall under the old regime when the propertied classes ran the show.

After Stalin's death, with the coming of the more liberal era of Khrushchev and Nagy, my father had hoped for an improvement in the Communist regime — no more than that. He, like me, hoped that Rakosi himself would improve, that in the name of "Communist justice" he would adopt a more democratic policy, in line with what the Soviet Union was now prescribing.

He wasn't a stupid man, far from it. He was a cultivated and sensible working man. But when you pass an entire life in the service of an ideal, that ideal, whether true or false, has a hold on you. For my father, the party was always right, simply because he knew too well its detractors who so often were wrong, especially during the war against the Nazis.

During the 1956 revolution, my father, who was then in his fifties, was mayor of the fifteenth district of Budapest. He had left Diosgyor six years earlier, originally to become director of a technical school in the capital. He was happy in his work. Demonstrating the same courage he had shown during the war, he confronted party authorities daily on behalf of the people in his district who deluged him with their problems.

Curiously, the days of insurrection did little to change his opinions or his activities. Comrade Joseph Kopacsi was at his desk every day. All that changed were the subjects that he had to deal with. Such and such a revolutionary committee called him to procure transportation to bring in fresh supplies. An old party comrade, about to be thrown into the street by his neighbours, begged him to make them listen to reason. (And they listened, not because he was mayor, but because they knew his integrity.) During the revolution, my father was just as busy as I was, if not busier, and often his activities were far more useful.

We spoke to each other on the telephone several times a day. The telephone service functioned almost everywhere in Budapest, even after furious artillery battles. Our hasty conversations usually ended the same way: "Take care of yourself, take care of the child."

We knew we wouldn't be able to meet until, as he said, "this party is over". But on the day before Operation Sunday, my father and I arranged a rendezvous.

"Sandor, the guys at the Siemens factory gave me six chickens. You don't want them to spoil, do you? Rain or shine, Monday at noon, you're eating at our place with Ibolya and the kid. All right, my boy? I want to talk to you face to face."

On Monday, we would eat chicken paprika, sprinkled with a little white Tokay wine from my own modest cellar. What did he want to say to me "face to face"? Did he want to speak of the important truths he had learned during fifty years of struggle and during these twelve days of revolution? Or would he simply have been content to place his hand on my head as before?

But on Monday, November 5, 1956, we did not eat chicken paprika together. Nor on Tuesday nor on the days that followed. And at our next meeting, eight years later, it would not be he who would place his hand on my hair, but rather I who would smooth down his while the Hungarian and Soviet officials on the other side of the catafalque looked on. They had made it impossible for us to hold our little family reunion to celebrate the end of the revolution. Instead they accorded us this final rendezvous.

"Sit down, Comrade Kopacsi, I have to talk to you."

Imre Nagy had taken off his pince-nez and he looked at me with tired eyes that had been sleepless for days and nights. Joska was in the room, a telephone to his ear.

"My question is simple: do you have any idea where the Minister of the Interior is?"

I had to say that I had none. As of the day before, I had been unable to reach Ferenc Munnich. He had deserted the ministry. I had looked for him all morning at the national police headquarters, where he and his friend Pocze liked to play a two-handed card game called kalabrias. There was no trace of him there or at his home.

Nagy and Joska exchanged glances.

"You should know that the first secretary of the party, Janos Kadar, also cannot be found. Yesterday he took part in all our deliberations. Today, he's disappeared without a trace."

I was dumbfounded. Without further comment, Nagy told me he was counting on Bela Kiraly and me to ensure public order.

His face bore an expression of almost insane hope as he said, "Nothing must disturb the atmosphere of the country at this crucial moment. Can you and Kiraly guarantee nothing will happen that could be labelled an anti-Soviet provocation and used as a pretext for breaking off the negotiations?"

We were ready for the next day's operation. We could concentrate the major part of our forces in different parts of Budapest from this evening. We had 20,000 rifles and they could be distributed tonight, I told the Prime Minister.

Nagy turned to Joska: "Bring in all the delegations that are waiting in the halls. Armed force is one thing, but to avoid any incident, the population must understand the seriousness of the moment and act accordingly."

As usual, Nagy's door was wide open. The people who were

waiting in the anteroom came in, along with Maleter and other members of the government delegation that was about to leave for Soviet general headquarters. The greater part of the agreement on troop withdrawal had been worked out on our turf, in the Parliament building. There remained only technicalities to be decided — what to do with the burnt-out tanks, whether the departing soldiers should be presented with bouquets by schoolchildren — and these would be talked over twenty-five kilometres from Budapest at Tokol, where Soviet headquarters was located, surrounded by Russian ground and air forces. Because the talks had been so amicable and the Russians had seemed so sincere, we had agreed to this request.

"Comrade Nagy, the government delegation is ready to go."

The room fell silent. The young Maleter, Minister of Defence with the new rank of Major-General of the Hungarian Army, glanced around.

"Comrade Nagy, I see that the tension is great."

"That's because the moment is decisive," replied Nagy.

What he said was serious, but Nagy couldn't help smiling to see the confident expression of the young minister.

"It'll turn out all right, you'll see," Maleter said. "The head of the Soviet delegation, General Malinin, is a great guy. The two other generals, Shcherbanin and Stepanov, also seem fine. You know that this morning we finished the first phase of the negotiations, here at Parliament. These military men are faithful and loyal negotiating partners. We've had to discuss delicate problems, dates, difficult formalities such as the military music and farewell speeches to be made at the moment of departure. Don't laugh, comrades, the Soviet government insists on it and together we had to discuss mass psychology and other problems. Tonight, we'll clear up the final details."

"Let's hope," sighed Nagy.

He ordered Maleter to inform the government by phone of their arrival at Tokol, then to report by telephone on the progress of the negotiations every half hour. He shook hands with every member of the delegation. In addition to Maleter, there were three: Ferenc Erdei, Minister of State, Major-General Kovacs, the military chief of staff, and Colonel Szucs.

"Good luck, my boys," said Nagy. "I won't budge until you get back. I can't wait to squeeze you in my arms again."

Maleter put on his kepi, saluted, and smiled. Nagy made a sign of encouragement with his hand. The man was smiling, but behind the smile was a profound fatigue. I thought it was lack of sleep. At the time, I didn't know that at that moment he had no more illusions. This man who had spent more than fifteen years in the Soviet Union knew that with the Russians there was always a difference between words and acts. He adjusted his pince-nez.

"Well, Joska? Send in everybody who has problems. We're not going to laze about, are we? The night is long."

As the new military commander of Budapest, Bela Kiraly made a tour of the Ministry of Defence before rejoining me at police headquarters. He came back with discouraging news.

"Sandor, there are troop movements. Everywhere. And these reports aren't just from our observation posts, they're from individuals, from hundreds of phone calls coming from every part of the country. Here's a map of the invasion, drawn up from the reports."

He spread out a map of Hungary, with multicoloured arrows, on my desk. From the reports, we knew that ten divisions were on the move in key areas of the country. At least five armoured columns were converging on Budapest. Kiraly called Joska on the direct line.

"Has the old man seen the map of the invasion?"

"He has it."

"What does he say?"

"He believes in a miracle. 'The negotiations, the negotiations.'"

"Maleter?"

"Arrived safely. We've had two reports. They're optimistic. I'd even say very optimistic."

"Damn it, maybe the old man's right after all. Miracles exist."

"Yeah," replied Joska. "You're lucky; you've got faith."

The red telephone from the Ministry of Defence was ringing every three minutes. As I took calls, I kept adding arrows to the map. For the first time in my life, I became a military strategist, drawing up plans for the defence of Budapest with Kiraly.

From time to time, we called Nagy's office for news of Maleter. At Soviet general headquarters, everything was going beautifully. An agreement in principle had already been concluded on the timing of the Soviet retreat. General Malinin was being exquisitely polite. Not only did he display a ready understanding of the Hungarian government's point of view, but he was proposing formulas to make the wording of the final protocol more flexible. I began to rally to the Catholic point of view — maybe there were such things as miracles after all.

At 11:00 p.m., a Soviet jeep stopped in front of police headquarters. One of our militiamen was at the wheel and he and another militiaman led two Soviet servicemen into the wing of the building that Kiraly's men had been occupying for the past few days. We heard voices raised in argument and hurried over. Colonel M, one of Kiraly's senior staff, was questioning a Soviet major and a little Kalmuk sergeant, both of whom belonged to an armoured division we'd never heard of. The two Soviets were dumbfounded, the sergeant visibly panic-stricken. The major claimed they had simply gotten lost; he had no idea that it was forbidden to venture into the outskirts of Budapest.

"I don't even know what's happening in Budapest, I was simply ordered to go to the Soviet general headquarters near here."

Colonel M had already ordered sandwiches, coffee, and rum for these two "lost" Soviet servicemen. The atmosphere became less tense. Colonel M described the past few days for our guests. The major listened, open-mouthed, while the little sergeant, who didn't seem to understand Russian, wolfed down his food.

Finally the major declared: "The Hungarians are not our enemies."

Colonel M ordered some cognac and we clinked our glasses. But our hearts weren't in it. I looked at Kiraly. Discreetly, he gave the order to consider the two Soviets as prisoners of war. We left the room to take stock of the situation. It was clear that the Soviet major was lying. He claimed to have come directly from the Soviet Union. We knew that the events in Hungary were being widely discussed in the Soviet media. His government had issued an official communiqué on the subject on October 30. Soviet radio broadcasts were preparing public opinion for a general retreat of the Soviet Army from Hungarian territory. However, this officer belonged to one of the columns that our information told us were converging on Budapest. It was more than probable that he was in the vanguard.

I called Joska and asked him to connect me to the old man, who came on the line immediately. I informed him that we were holding the two Soviets. His response was forceful and definite.

"Comrade Kopacsi, you know very well that Hungary has become a neutral country. We must avoid even the slightest incident with the Soviet Union. I want you to take a car and conduct the two Soviets under escort to their embassy. I want to be informed as soon as the order is executed."

Twenty minutes later I made my report by telephone: order executed.

But the black clouds were already piling up on the horizon. Joska called to tell us that Maleter had stopped phoning in reports on the negotiations. He was giving no sign of life whatever.

We tried to call the Soviet headquarters at Tokol. Without success. Nobody picked up the phone. It was just after midnight. Kiraly asked Nagy for orders. The Prime Minister's response was calm.

"I order you to re-establish contact between the Hungarian government and its representatives by sending mediators to the site of the negotiations."

Kiraly sent for a Hungarian Army tank. A large white flag was attached to the turret. A young major of the armoured forces was named mediator. His mission was to go to Tokol to try to re-establish contact with the Hungarian delegation. He was to give us uninterrupted radio reports until the completion of his mission.

The receiver was connected to the phone lines at police headquarters, allowing us to listen in on the most dramatic radio broadcast I have ever heard.

"The streets are calm in the city. . . . Now we're passing the Kilian Barracks. . . . The guards are waving to us. . . . Now we're heading toward Csepel Island. . . . We're crossing the main street of Csepel. The streets are full of people, the windows are lit up, it seems hardly anyone is sleeping. . . ."

In Csepel, site of the great steelworks, lived thousands of armed workmen. They weren't sleeping because they had the same premonition that we had. And, like us, all they could do was wait.

The young major's voice became animated.

"I'm leaving Csepel Island and coming into the outskirts of Tokol. . . . We're passing the first Soviet tanks — they're big Joseph Stalins. . . . Now two of them have made U-turns and are following us at a distance of about a hundred metres. One of my men is standing out of the turret to his waist, waving the white flags. . . . We're passing a barrier, without incident. . . . The two Joseph Stalins are still following us at the same distance. . . . We have the Soviet headquarters in view. . . . The barracks are surrounded by tanks, maybe 150, maybe more. . . . We're slowing down, we're approaching the gate. . . . They're signalling us to pass. . . . Some soldiers are running up to us. . . . Now I'm going to leave the tank for a second to notify their commander."

We heard a commotion, a few words in Russian, then the sound of the radio transmitter. Then nothing.

"Hello, Owl. This is Hawk. Come in, please."

The radio operator was shouting himself hoarse. Kiraly and I looked at each other, shattered.

Kiraly mumbled something and called Nagy.

"Comrade Prime Minister, there is something cockeyed at Tokol."

"What, in your opinion?"

"It is probable that the Soviet general headquarters is trying to separate the Hungarian government from its Minister of Defence and its military chief of staff."

Nagy was silent for a few seconds. "Thank you. I would like you and Kopacsi to assume the functions of the delegates until their return."

He hesitated for an instant, then he added, "Try to sleep for an hour or two, comrades."

We followed his advice, or at least pretended to. Kiraly curled into an armchair. I remained open-eyed in the darkness, arms on my desk, head on my arms. Just before 3:00 a.m., Death passed beneath our windows, mounted on a half-track. We raced to the balcony. There were three Joseph Stalins, huge beyond measure, travelling fast, faster than machines of that size are permitted to travel. With their infernal clickety-clack, they disappeared in the direction of the Ministry of the Interior.

Just then, I had a phone call from the ministry. It was Lieutenant-Colonel Szalma, a little squirt who had been an officer in the now-dissolved AVO. He spoke to me in a tone of unbelievable arrogance.

"Kopacsi?"

"Yes?"

"As second in command of the National Guard, you will immediately give the order to the counter-revolutionaries in the entire country to lay down their arms."

"I don't know any counter-revolutionaries," I replied angrily, "and I'm not interested in your orders."

I hung up. Kiraly, who had overheard the conversation, understood that the Soviet attack had been launched. He stood up, asked for a weapon (until then, he hadn't carried one), and declared: "We are going to wake up the head of government to request orders."

Of course, Nagy hadn't been sleeping. He replied, in an authoritative tone, "I refuse to give the order to resist by arms."

"As you wish, Comrade Nagy. Shall I continue to give you reports?"

"It's useless, my friend. Thank you. Thank everybody."

Nagy hung up and at the same time we heard the sound of the Soviet heavy artillery. They had encountered the tanks we had posted around the Solymar Avenue Barracks. The artillery fire was frenetic. All our telephones started to ring at the same time.

Kiraly looked at me.

"Are you going to answer?"

I refused.

He sent for the head of his general staff and ordered him to transmit the order not to resist the Soviet aggression.

Ibolya, who had spent the night on a camp bed set up in the entrance area, stuck her head through the doorway.

"Joska left you a message. You're to go to Parliament and bring as many policemen as you can."

She was dressed, combed, and made up. A policeman's cape was thrown over her shoulders as protection from the cold. For her, it was obvious that she was coming with me. Our daughter was at the Parliament building, with Joska's wife and children.

Kiraly checked his revolver's magazine and said, "Well, Sandor, our paths are going to separate now. I'm going to lead a company up to the belvedere on Mount Janos [the hill that overlooks Budapest]. It's not forbidden to take up a position as observers. After that... we'll see."

We went down together. The explosions were shaking the whole city. Kiraly tried to joke, calling Ibolya "Madame General". We did our best to smile and shook hands. Then Kiraly went to find his soldiers. At the head of fifty cold and disoriented men, I moved out on foot, "Madame General" at my side, in the direction of the Danube, toward the Gothic towers of Parliament that stood black against the scarlet early morning sky.

■ *To Parliament*

Hugging the walls, we made our way through the side streets. In an adjacent main thoroughfare, the noisy Stalin tanks were passing, firing broadsides as they went. Acrid smoke closed in on us. As we walked, I wondered, "Will Nagy be able to give the order to return their fire?"

Nagy had been a Communist leader for forty years. He had been educated in the Soviet Union. He knew the situation better than anybody. Perhaps he was still hoping for a compromise.

Besides, the old man had never spilled so much as a drop of blood. Because of his political views and temperament, he had been kept out of Rakosi's cabinet and had never been present when the dictator ordered innocent people sent to their deaths.

Finally, he was better informed than any of us on the international situation. He knew, as we didn't at the time, that while world opinion was on our side, the Western governments wouldn't lift a finger to help us.

Ibolya had her mind on one thing — the presence of our daughter at Parliament. Since we had never given anyone permission to take the child away from home, I was puzzled by it; still it cheered me up to know that I would see Judith again in a few minutes.

On the esplanade in front of Parliament, we found the Kecskemet armoured detachment. Our beautiful T-34s, flying the Kossuth emblem, were deployed around the seat of government, turrets closed, ready to fire. Three by three, four by four, their guns were trained on the adjacent streets and on the pedestals of the two large statues of Kossuth and Rakosi where an enemy might try to set up an ambush.

So it was war! There would be resistance after all.

At the head of my men, I entered the Parliament building.

Lieutenant-Colonel F, head of the parliamentary guard, confirmed the news.

"Kadar has formed a counter-government with Munnich. They're arriving behind the Soviet tanks."

Without asking more, I dashed off toward Nagy's office. The doors were wide open. I heard the old man's firm, calm voice. I stepped into the office where, instead of seeing Nagy in the flesh, I saw instead a tape recorder repeating, in a tragic tone, the chief of government's last proclamation:

> This is Imre Nagy, Prime Minister. Early this morning, Soviet troops unleashed an attack against our capital with the evident intention of overthrowing the legal and democratic government of Hungary. We are fighting. The government is at its post. I so inform the people of Hungary and of the entire world.

Ibolya stood behind me, at the door, white as a sheet.

The old man, Joska, and all the ministers were gone, no one knew where. As for our daughter, someone had seen her not long ago — maybe she was still here. But where? Finally, the guards informed me that she had left with certain members of the government. But where had she gone and with whom? No one could tell me.

Budapest's Parliament, built in the nineteenth century, is almost as big as the famous Westminster in London. Torn between anguish over the fate of our country and fear at not knowing where our child was, we raced frantically about this massive and luxurious maze. I entered the room that was used for radio broadcasts and there I found the famous dramatist and writer Julius Hay and his wife. Hay was a friend of Bertolt Brecht and a lifelong Bolshevik. He was in the midst of playing a recording that he had just made: "I call out to the whole world, to intellectuals everywhere. Help! Help us!"

We looked at this man and his wife, both of them pale and dishevelled. They shook hands with us, their expressions like those of condemned prisoners about to be led to their deaths. Then another recording started playing and we heard the following announcement: "Imre Nagy, president of the national government, calls Paul Maleter, Minister of National Defence, Istvan Kovacs, chief of the general staff, and the other members of the delegation who arrived last night at the general headquarters of the Soviet Army and have not returned. He orders them to return without delay and resume their respective posts."

But Maleter and the rest had little chance of resuming their respective posts. They had been taken hostage, the sort of thing that used to happen in Hungary when it was ruled by the Ottoman Turks. My comrade Bela Kiraly was at that moment the only military leader at liberty and at the head of an intact unit.

An officer of the parliamentary guard came up to me. "The Minister of State, Zoltan Tildy, needs you."

Zoltan Tildy, a man of integrity whose name and face were famous in Hungary, was a Protestant pastor and head of the Smallholders' Party during the Resistance. He had become president of the republic and then, in a typical Rakosi tactic, had been arrested and confined to his residence for many years. In Nagy's absence, he was now in charge of the government. I found him in discussion with the commander of the parliamentary guard.

"I don't know if you're aware of it, but the armoured forces of the Soviet Union are approaching Parliament," I told them. We had seen their panzers as we were *en route* there ourselves.

Some armoured columns had just crossed Margaret Bridge, while other units were on their way from other directions. From the windows overlooking the Danube, we could see several artillery batteries that had taken up positions along the embankment.

"My military friends, we must make a decision," said the minister.

I asked where the head of government was and pointed out that, in my opinion, the decision was his to take. But Tildy didn't know his whereabouts.

I crossed the offices of Sandor Ronai, an old social democrat devoted to Rakosi, and Steven Dobi, an alcoholic and a Rakosi-Gero stooge, and also the longtime president of the republic and former leader of the Smallholders' Party. In the neighbouring small room I saw Minister of State Stephen Bibo of the Peasants' Party. In these moments of unbearable tension, this tall man was sitting calmly before a typewriter, typing a document with steady rhythmic movements. As I would learn much later, I was watching the act of creation of a work of political philosophy that inspires the opposition movement in Hungary to this day.

These three men were the only government leaders still in the building. Tildy called them into his office.

"You do what you decide to do," said Bibo. "As for me, all I want is that the whole world and all the generations to come know what happened in Budapest in 1956. That is my sole task. If you can delay the invasion of Parliament, so much the better. If not, I will continue in the presence of the occupiers."

Ronai and Dobi said they would follow the judgement of Tildy and the military men. The decision was quickly made: any resistance would be useless because it would delay surrender by only a few hours and would surely result in the destruction of Parliament. With a heavy heart, I had to agree with this decision.

Lieutenant-Colonel L and myself were appointed negotiators. Looking out on the esplanade, we could see the head of the first column of Soviet tanks as it approached the Parliament building. Our mission was to make contact with its commander.

I kissed Ibolya. With L, I went out on the esplanade. As commander of the parliamentary guard, L had the duty of informing the men of our armoured units of our plan to surrender.

As soon as the men saw us coming, white flags in hand, an extraordinary thing happened. The turrets of the tanks opened and the men hopped up and began hollering: "We're not surrendering. You're crazy. We'll pass the Russkis through the mill!"

The turrets of some of the tanks pivoted so the machine guns were pointing in our direction. The situation was becoming delicate. We hurried back into the building.

Tildy was in tears. He had watched the scene and now he shook his white head in despair. "You must talk to the soldiers," he said. "They have to understand."

We went back down among the tanks. We took off our kepis and L said a few words. It was the shortest and saddest speech I ever heard. Perched on the tanks, many of the soldiers were crying.

My fifty uniformed policemen came out on the esplanade. Carrying the white flag and without their gunbelts, they moved out in a fan-shaped formation to meet the Soviet tanks, one of which came as far as the main entrance to Parliament before it stopped. Its turret opened and a soldier hopped out, followed by a Soviet colonel. The other tanks also stopped, with their long guns aimed at our units.

Several Soviet officers followed their colonel as he climbed the stairs and entered the Parliament building. Having learned with the help of an interpreter where the radio broadcast room was, he went there on the run.

"Open!"

There was no need to shout or to aim a machine gun at the door; it was open. A tank soldier kicked it down anyway. What disappointment on the face of the Russian colonel when, behind the smashed-in door, he found not the head of the Hungarian government but only his voice.

He unplugged the radio equipment. The guns were aimed at us.

"Where is Imre Nagy?"

We didn't know.

The colonel sent for Steven Dobi. The drunken president of the republic was red-faced and teetering. The colonel ordered him to sign the act of surrender of the armed forces. Maintaining one last spark of dignity, Dobi murmured something like, "If the representative of the Soviet Union wishes to speak to me, I am at his disposal in my office." He turned on his heels and departed, making an extraordinary effort to march as straight as possible.

With the help of his interpreter, the Soviet colonel issued his orders: "You will go out to the esplanade and order your armoured units to raise their guns toward the sky. Then, your men will descend and stack their weapons on the ground. Only the officers will have the right to keep their weapons. You will tell them that if the surrender is done according to the rules, no one will be punished. Everybody will be free to leave."

We obeyed. Abruptly, I was confronted with the history of my country and I could understand the feelings of the fighters in the 1848 war of liberation against Austria when, in Transylvania, they had to lay down their arms before the horsemen of the Russian czar who had come to the rescue of the Austrian emperor. The cold touch of his weapon gives a soldier an indefinable sense of security. To be stripped of it is a horrible thing. The soldiers cried with rage as they threw their machine guns on the pile. Apart from their weeping, silence reigned in the early morning and the only sound was that of the weapons falling to the ground. The pile grew higher and higher.

I stepped toward the cemetery of weapons, pulled the magazine from my revolver, and threw it down. I had the right to keep the empty revolver, and I stuck it in my jacket pocket.

But suddenly the atmosphere changed completely.

A Russian officer lined up the disarmed men and separated the soldiers from the officers.

Several soldiers started shouting, "We told you they were going to screw us."

With an interpreter's help, I protested politely to the Soviet officer that the colonel who had given us the orders hadn't said anything about this separation. The Russian looked at me with ill-concealed contempt and barked a few words at the interpreter.

"The comrade major says, 'When we get to Soviet Russia, we'll talk about all this again.' "

When we get to Soviet Russia?

Were we then prisoners of war, destined for deportation? Despite the colonel's formal promise, we were no longer free to come and go. Ibolya, who had come out to the esplanade, came up to me and whispered in my ear, "Sandor, we can't stay here."

At my side was an army liaison officer, a young sub-lieutenant. As if it were the most natural thing in the world, Ibolya slipped one arm under his and another under mine and, as relaxed as Sunday strollers — and it was Sunday — the three of us wandered off toward the edge of the esplanade. To escape in this confused situation, all one needed was presence of mind.

We passed near the statue of Kossuth, at the foot of which one could still see the thick layer of sawdust that the AVO troops had spread only ten days ago — though it now seemed an eternity — after perpetrating their massacre. It was cold. Snow had fallen the day before. The sawdust was frozen and we thought we could see human limbs under it. Or were we mistaken, was it just a hallucination caused by our distress?

"Stop! Who goes there?"

A small Russian non-commissioned officer held his submachine gun pointed at our chests. He commanded the battery containing several anti-tank units that had been hastily positioned across from Parliament.

Ibolya, unruffled by the fierceness of his shout, opened her coat to reveal the Resistance emblem that she wore prominently on her tunic. We did the same. Our friend, the sub-lieutenant, who spoke a few words of Russian, said: "We're going back to our posts."

The Russian NCO hesitated, then shrugged his shoulders.

"That's good, that's good."

He gave us a friendly tap on the back and motioned us ahead, across the demarcation line.

We took the first street on the left. From every side, we could now hear small-weapons' fire. The war was on again.

"Let's go to Szabadsag Square."

I did not want to wander unarmed in the streets. Szabadsag Square was the location of the nearest police station. It was also the address of the American Embassy.

At that moment, a strange-looking man accosted me. He had on a black cape beneath which could be seen the edges of a burgundy-coloured ecclesiastical robe. "My son," he said, "do you know where the United States Embassy is?"

I recognized Cardinal Mindszenty. He had been liberated several days earlier after seven years of captivity. Accompanied by his secretary, a layman, he was trying to find his way to safety through the invaded city and, seeing my policeman's uniform, had come to me for help.

I forget now whether I addressed him as "Father" or "Sir" or "Your Eminence" but, in any case, I told him he had only to follow us, as we were going in the same direction.

On the way, I asked him where he was coming from and he replied that he had taken refuge in the Parliament building and had gotten out through a service door.

"How did you get past the Soviet lines?"

"In the simplest way in the world. The Russians saw my clerical dress and let me pass without demanding an explanation."

When we arrived at the American Embassy, he pressed the doorbell. The door opened, and they went in. Cardinal Mindszenty would not pass through that doorway again for fifteen years.

I went up to the policeman on duty in the sentry box. Our police guards outside each foreign embassy had remained on duty throughout the uprising.

"Comrade, if you have one or two spare magazines, let me have them. I'm without ammunition."

"At your service, Colonel."

He pulled out his revolver, removed the clip, and handed it to me. I took it and loaded my gun. Then the three of us wound our way through the side streets to police headquarters, a good kilometre away.

It wasn't yet 9:00 a.m. Police headquarters was in a state of complete anarchy. The fifty agents I had taken with me to Parliament early in the morning had been able to escape through a passage to the Danube. That was some comfort; but most of my other officers were absent. My deputies scurried from one phone to another, without knowing what to do.

"Comrade Kopacsi, the Kilian Barracks is calling you."

These were the members of the National Guard. They had been attacked by Soviet armoured units. From point-blank range, the huge Russian tanks were bombarding the crumbly walls of the old barracks. The stairs that I had climbed several days earlier as a candidate for second in command of the newly created force were now littered with the corpses of youthful fighters, the same ones who had elected me unanimously "despite the fact that you are a Communist".

"Kopacsi, tell us what to do."

I could hear loud mortar explosions over the phone.

What would I do if I were in their place? What would I do when, in three hours, one hour, or even a few minutes, the Stalin tanks surrounded police headquarters and their cannons began to spray me?

"There is no longer a functioning government. Each of us is fighting for honour and his life. If you can't handle that, you'll have to give up."

They didn't give up. After the furious tank assaults, Maleter's former citadel came under aerial bombardment. It held out until November 7. When the Russians got in, all they found were the dead and severely injured.

Phone calls informing us of the Russian tank movements and of how the battle was unfolding poured in from the working-class districts of Ulloi Street, Marx and Kalvin squares, and the Corvin cinema. The famous Kobanya brewery, where in other times I had emptied bottles of Giraffe beer, had become an arsenal for the National Guard. The workers from the big iron and steel factory at Csepel inflicted heavy casualties on the Soviet tanks. The most tragic of the calls were those that came, furtively, from a corner of an invaded barracks.

"Comrade Colonel, I've only got a minute to talk.... The Russians arrived without warning, they rounded up our comrades while they were sleeping, those who resisted were killed, now they're making us march down the street, toward the prison camp, maybe to Siberia...."

Then came a list of soldiers whose parents we were asked to call.

Other calls came from ordinary civilians. "Send your men with their artillery right away. The Russians are slaughtering everyone, even our children. In the name of Christ, come quick."

In reprisal for Molotov cocktails that had been thrown at them, the Russian armoured units were systematically destroying whole buildings. Entire rows of houses were flattened because the Russians thought insurgents were inside. Several thousand civilians were killed in the streets or buried under debris. The severely injured couldn't be transported to hospital because the Soviet artillery on the hills of Buda and the tanks patrolling the streets prevented all movement.

And yet here at police headquarters we hadn't been attacked. It wasn't until noon that I began to guess the reason for this from the tenor of the phone calls I was receiving. I was being cajoled and threatened by people in the Ministry of the Interior to transfer my allegiance; there was still time, they said, to declare myself for the Soviets and avoid a bloody siege of the police station.

I could see that Soviet general staff had been fed exaggerated reports by overzealous Hungarian informers. The former minister, Piros, the present one, Munnich, and several other AVO officers who had taken refuge in Czechoslovakia or the Soviet Union, had probably warned them that police headquarters was a vast arsenal of heavy and light arms and that General Kiraly and myself were at the head of several divisions organized and trained for street combat. Because of these "facts" the Russians were doing their best to avoid direct confrontation before they had exhausted the path of negotiations. We did have some arms but nothing like the quantities our adversaries seemed to credit us with.

At that moment, Kiraly was in fact at the head of his men, but not at police headquarters. He was trying to inspire the resistance, using materiel recouped from the aggressor, just as the manuals of revolutionary warfare teach. Knowing that resistance would ultimately fail, he fought reluctantly, but not without ingenuity.

When his men found themselves surrounded on all sides by Soviet troops in the mountains of Buda, he lured the Russians into bombing the Nagykovacsi arsenal there. The arsenal was filled with TNT, which forms a mushroom-shaped cloud when it explodes in large quantities. Thinking an atom bomb had been detonated, the terrified Russians fled, giving Kiraly and his men the chance to escape across the Austrian border.

My duty was to dress the city's wounds, to help and to protect the civilian population. No one else could do it. Meanwhile, the Soviet Army was slaughtering them, and the reborn Hungarian security force, the AVO, was helping its masters.

One of its tasks was to pester me. A call from the sinister Szalma in the early hours of the morning, was followed by a series of calls from Colonel Kucsera, one of the most hated men in the former AVO.

"Kopacsi, we know about your crimes. You are holding our security officers *naked in their cells.*"

I almost fell over backwards with astonishment. Prisoners "naked in their cells"? I didn't know what he was talking about. Later, reading Solzhenitsyn, I understood: the guards in the Soviet gulags kept prisoners who were waiting for their executions naked. Kucsera had swallowed the brainwashing of the KGB and served it to me raw, as a way of terrorizing me.

"Kopacsi, you have one last chance to get yourself out of the mess you're in. Order the counter-revolutionaries to lay down their arms. We'll record it and broadcast immediately on the radio."

They'd learned nothing from history. Back from Russia and Czechoslovakia, the AVO leaders were as ignorant and brutal as they had been before the insurrection.

"Do you understand what you are suggesting? Do you want to label as counter-revolutionaries the same people that Kadar the day before yesterday called revolutionaries and patriots? Your idea is not only tactically and politically idiotic, it would also be ineffective."

"Are you ready to record the appeal or not?"

"I refuse and I do so indignantly. As for my so-called naked prisoners, they are in good health, at liberty in my offices, and ready to rejoin you...that is, if they dare to venture into the streets and risk being shot by your Soviet comrades."

"Watch out, Kopacsi. Comrade Kadar will be informed of your refusal. He'll know what to make of it."

Comrade Kadar. His attitude is still a mystery to me. I had missed his proclamation on the radio early in the morning. On my return from Parliament, my deputies had filled me in on the activities of Kadar and Munnich. According to a proclamation sent from an unknown transmitter that probably belonged to the Soviet Army, Kadar had announced the formation of a counter-government. He branded the armed population "terrorists and bandits of the counter-revolution assassinating our brother workers and peasants". He added that his "government" had asked the Soviet government "to help our nation to crush the sinister forces of reaction and re-establish order and calm in the country".

Several of my officers had written down this proclamation word for word. I read and reread it but found it hard to believe that it had been written by Kadar. In my opinion, it bore the hallmark of the KGB. Hadn't Kadar only three days earlier declared in the presence of Ambassador Andropov, "If your tanks come back, I'll go down in the street and fight them barehanded"?

Was Kadar a Russian prisoner? But how then to explain the simultaneous disappearance of Munnich, and of several Stalinists who had also signed the proclamation?

In Hungary, the Soviets were perfecting the same method they would use years later in Czechoslovakia: prolong the negotiations with the legal government of the satellite country while preparing a military intervention behind its back.

Kadar had been a victim of Rakosi and Stalinism and had fought against the illegal activities of the AVO. It seemed unimaginable that he would now change sides and put himself at the service of the Russian secret police.

I watched the clouds of smoke rising over different sections of Budapest. Why should I remain at my post? To keep which illusions? "Remain at one's post" is no more than a hackneyed formula, the rule obeyed by the famous sentinel of Pompeii, petrified under the lava, his lance at the ready. That soldier would have done better to flee; his flight would have had no effect on the eruption of Vesuvius.

What could I expect if I waited here? The dreams of my youth, the recent explosion of hope that we could create a socialism with a human face — all that was buried under the lava spewn out by the Soviet guns. I say "Soviet" automatically. But was this really the same army, the same regime that we had awaited so hopefully in 1944 as our liberators?

Six of the seven leaders of the new party had shared a common goal — to create a humanitarian socialism in an independent country. But the seventh, Kadar, had won. One against six, but the one had the Russian Army behind him. After so much disappointment, did life still have any meaning? As a soldier, I was dead. My death dated from a pale November morning when I stood in front of Parliament, a white pennant in my hands.

Despite the horror of the situation, there was a circumstance that offered a slight glimmer of optimism. The AVO officers who called themselves "representatives of the new Kadar government" were in fact Kadar's personal enemies. For instance, Kucsera, Szalma, the commander of the Fo Street prison, and Ferencsik were known as torturers. They had all been compromised in the Rajk and Kadar affairs mounted under Rakosi. At least one of them had taken part in the worst of the tortures inflicted on Janos Kadar.

Profiting from the current confusion, they were trying to pass themselves off as spokesmen for the "new government". These agents of the Soviet secret police had persuaded their Muscovite masters that they could subdue the Hungarian people. But their trickery couldn't continue for long. Once back in power, Kadar would sweep his administration clean of the most compromised elements of the AVO. After everything that had happened in Budapest, no one with an iota of common sense would want to re-establish the terror the country had known under Matthias Rakosi.

The telephone's ring interrupted my thoughts.

"Sandor, I'm happy to find you in good health."

I recognized the voice and especially the accent. It was Vukmirovich, a Yugoslav ex-Resistance fighter who was now military attaché in the Yugoslav Embassy in Budapest. We had become friends several months earlier during a celebration staged by our Partisans' Union on the Yugoslav border when we had presented medals to former fighters in the Yugoslav underground. Vukmirovich spoke Hungarian perfectly.

"I wasn't able to call you earlier, Sandor, but now it's urgent: you must come and join me immediately at the embassy."

"At the embassy? But why?"

"Because your little Judith is here."

I asked no more questions. I understood immediately what had happened. From Parliament, Imre Nagy and a few of those closest to him had been transported to the Yugoslav Embassy.

I simply asked if I could speak to my daughter. The attaché replied that it would be best if only embassy personnel spoke on the phone. But he assured me that Judith was fine and that she was playing with other children.

"Sandor, come quickly with your wife, we're waiting for you. You can count on our hospitality and friendship."

I replied that at the moment I couldn't leave police headquarters because I had urgent tasks to carry out. I asked him to reassure my daughter that we were fine and would do everything we could to see her very soon.

That morning, Judith had gone to Parliament with the Szilagyi family, undoubtedly because Ella had told her that her father would come there to get her. She adored her mother, but her feelings toward her father were another story. For this child, I was one of those heroes of the little Soviet novels that she read in which there were two sorts of men — the bad and the good. And the good were always heroes. (Heroines were much fewer in official Soviet literature; if they existed, they were kept in the background.)

She knew that Daddy was committed to the insurrection. He wanted the Russians out and he was for the Nagy government. After years of Stalinist education, the events of 1956 had been difficult for the little girl to comprehend; this new Soviet invasion and outbreak of fighting must have disturbed her deeply.

The Yugoslav military attaché had told the truth: it was urgent that the child see us again. But neither Ibolya nor I had decided to follow the government's example and seek refuge in an embassy in the middle of Budapest.

Above all, we had a horror of being confined in a building. This aversion was virtually physical and was certainly the result of having passed our childhood and youth in the northern woods. The feeling also no doubt stemmed in part from the fact that, since adolescence, we had always had a weapon within arm's reach. To listen to the battle then raging in Budapest from behind the windows of an embassy struck us as unthinkable.

To tell the truth, we wanted to rejoin Kiraly. We didn't know where he was. He hadn't found a way to communicate with us, but we felt that he was waiting for us, that he was going to call and invite us to meet up with him some place where it was still possible to fight.

It was clear that our daughter would have to come with us. The military attaché kept calling every hour with news of the child, who was fine but who "is waiting for you". From the tone of these calls, we understood that there was something else. Judith wasn't the only one who was waiting for us.

The leadership of the new Communist Party was at the embassy where it was trying to continue fulfilling its functions. There were five of them: Imre Nagy, Donath, Losonczy, the philosopher George Lukacs, and Szanto. The only ones absent were myself and Kadar, who was with the Russians. The others wanted me to be there to demonstrate that Kadar was a minority of one in going over to the Russians.

"Give us the night. If nothing new happens, we will rejoin you tomorrow morning," I told the Yugoslav.

After a night of battle — Ulloi Street was in flames, as was the South Railway Station, while artillery roared from the heights — rumours of all kinds began to circulate. One rumour had it that the United Nations Security Council had decided to intervene in Hungary, but could not go ahead because the French and British were preoccupied with Suez. Bulganin was said to have threatened to drop atomic bombs on London and Paris.

Meanwhile, our stations outside the capital were showering us with encouraging accounts of victorious battles by local garrisons or discouraging ones of loss of life among the civilian population. In certain places, the Russian Army had arranged with local authorities for the Hungarian workers' soviets to assume the direction of public affairs in the absence of a central government (Kadar and his men had not yet shown their faces in Hungary). The army was ruled by revolutionary committees; a general strike was declared across the entire country "until the total retreat of Soviet troops".

At police headquarters, we still hadn't been attacked by the Soviets. Meanwhile, the phone calls from Vukmirovich were growing ever more impatient. It was clear that I could no longer put off my decision about whether to rejoin the Hungarian government-in-exile.

That morning, at about 9:00 a.m., we made our choice. For the first time since the fateful day of October 23, I took off my uniform and dressed in civilian clothes. Flanked by Ibolya on one side and on the other by Geza T, a police major who spoke Russian, we walked out of the building.

George ran behind me.

"You're forgetting your revolver."

It was true. I was used to having it suspended from my gunbelt but I no longer had a gunbelt. George checked the clip and handed me the gun. He hugged me around the shoulders, a gesture he never would have permitted himself in normal times.

"Goodbye, Colonel."

He had brought a shawl for Ibolya. The radiant days of October were gone and Budapest was covered in frost.

▌ *"Men Sprout Like Weeds"*

To get to the Yugoslav Embassy, we had to walk along Budapest's equivalent of the Champs Elysées, the beautiful Stalin Avenue. It was our first chance to admire the plaques that the insurgents had made and installed at the crossroads: AVENUE OF HUNGARIAN YOUTH.

Rat-a-tat-tat! A blast of submachine gun fire riddled the plaque, four metres above our heads. We jumped back into the shelter of the entrance to a building. It was a bad choice. From the traffic circle were emerging three enormous Russian panzers firing broadsides at the windows of the buildings. Geza grabbed my arm and pointed to the courtyard behind us. Several boys and girls young enough to be high school students were running toward the service staircase. Others, carrying submachine guns, could be seen in the corridors overlooking the courtyard. They saw us; one of the boys bent over the guardrail and motioned us to clear off.

I'll never forget that boy. A long beanpole, eighteen years old, with brown, dishevelled hair and blazing eyes — it was a vision of me when I was sixteen, in a meeting, holding in my hand the "Molotov cocktail" of the period, an electric light bulb filled with tar, destined for the cops. His old clothes, the threadbare overcoat in winter, the way he gestured to us to get out — it was me all over.

"Beat it, get out of here, old man, because things are going to get hot."

With the long dirty fingers of a fighter who had been in combat steadily for fifteen days, he pointed imperiously to the service door at the rear of the courtyard. Ibolya and Geza tried to drag me toward it, but at first I wouldn't budge. What had gotten into me? Wasn't I an important member of the government, a father, on his way to see his prime minister and his daughter? Why was I rummaging about under my coat for my service revolver? Did I really want to stay here with these adolescents, to die with them in battle?

Already, the shells were putting holes in the bricks in the courtyard. The Russians weren't bothering to set foot on the ground in their war against the resistants; they preferred to stay in their tanks and knock down the buildings of Budapest. We escaped through the rear door. From one end to the other, the Avenue of Hungarian Youth was in flames. We took a small road running parallel to it and moved along, hugging the walls. At the crossings, we waited for a lull before hurrying to the other side. When we arrived on a street named Gorky Mall, the nightmare we were living through reached its height: we found ourselves nose to nose with an enemy patrol.

It was a small detachment, composed entirely of Soviet officers. Wearing helmets and carrying submachine guns slung over their shoulders, they were keeping watch on the immediate vicinity of the Soviet Embassy. I hadn't even realized that we were so close to it. Here, the houses were still intact, the streets calm. During the entire insurrection, not one armed group had come here to provoke the masters of the country.

"*Drug* Kopacsi!" Instead of the fateful "*Stoy*" or "Who goes there?" one expects from a patrol, we heard instead these warm words of friendship. One of the officers left the patrol and approached me, arms wide open. "*Drug* Kopacsi! My friend Kopacsi!"

Under his helmet, I had trouble recognizing the features of one of the Soviet counsellors of the Ministry of the Interior, the one called "Colonel Hussar". He embraced me, and began talking feverishly. My friend Geza translated.

"Comrade Kopacsi, thank you for coming. The comrade ambassador of the Soviet Union as well as Comrade Janos Kadar want to speak to you. We've been waiting for you since yesterday. Follow us quickly, we're going to find them right away."

Ibolya, the major, and I looked at each other. We were in a total quandary. We couldn't very well explain our true intentions; besides, the patrol had surrounded us and, with the playfulness of welcoming hosts, the Soviet officers were pushing us toward the door of the embassy.

The large courtyard resembled that of a barracks. War machines were lined up outside the buildings: several large tanks, some half-tracks, and even some howitzers. The place teemed with military personnel, all armed with submachine guns. The guards bolted the door behind us and signalled us to wait. "Colonel Hussar" had disappeared. He had undoubtedly gone up to inform Andropov of our presence. Ibolya had a slight blush on her cheeks. This would be her first encounter with Andropov since the two of them had danced in the New Year.

For a long time, we were left standing there in the cold, listening to the battle raging across the city. The soldiers standing guard impassively near the garden door paid not the slightest attention to us.

I thought I recognized one of the officers near the armoured vehicles lined up along the wall. He was a stocky, middle-aged man, wearing a greatcoat that was too big for him and the decorated kepi of the superior army officer. Noticing my stare, he moved toward us and beckoned us over.

"Hello, *Tovarishch* Kopacsi," he said in a hoarse voice that reminded me of someone — but of whom exactly?

He turned toward my friend, the major, and asked him to tell me that I couldn't have come at a better time because he was getting ready to go with his men to a Soviet Army operations base in the Budapest suburbs and that he would take us there. He pointed to one of the half-tracks.

"But damn it, ask him who he is and why he wants us to go with him," I said.

My friend translated. The officer turned towards me for an instant; because of the cold, the collar of his coat was raised, partly obscuring his face. His blue transparent eyes stared at me.

"*Tovarishch* Janos Kadar," he said. "Comrade Janos Kadar wants to see you for an exchange of views on the subject of the current crisis."

Ibolya squeezed my arm so strongly that I almost cried out in protest. Her features were twisted by fear.

"Please," the Soviet officer in the huge coat repeated politely.

He signalled to his men who handed each of us a Kalishnikov submachine gun. Automatically, I checked the magazine. It was full. We got up into the half-track, my wife and the major behind, myself next to the driver. The officer in the greatcoat was about to climb into a tank when Ibolya squeezed my arm a second time. I stood up and cried out, "Wait. There's been a mistake."

The unknown officer turned toward us.

At that very moment, the door of the embassy opened and Andropov, bareheaded and without an overcoat, appeared. He was wearing a well-cut blue suit just like the one he had worn on New Year's Eve.

A flicker of a smile passed over his face. He greeted Ibolya with a nod of his head and very quietly asked why I had shouted. Ibolya frantically asked the major to translate that it wasn't Kadar we wanted to see, that we were simply trying to be reunited with our daughter who was at the Yugoslav Embassy.

Andropov listened and nodded that he had understood. He gestured his agreement to the officer in the coat, who climbed into his tank. With him in the lead, us in the middle, and a second Stalin tank bringing up the rear, our convoy started up and left the embassy courtyard.

The lead tank headed for Heroes' Square, where the Yugoslav Embassy was located. For the first time, we saw the huge bronze boots standing alone atop a two-storey-high pedestal. After the events of October 23, this was all that remained of Stalin's statue. Further up, on the Avenue of Hungarian Youth, the battle was at its height. But here, near the municipal park, the atmosphere was strangely calm. Soon we saw the white building housing the Yugoslav Embassy, squeezed in the vice of the surrounding Soviet tanks.

Ten shots from the tanks and we would have no more daughter and the country's legal government would be gone.

The turret of the lead tank opened and the officer in the greatcoat shouted several words to us. Our interpreter translated. "The woman can get down."

There were several seconds of silence, of immobility.

Under the leaden November sky, trapped amid foreign tanks, near windows behind which our child was waiting and perhaps watching, a crack opened up in my wife's heart.

In a split second, she understood that her husband was the victim of treachery, that he was going to meet his death. One of the soldiers had already got out and was offering her a ladder. Ibolya clung to the edge of the half-track, and began screaming in a voice that froze the blood.

Never before had I heard such screaming. It's undoubtedly thus that the wives of deportees scream when their husbands are forcibly dragged away to the gulags. The wife of the police chief of Budapest,

Madame Colonel, holder of the order of merit of the Hungarian Resistance, screamed skyward like a wounded animal because Andropov's men were robbing her at the same time of her life, her husband, and her only child.

"Noooooo!...I'm staying with my husband."

Her cries reverberated across the square. The windows opened, including those of the embassy. Instantly, the tanks' automatic weapons were trained on the windows.

In the turret of the lead tank there was a brief conference. The Russians made a decision. They have a horror of scandal. For them, the worst atrocities must take place behind closed doors, otherwise heads will fall. The officer in the greatcoat signalled our little convoy to depart.

Ibolya's whole body was trembling. She had seized my hand and she pressed it frantically as if it was the last time she would ever touch me. The convoy crossed the square and turned into the path that bordered the municipal park. We hadn't come a hundred metres, yet we suddenly found ourselves in the midst of the biggest battle in Budapest.

It was an attack by insurgent units reinforced by a battery of anti-tank guns from the regular Hungarian Army. I had known that a strong Hungarian force had engaged the Soviet tanks at the edge of the park. But that was at daybreak. I hadn't expected to find the battle still in progress. Our men, waiting in the woods, unleashed their artillery the instant they glimpsed the nose of the lead tank. We were passing the party school at a relatively open spot. The lead tank charged ahead to find a less exposed position. Suddenly, the tank was hit and engulfed in flames. I was sure that its occupants were done for.

On our half-track, fifty metres behind the lead tank, the soldier operating the machine gun yelled: *"Agone!"* (fire) and *"Kaput!"*

It wasn't so. The flames were those of a fragmentation shell, which can't penetrate ten inches of armour. The two tanks pivoted their turrets toward the woods and fired back. A fierce artillery duel broke out. The shrapnel pounded the exposed side of the half-track like hail. The gunner, miraculously still alive, mumbled incoherently as he let loose his volleys.

I looked at the soldiers with us. They were pale and terrified. These were certainly not the battle-hardened Russians of twelve years earlier whose combat against the Nazis I had so admired. These were youngsters, some of whom may have been experiencing their baptism of fire at that very moment. Some perhaps were thinking in their heart of hearts that this wasn't Stalingrad but Budapest, and that they were not defending their native soil against invaders.

As for me, I felt relieved to be exposed to death. I squeezed my wife's fingers tightly and prayed that a shell would destroy our vehicle. We would be dead and all the horror I felt would fade away.

The ferocious battle lasted only about four minutes. Soon the lead tank extricated itself, ground its tracks, and took off toward the Budapest stadium. We followed it.

The armoured convoy moved as quickly as a cortège of cars. Trembling with fear, the machine gunner continued firing. At one hundred kilometres an hour, we turned into an alleyway and were hit by two or three grenades tossed by some isolated insurgents.

Then we were at the edge of the Sashalom Barracks, which had for many years been occupied by the Soviets. It presented an unusual picture at the moment, with half a dozen columns of Stalin tanks surrounding it in concentric circles. Several dozen guns aimed at the city fired every two minutes. The salvoes filled the air with a terrible din and an intolerable stench.

Our half-track stopped in front of the one-storey building that housed the post commander. The occupants of the two tanks were already inside. We got down and were led into the hall. My wife and Geza were directed to the room on the right, but when I attempted to follow them a soldier stopped me, saying, "Wait here."

The rear of the hall led to a large room that was normally a banquet hall. The double doors opened and two soldiers armed with sub-machine guns came out. They tore the Kalishnikov out of my hands and pushed me toward the open doors.

I went in.

It wasn't Janos Kadar who awaited me there. Instead I found a dozen Soviet generals in their campaign uniforms, which were decorated with the distinctive insignia of their ranks. Each wore, suspended from his belt, a strange pistol case made of wood, about forty centimetres long, such as can be seen on engravings or photographs depicting scenes of the 1917 Revolution. I almost burst out laughing: these generals were disguised as revolutionaries; undoubtedly to prove to the world that we, the Hungarians, were the "whites", the "counter-revolutionaries".

In the middle of the group of generals, standing immobile in a theatrical pose, was the stocky little officer who had been in the lead tank of our convoy. Now he no longer wore his coat and I could see that he had the rank of General of the Army. Slowly, he pulled a Mauser, a First World War German pistol half as long as his forearm, out of its holster.

"You bastard, do you recognize me?"

"No," I stammered.

With one hand he pointed the gun at me and with the other he pulled off his cap and threw it on his desk. His blond hair fell on his forehead. The steel-blue eyes stared. It was "the new Soviet counsellor from Moscow", the same one I had met in Piros's office on the day of the student demonstration. He blinked.

"Bastard, I am General of the Army Ivan Alexandrovitch Serov, member of the Central Committee of the Bolshevik Party, president of the state security committee attached to the council of ministers of the U.S.S.R. [in other words, the boss of the KGB]. At the meeting of October 23, you treated me brutally and I'm going to have you hanged from the highest tree in Budapest."

As the interpreter translated, three generals moved behind me; two of them held my arms, and the third frisked me. He took my service revolver as well as several other objects in my pockets.

I realized that my fate had been determined. But I knew I must respond.

"I protest. I have immunity; I am a deputy of the Hungarian National Assembly. The commander of a foreign army has no right to arrest me."

From my inner jacket pocket, one that the generals had omitted to search, I pulled out my deputy's card and handed it to Serov. He refused to take it. I placed it on his desk in front of him.

He gave a phoney laugh and swept the document off his desk with the back of his hand.

The theatrical fever is contagious and I was its next victim. *"Vae victis* [woe to the vanquished]," I shouted in Latin.

Oh yes. Son and grandson of factory workers and student of law, I couldn't prevent myself from showing Serov (the son and grandson of peasants from central Russia) that his hangmen were going to hang an educated man.

Clearly, *vae victis* was Greek to Serov, his generals, and the interpreter. So I had to repeat "woe to the defeated", which didn't have the same ring to it.

Serov put his big revolver back in its holster and shouted at me, "You're crazy. All you had to do was leave your post and join us and we would have made you a minister."

It was hard to miss the allusion to Kadar and the blunt tone a colonial master uses to describe how he makes and unmakes his provincial governors.

I replied rather pitifully that I had tried to do my best. Besides, in staying at my post I had been able to save the lives of a hundred of his colleagues who otherwise would have been lynched by the mob.

He listened to the translation with evident disgust. But at the word "colleagues", he pricked up his ears.

"What colleagues is he talking about?"

I replied that I was referring to Hungarian security officers. He opened wide eyes that had seen whole populations depart for the far north.

"Idiot! Why did you protect them? They're replaceable. Men sprout like weeds."

His tone was so violent that his own generals felt embarrassed. I thought that he wouldn't wait for the ceremony of a hanging, that he would kill me on the spot.

He turned and signalled to the guards to take me away. I heard the fire of light arms in the courtyard. It wasn't the noise of combat; in the courtyard of the barracks, surrounded by a network of tanks, there were no enemies to fight. I was to find out later that they had been shooting some of their own men, as a way of maintaining discipline.

I was shoved into an empty room and the door was bolted from outside. There were ten beds. I thought I was living the last minutes of my life. My arguments, my pretentious *vae victis,* my whole life became meaningless. I was going to die deprived of my identity: loyalty to a party and an ideal had placed me in a contemptible position. I was no longer a human being. I had become a little loser whom the gang leader accuses of violating the laws of the underworld and who must therefore be punished.

The Man with a Skeleton's Fingers

The shooting resumed in the courtyard. A long salvo lasting about
ten minutes was followed by a pause, during which, no doubt, they
cleared away the bodies and lined up new victims in front of the
firing squad. I counted and recounted the beds. The number always
came to ten. At each volley, I stopped at the head of one of them.
Five times I changed places. Something told me that my turn had
arrived. I hardened myself inside, as if to offer a sort of shell to
the bullets, not to prevent them from killing me, but so that they
would *make a noise* when they hit me. I heard steps approaching.
I decided to refuse the blindfold. I had prepared my last words: "Long
live free and democratic Hungary." I thought of home, of the beech
groves and the factory. The bolt was pulled and my wife appeared
at the door.

"Ibolya!"

We rushed into each other's arms. She was in a pitiful state. She
had suffered a body search by an improvised commando of wives of
generals and counsellors. Ibolya knew one of them well from having
met her socially at many receptions. With a ferocious thoroughness
worthy of a seasoned jail guard, this woman had undressed her and
performed the most intimate gynecological examinations.

"Maybe we're seeing each other for the last time."

"Maybe," Ibolya replied slowly, caressing my cheek.

"You'll live. You and the child."

She sat down on one of the ten beds.

"I don't want to live without you. If you die, I want to die too.
Judith too must not live."

She said this with calm determination. I knew her. I knew that she was serious. With me dead, she was going to kill the child and kill herself. In the same situation, in her place, I might have done the same.

Love is a strange thing. Ibolya could have married her boss's son. But when her suitor and his parents came to visit her, she climbed out the window and went to find me — me, a little, eighteen-year-old, half-starved proletarian. And I had renounced my gang and its rule according to which all the "meowing kittens" (young girls) had to be kept at a distance under penalty of excommunication. Happily, we were accepted in the workers' movement. They called us "the best couple of propagandists".

And now, instead of saving humanity, we were listening to the noise of a fusillade and wondering whether we would survive.

Someone unbolted the door. Ibolya knew what I was thinking. She took my two hands in hers.

"We had an ideal. It was beautiful. But it's finished. Try to stay alive, Sandor, one for the other, both of us for the child."

The Russian soldier assigned to accompany me said that it wasn't to make me go "pow-pow": he was taking me to see a general, one of the ten generals who a little while earlier had played walk-on parts in Serov's little drama, but not one of the three who had held and searched me. The general was a large man with a stern manner, but he looked kindlier than the others. Twenty-four hours earlier, he may have taken part in an important war council in Moscow where the final plans had been made in case of the eruption of the Third World War. All things considered, the Anglo-French attack on Suez, occurring at the same time as the deterioration of the Soviet Army's positions in central Europe, clearly entailed a threat of world war. The general's first words, translated by an interpreter, contained the key to the situation.

"Colonel Kopacsi, I consider the recourse to force in Budapest to be morally wrong. But Suez caught us unawares. We were forced to take military measures in the Danube basin because of its strategic importance *vis-à-vis* any operations we might have to undertake in the Middle East."

I was astonished by the frankness and courteous tone of the Soviet officer. Why take the trouble with explanations when I was but a toy in their hands? I responded, in the same tone, that they ought to honour their promises to my people and withdraw their armed forces before the conflict became even wider. He reacted quickly.

"Would you agree to help put an end to the fighting? Our services have prepared a Hungarian language declaration in which the second in command of the National Guard asks his units to stop the fighting. Are you ready to read this proclamation on the radio?"

He handed me a typed text. I needed only to glance at it to know that it was just the same old *Pravda*-style rubbish, full of the crudest lies. The entire insurrection, according to this declaration, had been the work of Western imperialism, a fascist uprising guided by remote control by the henchmen of the old regime, etc. I handed it back to him.

"Impossible to use."

"Why?"

"Whoever wrote it understands nothing of the realities of our country."

The general gestured impatiently.

"We know your particular views on these so-called realities. You explained them in the presence of General Serov on the occasion of the famous meeting of October 23 at the Ministry of the Interior. Events have proven you wrong. Yet still you persevere?"

"General, I repeat: reading this declaration on the radio would be illogical and useless."

He looked at me, got up, and left the room, undoubtedly on his way to see Serov, the likely author of this bit of purple prose.

He returned quickly, this time without the text but with a piece of paper and a pencil in his hand.

"Write a declaration of your own."

I sat down and wrote the following: "People of Budapest, the struggle no longer has any meaning. During our history, Hungarians have often been in a situation in which we have had to give up our lives. But this time it is useless. After fifteen days of combat, we need calm. I ask everyone to end the armed struggle."

I handed the text to the interpreter who translated it immediately. The general turned to me.

"Would you agree to add one phrase to that?"

"What?"

"This: 'The Soviet Army will not shoot on the peaceful population.'"

"Yes."

"Here, please."

I marked with an asterisk the place where he wanted me to insert the sentence.

Then I was led to a room with a tape recorder as large as a work table in the centre. I had never seen one so big. Someone passed the microphone to me. I read the text with feeling, carefully articulating each syllable. With all my heart, I wanted an end to the bloodshed.

I learned later that my proclamation was never broadcast. The fighting had reached such proportions that the Soviet high command had decided on a military solution.

Again I was in the room with the ten beds, but without Ibolya. Two hours later, two soldiers brought her back. She collapsed in my arms. A general (yet another one — this barracks was crowded with generals) had grilled her, mainly on the subject of bringing divorce proceedings against me.

She wouldn't be consoled. The general had said, "Divorce him. If your husband is executed, you will be covered. You wouldn't be known as the widow of a traitor." Ibolya would have nothing to do with this suggestion.

The sounds of the firing squad in the courtyard continued all night and all the next day, which was November 7, the anniversary of the Russian Revolution. It was normally a public holiday in Hungary as well as in the Soviet Union. I don't know if they were executing Russians or captured Hungarians or if it was a charade to terrify the prisoners. Meanwhile, in the city, the battle was at its height and the noise was deafening.

On November 8, the noise of battle began to abate.

The next morning, the door opened and a Hungarian-speaking Soviet lieutenant appeared. "Take your things, you're leaving the barracks," he said.

We were certain that they were going to bring us to see Kadar. They had come to an understanding, we thought, with Imre Nagy. The fighting had stopped, Nagy wanted us, and Kadar had sent for us.

The officer pointed to a half-track parked in the courtyard.

"Get in; your friends are waiting for you."

We climbed into the vehicle and, to our great surprise, found the Minister of Defence, Paul Maleter, and the other members of the government delegation that had gone to negotiate with the Soviets. There are happy moments, even when one is a prisoner.

"Paul!"

"Sandor!"

We fell into each other's arms. The Russian soldiers in the half-track didn't stop us. As long as there is no officer with them, soldiers rarely go looking for trouble. We kissed the others, Major-General Istvan Kovacs, military chief of staff, Colonel Szucs, and Ferenc Erdei, a member of Imre Nagy's cabinet. The military men wore uniforms; they were shaved and in good spirits. Only Ferenc Erdei had a four-days' growth of beard and seemed to have fallen apart completely.

"Sandor, have you got a cigarette?" he asked me.

I had several and my package was passed around. The soldiers were busy piling files on the half-track. We took advantage of their absence to exchange news.

Maleter and the others didn't know that the Nagy government had taken refuge at the Yugoslav Embassy. They had been under arrest since the night of the negotiations.

Maleter and the delegation had arrived at the Soviet general headquarters on November 3 at about 10:30 p.m. On the way, they had felt a premonition of bad things to come. But at Tokol, after having been received by an honour guard commanded by Soviet generals Shcherbanin and Stepanov, their fears had dissipated. They all sat down to work. The preliminary problems having been debated, all that remained was to decide the final details of the Soviet departure: the farewell speeches, the flowers to be offered to the troops, and the onward shipment of damaged materiel. The atmosphere was cordial. The participants clinked glasses to the success of their deliberations.

But at about midnight, the door suddenly opened and General Serov erupted into the room at the head of a group of Soviet security officers. He was holding a huge Mauser pistol. His men immediately surrounded the negotiating table.

"You are under arrest," Serov told Maleter.

Maleter, who spoke perfect Russian, jumped to his feet and started to reach for his gun. But he realized the futility of that and stopped.

"So," he said. "That's the way it is."

The members of the government delegation were disarmed and then led into the courtyard of the barracks. From behind the central building, they could hear the crackle of machine guns. Convinced they were going to be executed without delay, they all embraced.

They were brutally separated and thrown into individual cells.

A few minutes later, the cells were reopened one by one. After each door was opened, the prisoners heard a salvo. The Russians were firing in the air to make them believe that their companions were being executed. Each of the prisoners thought he was the sole survivor.

On November 8, they discovered that they were all alive. The Russians piled them into a small plane and transferred them to the Sashalom Barracks.

And now?

Erdei, that writer of elegant prose, was trembling so hard he could barely hold the cigarette. A son of southern farmers, he declared: "Sandor, if we get out of this alive, I swear I'll never get involved in politics again. I'm going to earn my living as a gardener in Buda. Will you help me fertilize the soil?"

A few weeks later, he was the only one of us to be released, thanks to his connection with the influential Hungarian Stalinist, Revai. But he didn't earn his living as a gardener. He became president of the Academy of Sciences and of the so-called National Patriotic Front, a puppet organization controlled by the Communist Party that included former members of the Social Democrat, Smallholders', and other outlawed parties. He died in the 1970s of cancer, still a relatively young man.

A major of the Soviet security force climbed onto the half-track. He forbade us to talk. We protested, saying that it's the right of human beings to communicate with each other. The major pulled out his revolver.

"Talk, but in Russian. If not, I'll kill you."

Maleter turned toward us. "Guys, this animal has forbidden us to talk. But he can't stop us from singing." He started to sing a beautiful old song, the bitter song of the soldier who knows he is going to die.

The cemetery of Kerepes
Has many new graves
In the first grave lies
The little soldier of First Battalion

We all took up the song and a whole series of soldiers' songs followed one after another. Singing at the top of our lungs we crossed a Budapest lying in ruins before the half-track pulled up at the Soviet Embassy on Gorky Mall.

How many times had we crossed that portal, entered the brilliantly illuminated garden, ascended the stairs leading to the huge mansion, listened to the soft music that filled rooms perfumed with Russian leather?... "Hello *Tovarishch* Andropov.... How are you?... Very well. And yourself?"

This time, we were shoved like beasts into the basement, which was set up as a prison. Who would have thought that this building, which enjoyed the diplomatic right of extraterritoriality, housed a prison? Budapest was full of Russian barracks where they had all the room they needed to store prisoners. But no, they had to have one here as well.

We found ourselves in an L-shaped corridor, lined on both sides with eight large cells, each big enough to hold eight or ten prisoners. The cells were furnished with immense boards, but no mattresses or blankets. The prison was guarded by morose Russian soldiers and Soviet security officers wearing the blue-striped cap of the KGB. All of them were armed to the teeth.

The men were kept in separate cells, but Ibolya was allowed to stay with me. The cell had the usual prison stink. But the ordinary soldiers among the guards were kind. A lady! That floored them. At 5:00 p.m., a Ukrainian soldier opened the grille and passed several cigarettes through with his pudgy fingers. And since Ibolya thanked him with a smile, five minutes later he reopened the grille, and a piece of Hungarian sausage and some bread appeared.

Thank you, little soldier from the plains of Kiev. You see, I haven't forgotten you. As I haven't forgotten your finger placed in front of your mouth and your panic-stricken face as you whispered, "Don't say a word to the officer."

Apart from that, we were fed soup from the kitchen of the Russian regiment and black bread. The place had no heating and we shivered from the cold. And once a day we were led to unspeakably filthy toilets. On the main floor was the ballroom; four metres below, the gulag. That was as good an image as any of Soviet sovereignty.

I was taken from my underground cell and up a service staircase to a wing that was divided into offices with wire-mesh-covered windows. An interpreter of Ukrainian origin was waiting for me. He was a KGB lieutenant who spoke bad Hungarian and never stopped trembling.

"You are going to be questioned by the colonel in person," he told me, as awed as if the colonel were Stalin himself.

An unusual odour hung about the office. I couldn't identify it until the colonel, whose name was Karlissov, entered. He was a tall man, about fifty years old and wearing civilian clothes, who smoked continually. He smoked a tobacco unknown in Hungary; I learned later that it was *makhorka,* a coarse-cut Russian tobacco that is smoked in a cone of newspaper.

"Face the wall!"

This was his way of introducing himself. I was horrified when his fingers, bizarrely deformed and yellow from nicotine, roamed my body with the rough touch of a skeleton's hand. Later, I learned through an indiscretion on the part of the interpreter how the colonel got his horrible hands.

This great specialist in "national questions", recently arrived in Hungary at the head of a detachment of other specialists, had been maimed during the 1950s by a mountain tribe in the Caucasus. Already an expert in the uprooting and deportation of populations — today we call it genocide — our Karlissov had been captured by some mountain dwellers who weren't ready to die and who, to give him a lesson he would remember, pulled out all his fingernails.

My pockets were emptied, during which Karlissov showered me with insults while blowing the smoke from his disgusting *makhorka* under my nose.

"Dirty bastard, up to your neck in counter-revolution, you are going to confess your crimes."

The lieutenant translated in a trembling voice.

"Counter-revolutionary bandit dripping in blood! You tortured the comrades of the security!"

I protested vehemently.

"Shut up. Imperialist assassin, you're in the pay of the American warmongers."

Each of his words, each of his syllables, exploded from a mouth twisted in anger. He used his cigarette butt to light another cigarette.

"You should thank our valiant army and our loyal police."

I took the chance of asking a question: "Thank them? Why?"

Furious, he roared: "Because they are protecting you from the wrath of the people, you bastard. If not for them, you would be lynched. *Lynched,* you son of a bitch."

"By whom? By the Hungarian security perhaps?"

Wide-eyed with rage, spitting bits of *makhorka,* the specialist in genocide replied: "By the *people,* the Hungarian people, bastard. The Hungarian people have no pity for their enemies. And they know who their true friends are."

Their true friends — the Soviets who roamed the streets in their tanks destroying a good part of Budapest and decimating the population.

The interpreter trembled. This speech was so full of primitive hate that in any other circumstances I would have burst out laughing.

After me, it was Ibolya's turn to be interrogated by the appalling son of Frankenstein. She returned in despair.

"This is what he said: 'You're an honest proletarian woman, a member of the party. Your life will be saved; but first you must divorce your husband....'"

She couldn't continue. I guessed the rest: "Before I am hanged, right?"

Despite the horror of these words, or perhaps because of them, we burst out laughing. She continued: "You know what I said? 'It's not to the party that I swore fidelity, but to my man. If you kill him, kill me along with him.'"

As simple as that. Just like in the songs.

The man with the skeleton's fingers had recoiled in surprise. Ibolya may have been the first person to stand up to him since the mountain folk of the Caucasus.

"Even if your husband, that assassin, remains alive, which I very much doubt, when he gets out of prison you will be a very old woman."

The Russians' determination to separate us was easily explained: they needed scapegoats. They would have loved to gloat about one who had been "repudiated even by his own wife".

To Karlissov's surprise, Ibolya had the nerve to ask him for news of our little Judith. The tortured torturer replied with a tirade on the "just punishment of dishonest parents who are separated from their child".

Unimpressed by this moralizing, Ibolya asked if Nagy and his entourage were still at the Yugoslav Embassy and how the problem of their presence there was to be resolved. After a coughing fit,

Karlissov responded that the Yugoslavs were "mangy dogs" and Imre Nagy was "an agent of Eisenhower destined to be hanged from the cupola of Parliament".

■ *Operation Scapegoat*

During our second day of captivity, we were relieved to hear the voice of that bear, Paul Maleter. He was alive, apparently in the next cell — and not only alive but dressing down, in fluent Russian, a KGB guard who hadn't shown him the proper respect.

"Stand at attention! It's the Minister of Defence of a socialist country that you have the honour to push into this cell."

His voice reassured us. But still we heard the sound of guns. Just as at Sashalom, executions were taking place in the courtyard. Was it young Hungarians captured in the streets who were falling under the Russian bullets or was it their own men? Or both? Years later, certain of our writer friends recounted that during those dark days they had observed the embassy from the offices of the Writers' Union, which was located nearby. They had seen the arrival of dozens of trucks jammed with young civilians; these same trucks left packed with corpses, leaving long trails of blood on the street.

The guard brought us some sheets and blankets bearing the insignia of the Hungarian passenger trains. I piled them all on Ibolya, who was shivering with fever. "Judith. . .Judith. . . ." she kept repeating.

The fourth day after our arrival at the Soviet Embassy, the cell door opened noisily. It was the man with the strange fingers.

"Kopacsi, you whore, you bastard: *davay*, your time has come."

There was no need to draw a picture. I hugged Ibolya, who was still shivering with fever. "Farewell, my dear. Life was too short, but it was beautiful with you. Live, and raise our child."

She was incapable of saying a word. All she could do was watch me leave between two armed soldiers, accompanied by the monster of the Caucasus.

In the courtyard, I saw an apparently empty truck and a firing squad armed with machine guns. So I would be executed alone. Or perhaps the bodies of the others were already piled up in the truck?

I attempted to adopt — how should I call it? — the correct posture. I raised my head to face the firing squad. I no longer remember what I was thinking about. Perhaps my family, my country; perhaps simply the leaden November sky, the dirty sky that I would never see again.

With a snigger of pleasure that I will never be able to forget, Karlissov pushed me in a different direction.

"*Durak* [idiot]. You'll lose nothing by waiting your turn."

His soldiers heaved me like a sack of flour onto a half-track where guards were keeping watch over two Hungarian civilians: one was the editor of a small provincial newspaper, the other a young insurgent who had been captured in combat. The vehicle's engine roared into life.

"Who are you?" the young man asked me.

I opened my mouth. Then, to my great astonishment, I realized that I no longer knew. The police chief of Budapest? No. A young metalworker roaming the woods of the north? No. The devoted son of my father? The adored father of my daughter? A spy in the pay of Allen Dulles? A follower of Khrushchev and Imre Nagy? Or, indeed, of Janos Kadar? An empty snail shell? A snowflake, brother to the one that had just landed on my forehead?

The two young men looked at me in amazement. In the company of what great criminal or lunatic were they about to die in the sugar-beet fields in the suburbs of Budapest?

The Russian half-track headed toward the old sections of Buda, and I soon realized where we were headed. On the banks of the Danube, well off the beaten track, existed a large complex of prisons and offices known as Fo Street. Before the insurrection it had been the AVO's major prison, but since the last days of October all the officers and most of the guards had left. The political prisoners had been liberated by the mob, and the buildings were empty and abandoned. Had the Russians now found a use for them?

The answer was yes. In the absence of Hungarian staff, the sentry boxes and entry gates were guarded by KGB troops. Passwords were shouted in Russian and the documents that accompanied each prisoner were typed in Cyrillic characters. The corridors smelled of Russian gunbelts, which were made of a leather different from our own. *Stoy* and *Davay* echoed through the prison, shouted in the different dialects of the sixteen Soviet republics.

I was separated from the two young men and led to an individual cell in an isolated area on the third floor. The bed was a bare board with a straw mattress, the floor was cement, and bars on the window were reinforced by a triple layer of wire mesh. There was barely enough room to turn around. I had "my" regime to thank for this. Because it was indeed "my" regime, the one I had supported for so many years, that had created this prison, as bad as the worst Soviet hellholes.

As I was to learn later, I was in the area occupied by military chiefs condemned to death. In the neighbouring cells were Maleter and the other members of the government's delegation. The chief anarchist, Dudas, was in the cell next to mine. "Father Szabo", an old insurgent captain whom I had last seen in the meeting in Maleter's office to set up the National Guard, was passing his final hours across the corridor from me. Finally, two quite exceptional guests were installed at the end of the corridor. They were Farkas, former Minister of Defence, Rakosi's right-hand man and chief executioner for many years, who had been betrayed and imprisoned by the Stalinists themselves, and Gabor Peter, former AVO boss, whom Rakosi had accused of being a Zionist and had put out to pasture in 1953.

During my first hour in this new residence, I was taken from my cell and led away for interrogation. I was both surprised and horrified to be confronted once again by Karlissov.

"Did you expect to escape from Soviet justice?" he inquired.

"Soviet justice." The disgust I felt for the man gave me the courage to reply coldly that, as a Hungarian citizen, Soviet justice had nothing to do with me.

Karlissov had obviously expected this response. He sniggered and pointed his index finger at me.

"You're wrong. As an intelligence officer for the Yugoslav secret police, assigned to spy on the Soviet Union, you fall under our military jurisdiction."

So now I was a Yugoslav spy brought before "Soviet justice". This was truly original.

Karlissov opened a file and informed me, via his interpreter, that he had received "a letter from an old female party comrade" who stated that I had been an informer for Horthy's police. The Yugoslav security agency, the UDBA, had learned this and recruited me as an anti-Russian spy. My direct superior was Vukmirovich, military attaché at the Yugoslav Embassy in Budapest. At the beginning of autumn, I had met this man near the Yugoslav border. Since then, he had contacted me several times by phone at my office and had received information from me to be passed on to Tito.

Karlissov read all this in a raging voice, spitting out each syllable, his eyes darting at me between phrases, his hand on his revolver, which was placed in clear view on his table.

"You would do well to admit the truth," he said. "We've got all the proof we need right here." He tapped the file with his deformed hand.

The scene was so unlikely, so outmoded. Since Stalin's death, so many things had happened, so many victims of fabricated trials had come back among the living and detailed the criminal methods used by the security police.

"Your response?" Karlissov spat out the words triumphantly.

"My response is astonishment."

"What? What?"

"I'm astonished that you haven't found anything new, that you are reduced to repeating the old formulas thrown in the garbage by your own Twentieth Congress. The whole world knows this old tune of yours by now."

The man grew pale. I was reproaching him for being a bad policeman. If Serov, his immediate superior, learned of my reaction, he would call him to account for ineffectiveness.

"Cut the crap! Do you confess, yes or no, to the accusations that have been brought against you?"

"I don't confess to them because they're false. I was never arrested by Horthy's police, so they couldn't make me their informer. If your so-called old party comrade had had the slightest grievance against me, she would have come forward well before the recent events. As for Vukmirovich, along with the president of the Partisans' Union, I met him during a celebration organized by our cabinet. And he did telephone me, at my office, on November 5, to ask me to come and get my daughter at the Yugoslav Embassy. That's all. Your stories of espionage don't stand up."

"I'll give you an hour to think it over. After that, you're finished."

I was led back to my cell, where I lay down on the straw mattress.

Suddenly I realized that the peephole was open. I was under surveillance. According to the rule, the prisoner is supposed to remain standing from 6:00 a.m. to 9:00 p.m. The door opened and the guard, a Russian soldier, entered.

"You, lying down. Not allowed."

I stayed where I was. The soldier looked at me and shook his head. Then he handed me several cigarettes.

"*Kurit!* Smoke."

"*Spasibo.* Thanks, brother."

He gave me a light and looked behind him. Then he whispered: "*Zhena.*"

"What? What? Repeat."

He repeated: "*Zhena.* Woman. Your wife is here."

Before I could say anything else, he went out, closing the door behind him.

I pounded on the door.

The peephole was lowered.

"You, what you want?"

"You can take cigarette to my *zhena?*"

He looked at me in amazement.

The idea that a woman might smoke amused him enormously. He only half believed me. I took advantage of his confusion: "You, want to see how *zhena* makes puff-puff with cigarette?"

I handed him one of the cigarettes he had given me. With an end of pencil lead I had found at the bottom of my pocket, I had traced on the cigarette paper: "IBOLYA: SANDOR."

The little peasant accepted. He didn't want to miss the unheard-of and somewhat risqué spectacle of a young woman lighting a cigarette.

That was how my wife learned that I was still alive and close to her.

After an hour, the KGB guards again led me to see the man with the skeleton's fingers. His office stank of *makhorka* and he himself stayed histrionically hidden behind the clouds of smoke with the desk lamp turned toward my face. In a hoarse voice, trembling with contained anger, he repeated his question: "Do you admit that you are guilty of spying?"

Calmly, I repeated my previous response: I am not a spy and the accusations have nothing to do with me.

I couldn't see his face, only his hands. With a deliberately slow movement, they closed the file he had in front of him, the one dealing with my "espionage". The finger of bone pressed a button. Two non-commissioned officers in green caps entered. The colonel barked at them. From either side of me, they fastened a sort of leash, one to my left wrist, the other to my right.

As if to try it out, they pulled. I had to stand up. They dragged me out of the room, towing me along the corridor.

I was certain that they would stop at one of the neighbouring rooms, which were no doubt set up for torture. But they continued to pull me by the two leashes. Then they started running. I had to run to keep up with them to keep the metal points where the leather was attached from biting into my skin.

The corridor gave onto another corridor, forming a T shape. The two NCOs turned me around to face the direction from which we had come and sprang off, one to the right, the other to the left. I stayed, crucified by the leashes, at the junction of the two corridors and found myself facing a Soviet soldier, lying flat on his stomach behind a Maxim wheeled machine gun.

He was twenty metres away. Meanwhile, the two NCOs were pulling with all their might on the two leashes. The soldier was an Asiatic, a Kalmuk. With his finger on the trigger, he was aiming the gun at me.

My mouth became dry. I stared at the soldier's slanted eyes. The NCOs, still hidden from my view, kept pulling. The Kalmuk — or was he a Tartar? — kept aiming, without shooting.

I cried out, in Russian: "*Strelyay.* Fire!"

I screamed, my arms a cross, my wrists bleeding, my mouth dry: "Fire, fire, fiiiiire. . . ."

What is this diffuse light above my head? It's Niagara Falls. No, it's the moon. No, it's only the light bulb that burns night and day on the ceiling of my cell.

I am in my cell, lying on my back, senseless and numb. Have I been shot? I don't feel anything. My left wrist is bathed in blood. The metal teeth around my wrists left a deep wound. (Today, as souvenirs of the nails on the leash, I still have four scars on my left wrist.) I tear off a shirt tail and bandage the wound. Then I faint again into a deep sleep.

I was unaware that someone had opened the door, although the unlocking was noisy and complicated. The little Russian guard was standing at my bedside.

"You, sick?"

He looked at my arm.

"*Nichevo.* It's nothing. You. Get up, come with me."

He helped me stand up, which cost me considerable pain. We left, leaving the cell door open, and walked toward the other end of the corridor.

"*Bystro, bystro.* Faster, faster."

The guard stopped in front of cell number 357 and signalled me to approach. I thought he was going to switch me into this cell, but instead he gently lifted the metal disc covering the peephole and motioned to me to look.

Inside, I saw Ibolya.

She was sitting on her bed. The opening of the peephole must have been enough to attract her attention. The silence was profound — this was the section for prisoners condemned to death. She turned around. Her eyes had shadows under them; her expression was lifeless.

Then the little soldier did something for which we will be eternally grateful. Putting a finger in front of his mouth, he chose a key from his case, put it in the lock, and very quietly opened and pulled down the steel rectangle in the door.

Ibolya rushed forward. Her pretty young face appeared in the opening, like an artist's portrait in a metal frame. She saw me and her eyes lit up. She stammered, "Sandor!"

I bent over to kiss her, but I couldn't reach my head through far enough for our lips to meet. Ibolya put her hand forward and I lifted mine to meet it. She saw the blood-covered bandage; a brief cry escaped her lips.

"Shhh," whispered the guard.

"Sandor?"

"Yes, Ibolya."

"Does it hurt?"

Men are big weaklings. Childishly, I replied, "Yes, enough."

The guard came to close the window. I said, "You. To wait a second.... Ibolya, I love you."

"Me too, my dearest. We have to get out of this."

"We'll get out, the two of us. We'll live."

General Serov thought exactly the opposite. He hadn't forgotten his promise, solemnly made in the presence of his band of generals with their long Mausers: the deputy Kopacsi will be hanged from the highest tree in Budapest. During the first days of the "victory" in Hungary, however, another task had preoccupied him: organizing the deportation of Hungarian youth to central Asia. This was an unfortunate initiative. All along the railway tracks, the young people crammed into the wagons had tossed out messages, which were collected by the railwaymen and sent to the resistance organs in Budapest, the Writers' Union and the workers' councils. These appeals for help were then passed on to Western embassies and made their way finally to the United Nations. As a result, "Project Population Transfer" came to a sudden end.

Serov had to make do with his "Operation Scapegoat".

The two main figures destined to die for "having led the armed struggle of the counter-revolution" were Paul Maleter and myself. Our friend, General Bela Kiraly had already made his way, at the head of his troops, across the wooded mountains to the Austrian border.

We were given an incredible piece of gibberish titled "act of accusation" for which the sentence couldn't possibly be anything but death. The execution would surely take place before March 15, the anniversary of the uprising of Hungarian youth in 1848 against the Habsburg oppressors. A persistent rumour had it that on March 15, the youth of Budapest would rise up again. To dissuade them, our two heads must fall without delay.

On the other hand, Ibolya was informed that she was free. She thought I had been executed and refused to leave the prison before being assured otherwise. As usual, she caused a terrible uproar. Karlissov tried to reason with her. "But comrade, but comrade...."

"Don't comrade me, you public terror, you're going to show me my husband or the prison is going to collapse on your head."

Karlissov gave up and conducted Ibolya personally to my cell. The two of them came in.

"There is your husband. But it is forbidden to exchange even so much as a word."

Ibolya was as unimpressed as ever with Karlissov's orders. She clung to my neck and whispered, "Don't give up. I'll get you out of here, I promise."

Ibolya rushed to see my father and the two of them paid a visit to "X", as I will call an old comrade of my father's who had become a sort of *éminence grise* to the new regime. Seeing the expression on the faces of his two visitors, X grew pale.

"You don't mean to tell me that Sandor...?"

He didn't finish his sentence. Ibolya replied that I was still alive, but that it appeared the Soviets were planning a military trial for me and Paul Maleter and that we were scheduled to die before March 15.

"*Janos* [he was speaking of Kadar] will never permit Sandor to be killed," he said.

X knew of an incident that had taken place at the beginning of 1956 while Rakosi was still in possession of full power and searching for a scapegoat to shoulder the blame for the Rajk affair. Rakosi's choice had been Janos Kadar. Though Kadar was newly released from prison, by virtue of his having been Minister of the Interior at the time of the trumped-up charges against Rajk, he could believably be fingered as the murderer of his innocent comrade. (He hadn't been. On Rakosi's orders, Kadar had tried to persuade Rajk to save his skin by confessing, but it hadn't been his idea to accuse him.)

I had found out about Rakosi's scheme. I felt badly for Kadar, a former worker like myself who had suffered years of torture and humiliation. I had received a copy of the minutes of a meeting of the Politburo in 1949 at which Rajk had been condemned to death, and these clearly showed that Rakosi bore sole responsibility for the execution of Rajk and that Kadar's role had been a minor one.

Through Imre Mezo, I had let Kadar have the whole file for a period of twelve hours only. He had studied it and returned it as agreed. The next day, he had gone to the meeting at which he was to be accused with full knowledge of the facts. A single allusion to the file had been enough to stop Rakosi in his tracks. The dictator had been furious and demanded to know where Kadar could have obtained such ultra-secret documents. Kadar had refused to identify his informers and this setback had helped precipitate Rakosi's fall.

X picked up the red telephone and dialled Kadar's number.

"Janos, I've got the wife and father of Kopacsi with me. They say that Sandor is in danger of death."

The man's face slowly became covered in sweat as he listened to Kadar's response. "Yes, yes. I understand," he repeated mechanically in a soft voice. He hung up.

X looked at us.

"At this moment, the Russians can't be budged. Mao is harassing them."

The Russians were obliged to make a gesture to appease the Chinese, who were hungry for "anti-imperialist action". What gesture? Anything was possible.

At the news of the new complications caused by Mao's attitude, Ibolya broke down in tears. Calming herself, she said to X, in an even tone, "You tell Kadar: if my Sandor is killed, he won't die alone. I will kill my daughter immediately, and myself. I know it will be the same for Father. As the new boss, Kadar's hands will be covered in blood."

My father held Ibolya in his arms. He confirmed to X: "That is what will happen."

Our daughter, Judith, was already at my father's home. While at the embassy, she had contracted tonsillitis and her temperature had shot up. In response to my father's pressing requests, the Yugoslav ambassador had put the child in the trunk of his personal car and driven her secretly to him.

X was grim. "Everything is in the hands of the Kremlin," he said. "The fate of our families and of our friends, whether we have peace or whether the planet is destroyed. At this moment, everything depends on Moscow."

In a tired tone, he added, "Let's pray."

My father couldn't believe his ears. "Neither you nor I have ever been pious as far as I know!"

Writing these lines is painful for me. My father had too much invested in me, his only child. He finished by deciding obstinately that everything that had happened to me was his fault. But no, father. You know very well that we lived through a time in which an entire generation was trapped in the net, the big red net made in the U.S.S.R., full of sharks and naive idealists. *Nothing* was your fault — I wish you had understood that before your death so that you could have rested in peace.

General Serov's Sentence

He was thin and small with stooped shoulders, and he never took off his sunglasses. He was called George Vadas and he was a lawyer.

Ibolya had first engaged as my defence lawyer a former justice minister, a friend of ours who had lived in Moscow for several years. He was refused by the court on the grounds that he was "not on the list of defenders accredited by the AVO". Another well-known jurist, a professor of law at the University of Budapest, was rejected for the same reason.

A list of "authorized defenders" was pushed in front of me. I didn't recognize any of the names on it.

"Choose one anyway."

One of the names had an address on a street where I had lived at one time. My finger stopped on his name. That was how Vadas became my defence lawyer.

He came to see me one Tuesday morning, drenched from the snow. He didn't offer his hand. He looked at me scornfully and said without any transition: "Aren't you ashamed to have dirtied the good name of the armed forces by your criminal treachery?"

This was the tone he would maintain throughout our interview. I was above all curious to know what he anticipated for my case.

He replied coldly: "In your place, I wouldn't take any chances. Make your confession to the security organs and before the court. That is your task. The rest is up to justice."

I still wanted to know whether, as my defender, he could help me in some way.

"Yes. By transmitting your confessions to the organs of justice. That is the greatest service that I can render to the working people, whose interest is far more important to me than that of a traitor."

Through a special favour, I was able to ask my wife to try to rid us of this creep. She went to Vadas's office with my father, who was full of misgivings.

"Ibolya, I beg you, be careful. Choose your words carefully. This man could hurt our Sandor."

Ibolya knew exactly what measures the situation required.

"How much do you want to quit my husband's case?"

The man in the dark glasses was open-mouthed in surprise. But only for a moment. Then he shrugged his shoulders and said, "Two thousand forints."

That was the monthly salary of a qualified worker. My father was staggered. Ibolya didn't turn a hair.

"Very well. Here is your money. Write on a paper: "I resign as defender of Kopacsi.""

Vadas felt it would be imprudent to sign such a paper. He made out a receipt to a non-existent name created from the first names of my daughter and me. We have kept the receipt to this day as an example of the morality of the Hungarian security service and its appendages.

This adventure allowed us to find a new, sincere friend, a great jurist who would remain loyally at my side until the last moment of the trial. His name was Laszlo Bajor; under Rakosi, he had been public prosecutor for military affairs, which was why his name was on the AVO's approved list. But the revolution had shaken the man to his foundations. When the new Kadar regime wanted to reinstate him in his previous job, he had replied, "The rest of my life will be consecrated to defending the innocent."

Later, thanks to the indiscretion of the president of the tribunal assigned to our case, word got out that I had no one to defend my case. When Bajor heard of it, he immediately went to see Ibolya.

"I admire your husband. Ask him to place his confidence in me and I will do the impossible to save him. I do not ask for any fee. If necessary, I can even help your family financially."

Bajor was an excellent man, a moral man, and a fine counsellor. But no defender would have been good enough to save a head that Serov had sworn to chop. It would take powers greater than his to save my life.

In Hungarian prisons, unlike those in Western countries, the inmates don't play ping-pong, they don't watch television or get newspapers, and they don't have the chance to exchange information and marijuana with each other. The prisoner is alone in a cement cell whose only decor is a light bulb that burns day and night above the steel door.

Ordinarily, the guards are members of the AVO. Watched and informed on by each other, they testify against the inmates with a patriotic hostility, calling them "fascists" and punching and kicking them in the corridors. At least twice a day, the guards had the job of bringing us to see the AVO's "investigating officer".

This was a macabre ceremony. Fo Street prison in Budapest, like the famous prisons of Moscow, was equipped with optical and acoustic signals designed to prevent any chance meetings in the corridors. To keep thousands of innocent people in a state of total ignorance while their cases were "under investigation", the kilometres of corridors were equipped with recesses and sentry boxes so that, signalled by warning lights and sinister beeps, a prisoner could be hidden in one of them in case another prisoner approached.

The prisoners were thus kept entirely in the dark, without any chance of obtaining information, at the mercy of the "investigators" who could tell them any lie whatever and were happy to do so.

In the midst of this artificial solitude, I began to prepare my defence. My plan was simply to proclaim before the world the truth about the events of 1956 in Budapest. As one of the new leaders of the Hungarian party, it was my duty to provide an analysis of this historic period — including the deadly role played by Rakosi, whose tyranny was the direct cause of the explosion — and to examine the disastrous tactics of the Soviet authorities who, rejecting any political solution, chose instead a massive, brutal, imperialistic intervention by their armed forces.

I believed that the members of Kadar's government would listen to my words with respect, and I even hoped that they would pay heed to what I said in forming their own policies. My voice would come to them from the depths of prison through the intermediary of a trial. Before dying, I would have given cause for reflection to the new leaders of a country completely obsessed by the presence of the Russians.

I was naive. But, without information, alone in a cell, one can only build castles in the air. Fortunately, even Fo Street was not totally impregnable and my eyes were soon opened to reality.

"Psst. Psst."

One of the guards called me familiarly through the peephole. He whispered in Hungarian, "Colonel." What was going on? The key turned in the lock of the wicket, and a face that I knew appeared in the metal rectangle. It was the policeman with the scarred face, the sergeant who had arrived at police headquarters during the revolution and had accompanied me, along with my chauffeur, George, into the crowd assembled in front of police headquarters.

"Colonel. I've been transferred here as a guard. As soon as the officer buggers off, I'll be back to see you."

It wasn't only cigarettes and extra food that I would get, thanks to this man — let's call him Ferenc. I would also get news, and that was what I needed most of all.

In March 1957, about five months after my arrest, the Russians replaced the Russian guards and examining officers with staff recruited from among former Hungarian AVO personnel. Because they couldn't get enough ex-security police, they also hired Greek refugees who had been in Hungary since the end of the Greek civil war (their qualifications included not being able to speak enough Hungarian to get friendly with the prisoners), and several ordinary policemen like my friend Ferenc. The top management of Fo Street, however, remained in the hands of the Russians, headed by Colonel Shumilin, who held the post of "general counsellor for counter-revolutionary affairs".

I learned that my wife was earning her living selling pretzels in front of the elephant enclosure at the Budapest Zoo. Her position was better than those of the wives and children of the members of the Nagy government who had sought refuge in the Yugoslav Embassy. Fifteen high officials of the Nagy government along with their wives and some twenty-seven children had been transported to Romania. Included in the group were celebrated Marxist philosopher George Lukacs and Julia Rajk, the widow of the martyred Laszlo Rajk. The families of the accused weren't allowed to return until six weeks after the trial.

Their abduction was an operation worthy of Al Capone. After fifteen days of negotiations through the mediation of the Yugoslav ambassador and correspondence with Tito, the new Hungarian government guaranteed immunity from prosecution to Nagy and his friends if they would return to their residences in Budapest. The agreement was approved by Janos Kadar in a handwritten letter to Tito's Minister of Foreign Affairs.

Nagy accepted. Munnich, once again installed as Minister of the Interior, sent a bus to transport them from the embassy to their homes. But as soon as the government leaders and their families were in the vehicle, it was surrounded by Soviet half-tracks. Several Russian security officers entered the bus. The two Yugoslav diplomats assigned to assure that the departure of the refugees went smoothly were brutally pushed aside. Escorted by the half-tracks, the bus sped to the Soviet general headquarters. The occupants refused to leave the bus. They were pulled out by force, the children shrieking in fear, the women screaming. That same night, they were piled onto a plane. The next day a communiqué was published in the press to the effect that "Imre Nagy and his friends have left at their request for the Popular Republic of Romania".

The truth rapidly became public knowledge. A delegation from the National Workers' Council, a sort of Hungarian soviet sprung from the revolution, demanded an explanation from Kadar. On November 26, he replied on Radio Budapest: "We promised that the behaviour of Imre Nagy and his friends would not be subject to legal proceedings. We will keep that promise. We do not consider their departure as permanent. But, in our opinion, it is to the advantage of Imre Nagy and his associates and their families to leave Hungary for a certain period of time."

Several days later, at the plenary session of the United Nations on December 3, the Romanian Minister of Foreign Affairs declared: "The Romanian government assures that Prime Minister Imre Nagy and his group will enjoy the full benefit of the right of political exile. The Romanian government will observe the international rules regarding this right."

The workers' council reacted firmly to the kidnapping of Nagy. It ordered the factories to stop production until Nagy returned and the Russians departed. It was a general strike: all work stopped, and offices, schools, and service industries were closed right across the country.

The workers' council was the last bastion of opposition still operative in Hungary. Because it was an elected body, with representatives from each major workplace, it had great credibility, and both the regime and the Russians had to take it seriously. Despite the strike, the Russians still hoped to use this council to control the fractious workers. They had distributed travel passes to its members (for ordinary citizens, travel within the country was still restricted) as well as authorizations to carry arms. They even appointed their own delegate, a colonel, who took part regularly in the council's deliberations, which were also sometimes attended by Kadar and senior Soviet officials.

On November 23, a month after the beginning of the insurrection, many senior Soviets had shown up at the council's meeting. They wanted to know what orders the delegates had given to the population to mark the occasion. (Their own delegate had been absent from a previous meeting when the matter had been discussed.) A few minutes before 2:00 p.m., Sandor Racz, president of the council, stood up to speak. He was only twenty-three and a man of little education, but he was such a remarkable orator that he had been elected to head the council.

"Comrade interpreters," Racz said. "You may assure the Soviet officers present here that the population of Budapest is not about to resume the insurrection. But they will see something that they have never seen before. From this moment, and for the next hour, you will not see a living soul in the streets of Budapest. This is our way of commemorating those who fell in the battle for liberty. As for us, we are going to observe a minute of silence."

Everybody rose and sang the Hungarian national anthem. The Soviet officers also took part in this salute to the martyrs of the insurrection. For an hour, the streets of Budapest were as empty as the streets of a city might be in the aftermath of a nuclear war.

Abruptly, the Russians put an end to this game. Early in December, the council president was summoned to the Soviet general headquarters. Serov was waiting for him.

"It's finished. We don't want to hear any more phoney demands from you and you are not going to continue the strike. Consider yourself fortunate that I allow you to walk out of this room."

On December 9, the workers' council was outlawed and its leaders, who had been chosen by secret ballot by workers in every factory and business in Hungary, were arrested.

Meanwhile, communiqués were published assuring the public that Imre Nagy and his group were "enjoying the hospitality of the Romanian government in an excellent atmosphere marked by mutual understanding".

The Soviets decided it was time to clear up this ambiguous situation. They held a conference in Budapest of the Soviet, Romanian, Czech, Bulgarian, and Hungarian parties. The Soviet party was represented by Khrushchev and Malenkov. The conference lasted for four days and, on January 6, two days after it had closed, Kadar had the following communiqué published: "Imre Nagy and his government opened, by treachery, the road to a fascist counter-revolution in Hungary."

Several days later, Chou En-lai, the Chinese prime minister, arrived in Budapest. Immediately, the Kadar government issued a second communiqué in which Nagy was branded a renegade and henchman of Western imperialism. On January 18, Chou left Hungary. On January 19, during the night, 2,000 people were arrested, including workers' leaders, writers, and highly regarded members of the Communist opposition. That same night, death sentences were carried out in the courtyard at Fo Street against some Hungarian captives, including children as young as twelve. Total terror reigned in Budapest. The Soviet authorities could breathe more easily.

They also made a clean sweep among their own personnel. My friend Ferenc told me of horrendous butchery involving Soviet soldiers and officers at the Budapest central prison. Several hundred Russian combatants were confined in that prison. For the Hungarian common criminals who shared the prison with the Russians, it was paradise on earth: for a package of cigarettes, they could get a gold case, a gold ring, or a handful of rubles from the Russian inmates. The unfortunate Russians knew that they wouldn't need their valuable objects much longer. Within forty-eight hours, they were all machine-gunned to death in the courtyard of the old prison. This was a common scene in the Soviet Army: after a foreign campaign, for reasons difficult to define, the political section of the army imprisoned and often killed a goodly number of conscripts who had witnessed scenes they couldn't guarantee to forget.

I learned also of the tragic end in northern Hungary of several Soviet officers who commanded a column of tanks. Near the great steelworks on the road to Lillafured, the column was heading toward an area firmly in the control of the insurgents. On November 4, the women and children of the workers of Alsohamor and Felsohamor lay down on the mountain road. The Soviet commander stopped his tank column and told the women and children to move. They refused. After considering the alternatives, the officer chose to retreat. Two days later, he and his deputies were executed in the courtyard of the barracks in the town of Miskolc for the crime of failing to crush women and children under their caterpillar tracks. Where are the streets named after the women and children of Alsohamor and Felsohamor in Hungary and in the world? When will we learn the names of those officers martyred for having spared innocent lives?

Such was the news I received from Ferenc. After hearing it, I couldn't sleep for weeks. I had a new investigating officer, a Hungarian AVO major named Takacs. One day a civilian dropped in on us, a man with a personality as dry as a smoked herring. Wearing dark glasses like most of the KGB officers, he gave me a scornful look without speaking. Who was this character? He moved close to Takacs and whispered something in his ear.

"*Da, da,* yes, yes, it's definitely him," my investigator replied in a low voice. So the unknown was a Russian. And I was what for him? The chief assassin? The henchman of international imperialism? Neither, as I would learn later.

Soon after this puzzling interview, a remarkable construction project began in the prison. The halls on the third floor were divided in half by partitions from floor to ceiling: kilometres of partitions were erected in the corridors, on the staircases, and in certain offices and rooms. The noise of hammers and saws continued day and night. Cells were emptied and we were regrouped. Sound and light signals were installed. What we lived through in that prison was just like what Kafka described in his account of an imaginary trial in another time.

I was alone in my cell for a year. My friend Ferenc had been transferred. My one contact with the outside world was the visit, in the presence of a heavily armned guard, of Bajor, my defence lawyer.

For a year, I had been forbidden to see him. When we finally met, his seriousness and the nobility of his face inspired me immediately. He shook my hand, while bowing very low. It was the first time a man had bowed before me and I quickly understood why. I was no longer one of them. For those on the outside, I belonged to another world, that of the ghosts, perhaps of the martyrs. We sat down face to face in the ill-furnished room that was used for interviews between prisoners and their lawyers.

Bajor spread out his files in front of him. I wasn't allowed to look at these papers, but my attention was caught by one of Bajor's gestures. On several occasions, he placed eight of his fingers clearly in view, with the two thumbs bent out of sight, on the cover of the file, all the while looking at me insistently.

Obviously, the room was stuffed with microphones. The guard was an AVO non-commissioned officer, specially assigned to observe even the slightest gesture that passed between us and to listen carefully to everything we said.

"What are you wriggling about for there?" he asked belligerently.

Bajor eyed him with a superior air.

"Nobody is wriggling about. I am here to defend one of the principal accused in a *big, big* case and...."

The security man gave a start and interrupted the lawyer: "Shut up. I forbid you to speak."

Bajor turned toward him.

"If I understand you, you take it upon yourself to interrupt the proceedings?"

The guard was furious: "I forbid you to pronounce, to pronounce the...."

"The what? The adjectives 'big', 'large'? Is that what you don't like?"

The noise of the carpentry resumed outside the room, and in my little brain a light went on. In Hungarian, the word "nagy", the surname of Prime Minister Nagy, means big: Big, Grand and Co.

The guard screamed: "The meeting is adjourned."

Coldly, Bajor rose.

"The responsibility is entirely yours."

His eight fingers well spread out, thumbs bent back, he reached out his hands to gather up the documents.

The guard's face was covered with sweat.

"Continue. But if I see the slightest suspicious gesture, if I hear the slightest out-of-place word, you will pay dearly."

I no longer needed any explanation. Now I understood everything.

Bajor was predicting *eight accused*.

We were now looking at a much different trial from the one that had been previously planned for Maleter and me: instead of two death sentences, the Russians now planned a series. All the construction in the corridors and in the cells.... They had some distinguished guests, more important than us two.

Big, large, the big case: *Nagy*.

They had brought Nagy back from Romania and they wanted to kill him at the same time as us.

I scratched my hair with my eight fingers, thumbs conspicuously bent back. Bajor closed and opened his eyelids.

The AVO man screamed: "What is that?"

Bajor confined himself to looking contemptuously at the man. He continued to speak in an even tone of my case, the charges against me, the grounds for the defence. I barely heard. I was astounded by the news I had just been given.

So they had dared! After repeated assurances and safe-conducts, and multiple promises of immunity, the Russians had reneged: they had arrested the Hungarian prime minister, a man of sixty-one years, a Communist for forty of them. He would pass his last days hidden behind the newly erected partitions and die probably behind other barriers that would smother the sound!

"So? What is your response?"

Solitary confinement reduces the brain's ability to process new information. I hadn't heard Bajor's question. He repeated his proposition: "Your wife and I, we are going to do everything to improve your lot, but it's necessary that you be in agreement."

The AVO man came closer to us.

"What's this all about? What has the defendant's wife got to do with his defence?"

Now I understood what Bajor was trying to get across to me. Perhaps I would live to see my wife again after all. So long as I was to be part of a two-person trial, with Maleter as my co-accused, the death sentence was assured. But on a slate of eight accused, we would be ranked according to our importance; perhaps not all of us would be condemned to death.

I felt as if I were suffocating, as if the rope were tightening around my neck. The animal reflex told me that I had to get free. I had a horrible vision in which I saw the dignified form of Nagy strangling on the gallows. I heard him cry out: "Long live free and socialist Hungary" — the same phrase I was going to shout myself in front of the firing squad.

I saw the young Losonczy, so fragile (he had contracted tuberculosis in Rakosi's torture chambers and had had thoracic surgery a few months ago); I saw the great Maleter, smiling bravely, falling before the bullets; I saw myself on the ground, eagerly awaiting the *coup de grâce* from the revolver of this Boy Scout who was leaning over us at this very moment.

I began to scream: "Counsellor Bajor. Do something. For the love of God, do something!"

In a movement of impotent anger, the AVO man indicated the end of the interview.

Assassination of an "Unpresentable" Prisoner

I was transferred to cell 512a on the fifth floor and thoroughly frisked. I was not left alone for long; two guards came to get me and gripped me firmly, one on each side.

They led me into an elegantly furnished room — the office of Lieutenant-Colonel Joseph Szalma, commander of the Fo Street prison. Szalma was a slight fellow whom I knew well as an ambitious underling in the AVO. Seeing me, he couldn't — or wouldn't — stifle a snigger.

"So, the celebrated commander of the counter-revolutionary armies, Sandor Kopacsi! Glad to have you with us."

Another fanatic was seated on his left, an AVO colonel named Joseph Ferencsik, who would be the official responsible for the Nagy affair until the completion of the trial.

The door opened to admit a Russian in civilian clothes, Boris Shumilin of the KGB, the man delegated by the Kremlin to destroy Imre Nagy. He was about sixty, of medium height, and rather corpulent. Like Nagy's his hair was greying at the temples. But while Nagy's eyes sparkled merrily behind his professorial pince-nez, Shumilin's were obscured by the tinted lenses he wore, indoors and out. When emotion prompted him to remove them, he revealed eyes of glassy blue.

"Ah, Kopacsi."

He studied me, then motioned to someone to enter. It was

Sandor Rajnai, an AVO plainclothes officer. I had run into him dozens of times before at meetings connected with work. A small leathery-skinned man who radiated an air of deceitful intelligence, he had managed to slither his way up the ladder over the years. He had learned to speak fluent Russian and enjoyed the confidence of the Kremlin. It was he the Russians had sent to Romania to begin interrogating Nagy and his associates. Rajnai looked me up and down without a word of greeting, as though taking my measure for a coffin.

"Well, well," Shumilin said in Russian. The three Hungarian security officers leaned forward obsequiously as if better to savour these profound words from their Russian boss.

"Kopacsi, Colonel Shumilin knows all about you," said Ferencsik. "You have been misled by circumstances. One thing is clear. You are here because of Imre Nagy. He was the one who blinded you with his so-called philosophical writings masquerading as Marxism. He was the one who rejected the hand we extended to him. When he was still at the Yugoslav Embassy we offered a compromise: 'Practise self-criticism of both your views and your actions and you can take part again in political life.' He refused. Later, in Romania, the leaders of our party, Dezso Nemes and others, sought him out. He still refused to co-operate. He wouldn't give up his ideological views and wouldn't repudiate his stand before and during the counter-revolution. Had he done so, he would today be in an important position in government and you would not be waiting in Fo Street for a heavy sentence."

Shumilin's job was to duplicate the infamous trial of Laszlo Rajk in 1949, which had been rigged by Shumilin's predecessor, Theodore Bielkin (also known as Abakumov), whom Khrushchev had ordered shot shortly after the execution of Beria. I wondered if Boris Shumilin didn't fear he'd meet the same fate one fine day.

If he did, he wasn't letting it show. He was full of energy and eager to finish off Nagy and his associates. He employed two chauffeurs in shifts so that his car would be at his disposal twenty-four hours a day. In his new, eight-cylinder Chevrolet, Shumilin made the circuit from his luxurious house on Viranyi Street in Buda to Fo Street, and then to the Soviet Embassy where Comrade Andropov issued his orders. Andropov had just received a new appointment in Moscow; he was now in charge of "relations with fraternal parties". But he continued to make frequent trips to Budapest to keep the Hungarian affair in hand.

The survivors gave the following account of what had really happened in Romania. During his forced stay, a succession of Hungarian party representatives kept trying to persuade Nagy to recant. If only he would accuse his collaborators, vilify the revolution, and renounce his past, he could return to Hungary.

Then the formula changed. One morning, Nagy was handcuffed and put aboard a Soviet military plane where his ministers were already installed — in handcuffs and with welders' goggles over their eyes. These glasses were one of the KGB's standard accessories for special trips. Nagy, too, had to put them on. The prisoners weren't allowed to speak to each other. Each was flanked by a Soviet KGB guard and a Hungarian AVO officer.

The plane landed at the military airport in Budapest, and the group was taken to Fo Street. The transfer was made at night, in absolute secrecy, with only a hand-picked group of AVO officers present. But even so, an incident was inevitable.

An AVO captain, whom I shall call "Captain N", took delivery of the prisoners and had them installed in special cells on the fourth floor of Fo Street. When the guards took off the prisoners' welders' glasses, Captain N recognized one of the prisoners as his friend, Joska Szilagyi.

The captain had expected Imre Nagy but not Szilagyi. He had another officer relieve him and ran off to see the commander, Colonel Szalma.

"Listen, I just saw Joseph Szilagyi. I couldn't believe my eyes. There's been a mistake, a terrible mistake."

Szalma asked him coldly where he saw the mistake.

"But...Joska. He was my best friend in the underground. I know him from the east, from the city we were born in. He's the most courageous man, the best Communist on earth! The way he handled himself before Horthy's tribunal is legendary. He spent three years in Horthy's jails with fabulous courage. Maybe he was in Imre Nagy's group, but he doesn't belong in a cell."

Szalma listened patiently right to the end. Captain N was one of his friends. He asked him to sit down, to calm himself, to have a drink, to smoke a cigarette. He began to explain, point by point, why Hungarian justice had to act ruthlessly against "the counter-revolutionary group of Imre Nagy".

Captain N lost his temper.

"Listen, Szalma, I'm a good security officer, an old party comrade.

I'm your friend. And I'm telling you: this is a fatal error. Either Joska shouldn't be here or I shouldn't. This has got to be cleared up and right away."

Szalma furrowed his brow.

"You're right. I'm going to look into this closely. Wait here."

He went to see Colonel Shumilin.

The whole thing was settled half an hour later. The person who was at Fo Street "by mistake" was Captain N. Two armed guards escorted him to the exit and shoved him into the street. One of the guards tossed his briefcase after him. It landed in the middle of the road.

Shumilin urgently desired the death of Minister of State Geza Losonczy before the *in camera* trial could take place. Losonczy, it seems, was "unpresentable".

In all probability, the man had lost his mind. His physical and mental health had begun to deteriorate years earlier, as far back as his imprisonment with Kadar in the torture chambers of Rakosi and Bielkin. In addition to pulmonary tuberculosis, for which he had been operated on during his first imprisonment, Geza suffered from paranoia: he imagined that everyone in the world was a KGB agent and that his liberation, after four years in jail, had been a farce staged by the Russians and by the AVO.

His involvement in the opposition movement was Losonczy's route back to mental health. As Nagy's right-hand man, he became his old self once again, a great debater and organizer, full of energy and imbued with humanism. Rapidly, he gained a reputation as the key person in the opposition movement within the party.

It was too good to last. Before long, this unfortunate man fell once more into the clutches of the Kremlin. Locked in the same cell, accused of the same phoney crimes as he had been under Stalin ("traitor to the workers' movement, supporter of western imperialism"), he must have imagined he was watching a rerun of the same old horror show. Others have gone out of their minds with less provocation.

The rest of the accused were given a transcript of Losonczy's interrogation a few days before the trial. We were stupefied to read his answers. They were identical to the ritual responses that the victims of the Moscow show trials were made to recite. "I admit to being a paid spy of Josep Broz Tito and of Eisenhower. I admit to fomenting a fascist counter-revolution against my people and against the glorious army of the Soviet Union, the country of all the workers of the world." And so on. Losonczy gave it to them wholesale. The statement proved only the poor man's derangement; his captors had crushed his intelligence and destroyed his sanity.

During this second and final captivity, Losonczy refused to eat. It wasn't a hunger strike; he was convinced that his food was poisoned. This fear was groundless. The inmates in the neighbouring cells, including myself, took whatever we could scrounge from the guards and, although we didn't know it at the time, this included the food Losonczy had rejected.

This former minister of the Hungarian government was no longer good for any of Shumilin's purposes. In court, he was certain to give harebrained responses. The falseness of his trial would stink from a hundred leagues away. He was no longer presentable before public opinion, even as a permanent inmate of a psychiatric hospital. "How dreadful," would be the reaction. "The Russians have driven him mad a second time!" On the other hand, his depositions, carefully pruned and abbreviated, could serve the court very well. Shumilin, the director of the play, cut to the heart of the matter. For this stage production to be a success, Geza Losonczy must die.

The murder was perpetrated in Losonczy's cell, just a few steps from my own. It was a cold evening at the end of December 1957, several days before the trial was to begin. Suddenly, I heard a hubbub in the corridor. Normally, the guards moved about in felt slippers, the better to look in on us unawares through peepholes in the cell doors. Now we heard the stamping of many pairs of studded boots. Soldiers gathered before Losonczy's cell. The iron door opened noisily, and the detachment barged in.

It began immediately — the sound of struggle, the smothered screams, the bed clattering onto the cement. The cries became more and more anguished. There was a way to slide back the piece of steel that covered the peephole from the outside. I did so and was able to look at Losonczy's cell. In front of the open door stood two soldiers.

"Murderers! Fascists! Murderers!"

Those were the final words of Geza Losonczy, a minister of the Hungarian state, killed in his prime, not in the middle ages in a castle in Spain, but in the second half of the twentieth century, in the heart of Budapest, by order of the Communist Party of the Soviet Union.

"What the hell are you doing there?"

The door of my cell was opened brusquely to reveal an AVO captain, strapped up tight in his uniform, cap on his head, revolver in his hand.

Luckily I had jumped back, an animal reflex. If I had been caught in the act of spying, I wouldn't have escaped lightly.

The captain closed my cell door. I saw a stretcher brought to Losonczy's cell and his body carried out. The detachment left.

The actual killing had been performed by the prison barber, who, for about a week, had been force-feeding Losonczy on orders from the prison doctor. That night, his assignment was not to feed but to kill, by plunging the rubber hose into the windpipe of the victim. Some accounts claim Losonczy's death was accidental. But Losonczy had not screamed on the other occasions when he was force fed, nor had his cell been filled with soldiers. The gruesome manner of his death was designed to allow it to be presented as an accident.

After Losonczy's death, the barber disappeared. He was a fat, red-headed, none-too-clean non-commissioned officer who shaved us once a week in our cells and stank up the atmosphere. We weren't shaved for a month. I asked a guard, a former policeman, what had become of the barber and was told: "He killed himself with his service revolver."

As far as I knew, however, the civilian prison employees weren't armed. The barber, a man who knew too much, undoubtedly *was* killed with a service revolver — but not his own.

We were summarily prepared for a new type of trial. The pretrial statements, written in Russian, were in the old-fashioned style — "spy of Tito, agent of Eisenhower", and so on. The new style was represented by Captain Istvan Metelka, whom Shumilin had chosen specially for me. Shumilin couldn't use Russians to take statements from us because we were refusing to sign transcripts that were drafted in Cyrillic script; Maleter, who spoke the language perfectly, declared that he had "forgotten Russian".

The choice of Metelka was fortunate for me because, unlike some of his colleagues, he behaved more or less as a human being. At the outset he declared that before the uprising he had not been a member of the AVO but a simple schoolteacher in the provinces. (I learned later that this was a lie; Shumilin had ordered him to hide his past security service.)

He called me by my first name from the third day of our

acquaintance. "Sandor, do you know that your team won on Sunday?"

Decidedly, he did not mean the opposition team in the party. That team was rotting in jail. He meant the Dozsa soccer team of Ujpest, the police team of which I had been the president.

Ah, the Dozsa team! The afternoons of pleasure and delight came back to me in waves. I knew all the players; I had watched them hundreds of times confronting Hungary's best teams, including the national team, which during the revolution had departed for the Olympic Games in Australia. Several of its members had chosen to stay there and live in freedom.

I couldn't stop myself from asking who had scored the goals. Metelka, who knew as much about soccer as I, gave me a detailed and expert description of the highlights of the match, and for a brief quarter of an hour I forgot my troubles. But worry soon returned when Metelka steered the conversation back to the events of 1956.

"Let's speak a little, if you will, of the Red Cross vehicles that brought the first foreign armaments into Hungary from the West. Did you see them, how, and in what circumstances?"

This tale of "arms brought in from the West" was their latest invention. Following the Stalinist formula, Shumilin had outlined this scenario: arms imported from the West, insurrection by remote control guided by vengeful West Germans and the Pentagon. But the new style of investigation demanded that accusations be supported by at least a modicum of proof, and for this fiction of Western arms and remote control there was none.

"Yes, I saw the Red Cross trucks."

"Sandor, try to remember: were the machine guns under the medications or on top?"

I could only respond, truthfully, that there were no arms whatsoever in the trucks bringing blood plasma and penicillin from West Germany for the thousands of civilians who had been wounded in the streets of Budapest.

"But the ammunition! What sort of fake packaging was it in? The packages marked 'antibiotics' or the ones that said 'first aid'?"

It was ridiculous. The Soviets would have been better off if they'd immediately produced phoney photos of American aggression as they had in Korea. And this nonsense about the imported arms wasn't the only sign that the Soviet show-trial machinery was seizing up.

One day, Metelka said to me point blank, "Your friend Joseph Szilagyi is making a fool of himself. He calls the interrogators 'bandits in the pay of Moscow'. You wouldn't want to talk to him a bit privately, would you?"

Privately, oh my, my! "Talk to him a bit...." This gentle approach had nothing in common with the style of the classic Moscow trial.

"You see, Sandor, your friend totally refuses to co-operate with us. He refuses to recognize the legality of his arrest. He's not a bad fellow, he's done practically nothing that could lead to his being sentenced to more than five years. But if he continues like this, he's on the road to ruin. Colonel Shumilin has had about enough."

Joska had been on a hunger strike for several months. He was refusing all food, including the vitamin-laced medications the prison doctor had ordered for him. Shumilin was beside himself. He had already had an "unpresentable prisoner" killed. The editor Gimes was also on a kind of hunger strike; by eating only a single tea-spoonful of food at each meal, he had lost twenty-five kilos. And Shumilin was having a terrible time with Imre Nagy, who obstinately refused to admit to even the smallest point in the accusations against him. Shumilin couldn't confront the Kremlin with a collection of Auschwitz inmates at the Budapest trial; nor could he kill everybody before a verdict was even pronounced.

Metelka asked me if Joska had any children — as if the AVO didn't know every last detail about the lives of its prisoners. But the question had its desired result. I agreed to serve as intermediary between the interrogators and my friend.

I had prepared my arguments in advance. They were roughly the same as those Ibolya had made to me when we were captured by Serov: we had an ideal and it's lost forever. Now you must live for your family; you've got a wife and three kids. Five years will pass quickly. And so on.

Perhaps I was also going to add, "Look here, my family is also going to need you because I'm not going to get out of here alive."

But Joska would have none of it. Metelka informed me that, unhappily, the meeting between Joska and me would not take place.

"Your friend is stubborn. He refuses to see anyone. He demands to be left in peace and says that each one should follow the path he has chosen."

I was astounded by Joska's courage, although I could have predicted it. Men of his mettle aren't accustomed to compromise. The "new style" trial excluded physical torture. But even under torture Joska would have refused to cave in to a power he despised profoundly.

"At least write him a note and ask him to chew a little paprika," Metelka asked pitifully. Popular belief has it that Hungarian paprika contains the vitamins necessary to combat scurvy. Joska's gums were inflamed and his teeth were falling out one after another.

I wrote the following note: "Joska, dear friend, don't commit suicide." But he was no more receptive to that than to our proposed meeting. He threw the note away without looking at it.

I agonized over what would happen to us at the trial, which now appeared to be imminent. In the courtyard at Fo Street, others who had been swept up in the revolution, many of them ordinary workers, were being exterminated. After farcical trials, they were executed Soviet-style, their final cries drowned out by the deliberate gunning of truck motors. Almost every morning, we were awakened by this horrible din. It's not difficult to imagine the depths to which our spirits had sunk.

At the last moment, Metelka indicated that "it won't be catastrophic". What did he mean by that? That we wouldn't be sentenced to death? Laszlo Bajor, my defence lawyer, came to see me. We were kept under surveillance as we talked. Bajor told me that the secrecy surrounding the trial was such that even our wives hadn't been told when it would be held. He said that the only extenuating circumstances that could be put before the court were our past services to the workers' movement. From these words, I understood that the verdict had been decided by Moscow before the trial, and that nothing short of a miracle would change it.

A miracle did occur but, unfortunately, not quite as we the accused had hoped.

■ *In the Labyrinth*

On the morning of February 6, 1958, the cell doors opened one after another. Got up in our cleaned and disinfected suits — I in a tie the AVO had chosen specially for the occasion because, according to them, my own didn't match the rest of my outfit — we were lined up in the corridor. Right away I noticed many uniformed police officers wearing the blue-grey that was dear to me from my years of service. It was nothing but a masquerade. Colonel Shumilin had required that, for the ceremony, the handpicked AVO officers don the uncompromised uniform of regular policemen. With pleasure, I saw again the tall figure of Paul Maleter, always cool and collected, standing straight and serene, greeting me with a loud *Servus!*, the greeting Hungarians reserve for their close friends.

We hadn't seen each other since we had crossed Budapest, singing, on a Soviet half-track, more than a year previously.

I was stunned to see a face that could have belonged to the great journalist Miklos Gimes if it hadn't been starved into the face of a child. But he looked at me confidently and smiled: *"Servus, Kopi!"*

To my great surprise, from the third cell emerged old Zoltan Tildy, former president of Hungary, former Protestant pastor, minister in Nagy's government, and the one who had negotiated the surrender of Parliament to the Soviets. He must have been seventy. I had known that he would be implicated in the trial, but I had difficulty imagining that this old gentleman, whose only crime had been to get mixed up with us Communists, would be imprisoned after having been under house arrest during almost all of the Rakosi regime.

The door of the fourth cell stayed shut. It was that of the cabinet minister Geza Losonczy. We looked at each other unhappily. All of us knew about the murder.

The little cortège set off. We were introduced into a labyrinth artfully created by the partitions. Here we were, already on the path to death, like cattle in a stockyard, entering into a huge system for manufacturing canned meat. We were ordered to stop. Five other cells were opened. Out of them came Miklos Vasarhelyi, Gimes's colleague and the former editor of the central party newspaper; Ferenc Janosi, Imre Nagy's son-in-law; Ferenc Donath, a respected adviser for agricultural affairs, and then...my friend Joska Szilagyi.

He hadn't noticeably lost weight, despite the hunger strike. He still had the stature of a huge peasant. We could read his determination in the solemn way he looked at us.

"*Servus*, Joska."

He didn't hear my greeting or return my pale smile. His attention was turned toward the fifth cell, which the guards were putting off opening.

It was Nagy's cell, and now all of us waited to see in what state we would find the man we all venerated and who, against all ethics and written agreements, was in the hands of our worst enemies.

He came out of the cell as if he were coming out of a meeting room, his face preoccupied. I found him a bit thinner, but the build was the same: the peasant or the sixty-year-old blacksmith, the village strongman in the most commanding period of his life. The legendary pince-nez straddled his nose as before. For an instant, he turned toward us and his glance passed us in review.

He gave each of us a brief, friendly nod. Our presence seemed to reassure him. I thought I read in his eyes the same astonishment that we had all felt: *What have they done to Geza Losonczy?* Then, Imre Nagy at its head, the cortège set off again.

We moved quickly through the labyrinth at a military pace. Then I glimpsed something that none of the others in the cortège could have seen.

I was third in the line. I noticed that the door of an office we were passing was slightly ajar — a piece of carelessness that, in a prison swarming with Moscow-style cops, could not be accidental.

After a few more steps, I turned around as if I were trying to catch a glimpse of my friends at the rear of the line.

"Look ahead," shouted a guard.

Too late. The door was now half-open and I saw clearly the burly form and dark glasses of Colonel Shumilin. Behind him, I glimpsed two shadows. Damned if the first didn't have the blond hair and steely blue eyes of that human hawk, Serov, head of the KGB.

The other was probably Andropov. No longer ambassador, he was now the top Soviet official in charge of relations with the satellite countries. It was he who had suffered the affront of being told that Hungary was withdrawing from the Warsaw Pact and declaring itself neutral. Now he had been assigned to make the head of the Hungarian government confess his sins. And here he was to observe his humiliated adversaries on the way to the scaffold.

A guard hit me a solid blow and dragged me forward.

I was on the verge of shouting, like Pereobrajenski, an officer of the guard who had been dragged to the scaffold by the hangmen of Ivan the Terrible: "Tyrant, you won't die in your bed either."

We were to be tried by the Supreme Court in order to rule out the possibility of an appeal. The judge was Zoltan Rado, a seasoned man, fat and rather friendly. He was forever taking off his glasses, wiping them with a large white handkerchief, and putting them back on.

"I ask everybody to speak loudly and distinctly, because I have problems hearing."

This was a discreet way of drawing attention to the microphone hidden behind his head, in the centre of the newly devised national emblem, an awkward mixture of the Rakosi emblem and the symbol of the 1848 republic. (Several months later, during the real trial, they wouldn't go to so much trouble. The microphone would be on the judge's desk and a movie camera would roll continuously.)

But at the time we didn't know that this was a dress rehearsal. Maybe the prosecution didn't know it either; Moscow's order to interrupt the proceedings wouldn't arrive until the next day.

In the Hungarian legal system, there is no jury of one's peers. The jury's function is filled by a panel of five appointed assessors who assist the judge (called the president of the court) in his deliberations. I couldn't stop looking at one of the assessors, a woman. Hate was written all over her face. She was the widow of Peter Lakatos, one of the victims of the siege of Koztarsasag Square. She wore her thirst for vengeance like a theatrical mask.

The one who would attempt to demonstrate our guilt was a man I knew very well from having worked with him many times during the first Nagy government. It was Joseph Szalay, the deputy public prosecutor. He was a distinguished man with white hair and a caustic way of expressing himself.

We were all accused of having established an illegal organization and of having fomented a plot aimed at reversing by force the legal order of the Republic of Hungary. In addition, Nagy was charged with high treason, and Maleter and myself with mutiny.

It was clear from the very beginning that this trial would be a lively show.

"Profession?"

Standing, Imre Nagy adjusted his pince-nez and declared calmly: "Prime Minister of the Republic of Hungary."

The prosecutor started. The assessors winced. Imperturbably, Rado corrected the "error", turning toward the court clerk and saying, "*Former* Prime Minister."

Nagy took off his pince-nez.

"Not as far as I know. My nomination to that position dates from October 24, 1956. No legal organ has called my nomination into question."

The president stared open-mouthed for a moment. It was as if he were saying to himself, "It's true, but what can we do? We're not here to tell the truth, but to execute a sentence."

"We'll deal with these questions at the appropriate time," he said. Then he asked Nagy if he considered himself guilty.

Nagy put his pince-nez back on. He looked severely at the president of the court. Head held high, he replied. "No. I am not... guilty."

Rado was no luckier with Maleter.

"Profession?"

"Major-General of the National Army, Minister of Defence of the Republic of Hungary."

"Former Minister of Defence."

"No. Comrade Imre Nagy, Prime Minister of Hungary, has never indicated to me that I have been relieved of my post."

The young soldier smiled at the old prime minister, who smiled back and smoothed his moustache with satisfaction.

The worst was yet to come. It arrived with the call to the witness stand of Joska Szilagyi. Instead of stating his identity, he said in a booming voice: "Mr. President, I have two questions to ask you."

Rado called him to order but was drowned out by Joska's thundering voice. "The first question is this: During the investigation, your men always referred to a Nagy-Losonczy group. I want to know where is my friend and comrade Geza Lonsonczy. My second question is: what has happened to my wife and three children who were deported to Romania?"

There was total silence for three seconds. Rado opened and closed his mouth several times without getting a sound out. Finally, he stammered: "The questions of the accused will be answered at the appropriate time. Do you acknowledge your guilt?"

"In this country, the only guilty one is a traitor named Janos Kadar. Supported by the bayonets of the Soviet imperialists, he has drowned the revolution of his people in blood."

There followed a bitter exchange between Joska and Rado.

RADO: How you must detest the Soviets to speak like that.

SZILAGYI: No. I like the ordinary Russian or Ukrainian. I like any ordinary person of whatever ethnic group in the Soviet Union. But I detest the imperialist power that, under the mask of Marxism, creates a world of slavery and colonization.

RADO: Those are your views....

SZILAGYI: Those are facts known by the entire world.

RADO: The entire world knows that the U.S.S.R. is the homeland of the workers, the working class is in power there and....

SZILAGYI: I pity you. You are forced to recite nonsense. You know well that the working man's life is a hundred times easier in the liberal countries than under Soviet dictatorship.

When this verbal duel was over, Szalay read the charges against the defendants. Nagy and the military leaders were charged with high treason (Kiraly *in absentia*); my crime consisted mainly of having distributed 20,000 firearms to the insurgents (the weapons were distributed to arm the new National Guard) and of having had dealings with "bandits and assassins" (in fact, they were patriots and I was acting on the orders of the National War Council).

"Guards," Rado ordered, "take the accused back to their cells, with the exception of Imre Nagy."

How I would have liked to stay to watch and listen to Gulliver fending off all these Lilliputians.

The next day, Rado was exhausted. In a faint voice, he replied to Joska's question.

"The accused Losonczy died during the investigation. According to the medical report, the cause of death was a pulmonary embolism."

Yes, milk directed into his lungs, the classic mode of execution in totalitarian jails.

As for the fate of the deported wives and children, the president gave no response. The accused would remain without any news of their families, who themselves would hear nothing of the trial and verdict until six months later.

The hearing had barely begun when the president of the court, who was visibly suffering, suspended it a second time.

At the third session, the prosecutor suggested adjourning the trial for "supplementary inquiries". His suggestion was accepted. That was the last time we saw Rado.

My investigator summoned me to his office where he declared, with an ambiguous smile, "The judge has a cold." This cold must have lasted for four months. In fact, it wasn't a cold but a coronary thrombosis. During two days of hearings, the Kremlin had changed its mind four times as to what verdicts would be pronounced.

I was to learn later that Khrushchev had been in an awkward position at the time. His policy of reconciliation with Tito was shaky. At the time of its second intervention in Hungary, the Kremlin was still counting on this friendship. Vielko Mitshunovich, a former Yugoslav ambassador to Moscow, has since described in his book, *The Moscow Years, 1956-58,* a visit by Khrushchev, on the night of November 2, to Tito's home. The Yugoslav leader didn't oppose the Russian intervention in Hungary, which by then was already well underway, and Khrushchev asked for neither Yugoslav participation nor agreement, but contented himself with informing Tito of the choice he had made for the new leader of Hungary. It was to be Munnich, a former Hungarian ambassador to Moscow. Tito vehemently urged Khrushchev to choose instead the much better known Kadar. The meeting lasted until 5:00 a.m. When he left the Soviet leader was jubilant and kissed Tito effusively.

The next day, the Soviet tanks entered Budapest, and forty-eight hours later, on November 6, the Yugoslav ambassador was summoned to the Kremlin. There he met a Khrushchev drunk with his international success in Suez and Hungary. Bluntly Khrushchev demanded the extradition of "this counter-revolutionary Nagy" and "his gangster-in-chief Losonczy".

On November 11, Khrushchev summoned the Yugoslav again. This time, he was insistent. "This bandit Imre Nagy can't stay at your embassy in Budapest. He's got to get out of there." He added: "The Romanian comrades will do what's necessary to get you out of this tight spot."

Although the Yugoslavs offered only moderate resistance to the

Soviet demands for the arrest of the Nagy group, relations between Moscow and Belgrade deteriorated. In November 1957, during a conference of world Communist parties, Yugoslavia, unlike China, refused to sign the final communiqué recognizing the total hegemony of the Kremlin over the "fraternal parties". Khrushchev made a final attempt, interrupting the Nagy trial and sending Kadar to Belgrade to negotiate with Tito. Instead of the hoped-for conciliatory gesture, Tito amused himself by corrupting Kadar, telling him: "You have to do like Gomulka. Fight to get the maximum of independence *vis-à-vis* the Russians and we'll support you."

At the beginning of 1958, Khrushchev went to Budapest to see if his reoccupied province was sufficiently pacified. He especially wanted to hear Kadar's account of his meeting with Tito. When Kadar recounted the seditious advice he had received from Tito, Khrushchev was furious. He summoned Shumilin to find out when the heads of "the dog Nagy" and his group would roll for the edification of "the dog Tito".

"Tomorrow," Shumilin replied.

The Hungarians timidly asked for a delay, pointing out that in the current state of world opinion, it would be preferable to lend at least a semblance of legality to the proceedings.

But the impatient Khrushchev ordered Shumilin to do something right away.

What could be done right away, without preparation, was to put to death the horrible Kopacsi and the cumbersome Joska Szilagyi. Tomorrow they would be shaved. The day after, they would appear before a semblance of a court. In three or four days, at the most eight, they would be hanged — to the astonishment of Tito.

This would be Khrushchev's way of sending a message to Tito: "We Soviets are ruthless. If you stray too far, we'll know how to tighten the reins." The desire to teach Tito a lesson explains why, two years after the Hungarian uprising had been quelled and the population "pacified", the Russians relentlessly pursued the trial of the Nagy government.

My lawyer, Laszlo Bajor, is now dead, taken in his prime by cancer. What I write can't hurt him. Armed with confidential information about the pressure Khrushchev was putting on Shumilin, information gathered in government circles where he was naively taken for an old "unconditional" of the military tribunals, Bajor went secretly to see my wife.

He had taken a thousand precautions, as in a detective novel, to shake anyone following him on his way to the zoo to see Ibolya. The act he had made up his mind to perform — "divulging a state secret" — could cost him fifteen years in prison as well as the loss of the right to defend me, which he seemed to value above all else. He sat down next to Ibolya on a bench and said in a low voice:

"Mrs. Kopacsi, we cannot afford to hesitate. If you want to see your husband alive again, now is the time to act."

My wife had her basket of pretzels on her arm. There were black circles under her eyes from sleepless nights spent worrying about me.

"Why do you risk your freedom for my husband?" she asked him.

The lawyer smiled. "During the revolution last year, I came to understand that the new fascism is called Soviet Russia. The rest of my life will be dedicated to serving the victims of this new fascism."

Ibolya, accompanied by Kopacsi senior, paid a visit to our northern homeland. My old comrades remembered how my father and I had fought for them and for our country. Ibolya returned to Budapest with a precious document, a series of signatures at the bottom of a petition addressed to Janos Kadar. In it, veteran party officials pleaded for the life of Sandor Kopacsi. The signatories noted that they had together passed "750 years in the workers' movement".

The north had acted. The north was the great steelworks at Diosgyor, the blast furnaces at Ozd, the coal mines at Borsod, and the mechanical engineering industry at Miskolc. It was perhaps half of Hungary's entire industrial production.

Of course, those who signed the petition were not threatening a strike. Under the terror of "normalization", a party official could no longer make demands, much less threats. The signatories who had spent "750 years in the workers' movement" were begging the autocrat, just as they would have had to do in Czarist Russia.

Nevertheless, the petition arrived on Kadar's desk at the right moment, plunging him into bitter reflections.

Two years earlier, I had saved his life, and now Kadar wanted to do something for me. But what?

Despite his status as a Quisling, Kadar wasn't a saint in the eyes of the Kremlin. One day, after I had explained to my investigator, Metelka, that I hadn't done much more than Kadar, who had told Andropov that he would fight the Soviet tanks with his "bare hands", the man called his boss in.

"Listen to what Kopacsi says."

The boss, Colonel Ferencsik, frowned as he listened. "My man, you're wrong to bring up Janos Kadar. Comrade Shumilin hasn't yet decided if this dog Nagy will hang by himself or in the company of Janos the shit."

Janos Kadar had spent four years in the clutches of these AVO officers. They rightly feared he would want to settle accounts with them once ensconced in power. They despised Kadar with all their hearts, blaming him for the decision to disband the AVO during the revolution; they were using all their influence with the Soviets to include him in the "package".

It is never wise to maintain in the palace a prince whom one has beaten every morning for four years and in whose mouth one has urinated — as one of the Fo Street commanders once did to Kadar.

Ibolya and my father were urgently summoned by Kadar's personal secretary, who was a close friend of my father's.

"Joseph, above all, you must go back up north."

"To do what?"

"Those people must withdraw their signatures."

"But...it's a petition, 750 years in the workers' movement."

"The 750 years, the petition — they don't matter. Kadar wants to try something for your son, but on condition that nobody forces his hand."

That's how things happen in a "socialist" country: a humble petition from old comrades is seen as intolerable pressure. Imagine the position of the millions of unknowns with no connection to the regime. What possibility have they to express their needs?

My father and Ibolya went north and the signatures were withdrawn. Kadar was no longer being pressured.

Kadar and Munnich, who was Kadar's deputy and the top KGB official in the country, dialled Khrushchev's secret Kremlin number on the red telephone. The conversation took place in secret; what was said isn't known exactly. But it is known that the conversation lasted for sixty minutes. Kadar and Munnich employed all the quibbling over details the international workers' movement allows between master and serf. Khrushchev and Mikoyan, at the other end of the line, would not budge.

"This police chief should be hanged."

It had been arranged with Shumilin, during Khrushchev's visit to Budapest.

By the end of the conversation, however, the matter had become more nuanced. Khrushchev realized that he was risking the loss of Kadar at the head of his Hungarian province. He sighed.

"Okay. But in exchange, Kopacsi has to help us."

In the language of the highest levels of international diplomacy in eastern Europe, that meant that I was to make it easier for the Russians to execute Prime Minister Imre Nagy.

"You Will Be a Witness"

My friend Joska Szilagyi had to be executed without delay. Even though the trial was behind closed doors, a man so impulsive and so uncompromising could not be allowed to stay on the team.

Szilagyi had to disappear, and the judge had to be replaced. Not only was Rado gravely ill, he was unpardonably soft to boot. The authorities decided to kill two birds with one stone and appoint a firm-handed man named Vida as judge. He would make his debut with my friend Joska alone. If he managed to get Joska hanged without too much fuss, he would have passed his test and would be a good candidate to preside over the new Nagy trial.

The man studied the result of the investigations for fifteen days. He was a peerless jurist and a faithful Communist. Before the war, he had served several years in Horthy's famous prison in Szeged. After he had studied the documents he asked to see the justice minister, Ferenc Nezval.

They knew and liked each other. They had been together all their lives in the movement.

"Feri, old friend," said Vida. "I've got bad news for you."

"Oh?"

"The Nagy material is worthless."

"What are you talking about?"

"I've studied it for fifteen days. I know it by heart. Not only is it impossible to convict him of anything serious, there isn't even material there for a trial."

The justice minister went deathly pale. He stood up.

"Tunis" — because of his dark complexion, Tunis was Vida's *nom de guerre* during the party's illegal phase — "you are mad. The Russians will hang us side by side."

Tunis looked at his friend. He was an anonymous soldier of the Communist movement just like his comrade, the minister. He knew as well as the minister that, in the movement, an order was an order, especially when it came from the Soviets.

"There's no point getting upset. I thought you were asking my legal opinion."

Feri Nezval had acquired his university training only recently. The man had been a simple artisan faithful to the party, but he had good judgement. During the summer of 1956, at a party celebrating Nagy's sixtieth birthday, he had come to shake the old leader's hand, although he knew, as did everybody, that AVO photographers were collecting shots of all the visitors from the windows of the house across the street. Obviously, the Russians had a complete set of photos. As for Vida, his relations with Joska Szilagyi were widely known. The two men belonged to the same party cell, and the two families mingled socially. After Joska's anti-Rakosi speech at a party meeting, Vida had kissed him in front of everybody, congratulating him for his "exemplary courage".

So the minister was quite right to remind Vida, "You'll go along or the Russians will hang the two of us side by side."

Vida's final test was scheduled for April 23, 1958, the date of Joska's trial. He had already had a warm-up during the "writers' trial". Apparently without any valid grounds, he had condemned the old novelist Tibor Dery to nine years in prison and the Communist dramatist Julius Hay to six years in prison. This time, he was to impose the death penalty against a friend simply because the man's existence irritated the Russians.

The thing had to be done quickly. On the morning of April 23, I was taken from my cell to an office set up specially as a hearing room. My investigator was waiting for me in the corridor.

"You will be a witness."

"In what?"

"In the case of your friend, Szilagyi."

I couldn't believe my ears.

"Szilagyi is one of the accused in our group. Have you separated him from us?"

"Don't ask useless questions. You will go before the court and you will respond to the questions the judge asks you, that's all."

I was led into the improvised hearing room. I saw Tunis behind the desk and my friend Joska Szilagyi on the bench of the accused. For an instant, I thought to myself, this is a joke, it's a reconstruction of a party meeting. Then Vida's voice brought me back to reality.

"Defendant Kopacsi, you are here as a witness. You must say what you know, first of all concerning the anti-party attitude of the accused."

I looked at Tunis, I looked at Joska — two destinies flying off in opposite directions. I felt like saying, "Listen, Tunis, don't be an idiot. You know him as well as I do, our friend Joska is the most upright man and the best Communist ever to walk the earth."

Instead, I said, "Yes, as far as I know, Joseph Szilagyi was opposed to the views and methods of the former first secretary of the party, Matthias Rakosi."

Vida grimaced. He didn't like my answer. No matter. The thing had to be finished on the double. He gave the floor to Joska.

My friend approached the witness box. He was very close to me, so close that I could feel the warmth of his body. He looked at me for an instant. His expression was inscrutable. He spoke slowly, seriously.

"The former first secretary of the party, Matthias Rakosi, was a shady politician, in the sense that one talks of a shady banker or an unreliable doctor. He wasn't a Communist any more. He had degenerated for the same reason that the leaders of the fraternal parties have degenerated: allegiance to a foreign colonial power, that is, Soviet Russia."

"I order you to be silent," thundered Vida.

It was as if Vida hadn't spoken. Joska continued without even raising his voice.

"A flunkey with bloody hands, that is what our Matthias Rakosi had become. Just like Janos Kadar, the new usurper of the Hungarian party."

"Silence! I forbid you to. . . ."

Joska looked at the judge and raised his voice.

"Mr. President, people's assessors. It is possible to be a Communist without spilling blood, without destroying the dreams of mankind. I deeply believe that."

There was silence. Then Joska continued. He spoke very quietly but we could hear all the inflections of his serious, ardent voice.

"It is to illustrate that truth that I am going. You who stay behind: get rid of the Russians and their methods. That is the first step to take on the road to the rehabilitation of a movement that has been sullied but still can become a great force for the good of humanity."

The verdict was pronounced that night: death by hanging. Joska refused to ask for clemency. "I don't want to breathe the same air as the executioners of my people." Through his lawyer, he asked for death by a firing squad instead of hanging. Vida rejected the request on the grounds that Hungarian penal law prescribed the rope.

That same night, Joska was transferred to the Budapest central prison. Until dawn, he wrote his wife a long letter that she would never receive. On April 24, 1958, early in the morning, he was led to the gallows that had been set up in the prison courtyard. He climbed the scaffold, head high, declaiming, "Long live free and independent Hungary!"

Obviously, I was too dumb to understand immediately the meaning of Metelka's latest manoeuvre. In the morning, he arranged for me to get croissants. Half an hour later, I was brought to his office where he received me with a serious expression on his face.

"Sandor, your daughter is better...."

"What! What is wrong with my Judith?" I stammered.

"Your daughter is particularly subject to the fear that she feels because of... because of *your future.*"

He didn't want to say another word.

Because of "my future"? I didn't have any. From the moment that I was arrested by the chief of the KGB, imprisoned and charged along with Nagy, Szilagyi, and Maleter, my future had been identical to theirs. They had committed no crime and neither had I. We were toys in the hands of a foreign power that would decide our fate.

I said as much to Metelka, who became unusually talkative.

"I don't agree," he said. He stood up and stepped to the front of his desk. "Your case is not completely identical to those of the other accused," he continued.

It was the first time I had heard this subtle distinction. It is difficult to suppress the beating of a heart that, despite all the reasons advanced by the brain, begins to hope to live. My dog, Tango, jumped for joy in the little scene that suddenly lit up my imagination. I saw my daughter running behind the dog and Ibolya calling to her to be careful not to trip on the stones in the garden. Mammy was embroidering on the terrace. The sun was shining.

"No, your case is not completely identical to those of the other accused," continued Metelka in an inspired tone.

From the top of his desk, he lifted a bundle of papers that I hadn't previously noticed.

"Do you know this manuscript?"

The manuscript had a title, but from four metres away, I couldn't make it out.

"Here, I'll pass it to you," said Metelka.

It was a copy of *Morals and Ethics*, by Imre Nagy.

"Do you know it?"

"Yes."

"Is it really the pamphlet that Imre Nagy had secretly circulated at the beginning of 1956? Look at it closely."

I opened the manuscript, glanced at the pages, and answered: "This is the manuscript that I read. But it did not circulate in secret. From what I know, Imre Nagy had it sent by mail to the members of the Central Committee of the Hungarian party so that they would be familiar with his ideas at the time that Rakosi had him excluded from the Central Committee and the party. He even left a copy at the Soviet Embassy addressed personally to Andropov."

Metelka let this remark pass and offered me a cigarette.

"You know what you are going to do? You are going to read this text again. I will give you enough time. I'm curious to know if after the events of October you will appreciate it differently. Read it, read it calmly."

I read it calmly, becoming more and more absorbed in what I was reading. Little by little, I came to forget where I was and why; I was listening avidly to the words of my compatriot who, for the first time in the history of the Hungarian Communist Party, was saying out loud and intelligently what was cockeyed in the workers' movement, and was proposing a way to remedy it.

Morals and Ethics meant, in Nagy's mind, *Communist* morals and ethics. He deplored the replacement of such morals and ethics by pragmatism. He spoke of the deep disappointment of hundreds of thousands of militants who, having been filled with hope when they found a movement wherein ethics dominated, saw their hopes dashed as the years passed.

What followed was even livelier. The changes that had occurred over the years in Communist practice had led to a wide separation between words and acts, had created a gulf between principles and their practical realization. "This contradiction," wrote Nagy, "shakes the popular democracies [the Soviet bloc countries] to their foundations."

Did I read these words differently now than before the events of October? Yes, Mr. Investigator. I saw them with a new eye. I saw them lit up by the thousand spotlights of the revolution.

Metelka's seedy office disappeared. I had been set free, liberated by the crystalline thought of a great man. The manuscript spoke of the changes undergone by the Communist power. It was the debasement of this power that had led, in June 1953, to the troubles in East Berlin and elsewhere. It was the abuse of this Communist power that had triggered the uprising of the prisoners in the Vorkuta camps in the Soviet Union and had sparked resistance movements in the industrial centres of Hungary. Communist policy was detached from the people. Not only the middle classes but the working class as well were filled with doubts.

And Imre Nagy rang the alarm. He wrote:

> To serve the interests of the people, to serve socialism, progress, and the national well-being, it is impossible to rely on the force of bayonets. Socialism and dictatorship do not make a good couple. Tyrant and people aren't made to go together. The owner, the master of a country, is the people and no one else, no matter what label the tyranny wears. *We must democratize!* There is still time for the popular democracies to prevent a general crisis for their regimes by taking energetic measures of democratization. Tomorrow? If these measures are too late in coming, it could happen that the very principle of a state-controlled structure will come under question.

I heard, almost physically, the tocsin. "To arms, to arms," cried Nagy. "Act quickly or else there'll be an uprising." Rather than wishing for violence, as his jailers claimed, a year before the uprising this man was recommending a way to avoid it.

I began to rethink the sometimes confused events of the last year. I saw myself and my comrades who thought as I did exchanging doubts. We had wanted what Nagy had wanted — to repair the party from within in order to avoid a catastrophe. It was for this reason and no other that we had talked with Nagy about change; it was for this reason that we sought out Janos Kadar. Both party leaders recognized the same danger.

I saw the words "too late" shrouded in cries, smoke, and human blood. Because Nagy's warning had gone unheeded, the nation's youth rose up, Stalin's statue was destroyed, and the tyrant's troops entered our land.

"And what do you think of this sentence?"

Metelka's smooth voice interrupted my thoughts. He pushed another Nagy manuscript under my nose, entitled *The Five Principles of International Relations,* in which the agent had marked several lines in red.

"Read."

I read: "The people cannot be free when the nation is not in possession of all its sovereign rights — just as any national sovereignty is illusory without the full enjoyment by the population of all rights and liberties." What sublime words.

"What do you think of it?"

"I am... captivated by it."

"Hold on, hold on. Read this sentence, underlined in blue pencil."

I read: "The material destiny of a people depends on its national independence: a country without independence is a population without well-being."

"Do you understand, Kopacsi? All the criminal policy of neutrality is present in embryo in that sentence. Look at the date on the manuscript."

It was January 1956. A month before the famous Moscow congress that heard the "secret" report on Stalin. Nine months before the Budapest uprising. More than twelve years before the famous Prague Spring. Two decades before the appearance of "Euro-communism". A great Communist leader of central Europe, in solitude and obscurity, was crying out the truth about the perils of allegiance to Moscow. And now he was in prison and was going to die.

This time, we took a different direction. We were paying a visit to the upper echelons of the administration of Fo Street prison. Colonel Shumilin's office was in what was known as the presidential wing of the prison. We entered and I found myself in the presence of the senior members of the team charged with managing the trial. The Russian officer was seated behind his desk surrounded by his closest colleagues: to his right was Colonel Ferencsik of the Hungarian AVO and to his left the bilingual Colonel Rajnai of the KGB. All three were in civilian dress. Nobody was smoking. The atmosphere was tense. Shumilin gestured to the guards, who left silently.

The Soviet officer took off his dark glasses, and for an instant I saw his steely blue gaze riveted on me. He motioned to me to approach.

"Kopacsi...."

He pronounced my name with a Russian accent so that it came out "Kapassi". That was how Iemelianov had pronounced it and Andropov, Petofi, and Magyar-Miska, the Chaplinesque counsellor to the police department.

Shumilin put his dark glasses back on and made a barely perceptible gesture to his Hungarian colleague, Ferencsik, who said: "The colonel knows who you are. He considers you a victim of circumstances."

This was typical of a Stalinist trial: the alternation between torture and kindness — one day the threat of death, another the promise of life; a cold shower, then a hot one. I said nothing. Ferencsik then got to the reason why these superior officers had summoned me:

"Look, Kopacsi, you must recognize one thing: if you are here, it's because of Imre Nagy."

The Russian eyed me over his dark glasses. The Hungarian continued: "I see at least two reasons why Nagy is responsible for your situation. The first: his so-called theoretical writings, dressed in Marxist clothes, dazzle you. The second and by no means less important reason for your presence here is that your Imre Nagy refused our outstretched hand when he was at the Yugoslav Embassy. He had been called on to perform self-criticism of his theoretical views and his practical activity so as to be able to participate once again in public life. He refused. Later, in Romania, officials of our party visited him, in the persons of Dezso Nemes and others. (Dezso Nemes — known as six-finger Nemes because of a malformation of his hands — was a second-rate civil servant, one of Rakosi's buddies and an overt KGB agent generally detested by party cadres.)

The colonel continued: "From Imre Nagy, yet another refusal. He didn't want to give up his theoretical positions, and he refused to renounce his role before and during the counter-revolution. If he had done so, today he would occupy an important role in the government and you would not be in Fo Street awaiting the serious verdict which is inevitably going to be pronounced against you.

Colonel Shumilin, the representative of the Soviet Union, and us, we would like to know your reaction to what you have just heard."

Yes. Deep down, I regretted just a little the old man's intransigence. If, despite everything, he had accepted this six-fingered hand....

An instant later, I got a grip on myself. Imre Nagy could not renounce his life and his work. A step on the road to concession and, doubtless, he would live. But what is a life of dishonour worth? After a cataclysm such as we had lived through, it was natural that the Janos Kadars would appear as instruments of Russian "normalization". It was no less necessary that there be Imre Nagys, Maleters, and Joskas to give their lives for principles that would emerge again one day in the nation's political life. Myself, I had chosen to share the fate of the latter group.

The *six-fingered man* appeared almost materially before my eyes. With an instinctive movement, I turned away.

Shumilin, who was staring me, sat up straight and whispered several words to his intermediary.

Colonel Ferencsik said: "The Soviet comrades think you needn't give an immediate response. You are going to be led back to your cell and you will reflect on what you have heard."

The guards appeared behind me. They led me through the labyrinth and back to my cell. It wasn't yet 7:00 a.m. The black brew they called coffee hadn't yet cooled off in the mess tin.

It was clear that the Russians were trying to cut me off from my comrades. This was part of the Stalinist rite of having one or two persons in each batch who would add a bit of variety to the proceedings, alleviating the monotony of all the other cases of "absolute guilt". A deceived worker: that was a role perfectly suited to someone like me. I was built for it. Hadn't Rakosi asked Hazi, his minister of the interior, before appointing me police chief and colonel, "Is he tall? Is he Aryan?" (He hadn't thought to ask if I had a brain or was of good character. For the lords of the movement, the worker is a two-dimensional caricature.)

This was the role imagined for "Kapassi" by Moscow. What do we do with Kopacsi? Well, he can be the "deceived worker". His head is going to fall, just like those of the others, but his testimony would bear witness to the nature of his class: workers, people without gumption, destined to fall in the enemy's traps as soon as they turn their backs on their true leaders.

I had nothing but contempt for this sinister farce. A year and a half in solitary confinement, Joska's heroic attitude, the greatness shown by Imre Nagy, because of all of these I had resigned myself to the idea of death. During the sessions of the "inquiry", Metelka sometimes repeated in an inspired tone that "all the penalties won't necessarily be capital", that some of the accused "would get out of this". But this was no longer having any affect on me. The dog Tango no longer appeared in the company of my daughter and my wife. I no longer imagined Mammy sitting in the sun. I was resigned to death.

I anticipated the sentence that I was going to say at the crucial moment — "Long live Hungary, long live the working class." By tying my shirtsleeve around my neck, I tested the sensation of the slipknot compressing the artery. I imagined a hundred times the brutal dislocation of the first vertebra and the severing of the spinal cord at the neck. I had seen executions during the war; I simply told myself that my time had come.

October 1956 had been eradicated from history. Now it was the turn of those who had been part of it.

The thing happened without any transition. From one day to the next, the guards began to bring us beautifully prepared dishes, not from the officers' mess but from Budapest's best restaurants. Chocolate croissants with jam in the morning, roasted meat at noon and in the evening, fresh fruits, and Viennese pastries. We were being fattened up, and we would soon understand why.

On the fourth or fifth day of this gourmet diet, the duty guard brought a glass containing a suspicious-looking liquid.

"What's that?"

"A tranquillizer."

"Until now, we've been getting tranquillizers in the form of pills. Why in liquid now?"

"Don't ask so many questions, Kopacsi, drink. You're not the only one to get this. Your comrade Imre Nagy has already drunk his without making a fuss."

Of course, Nagy had taken his "without making a fuss". For months now, he'd been used to a steady diet of pills, tablets, and drops for his heart. At the age of sixty-two, he had already suffered two coronaries.

The beverage had an indefinable taste although it smelt of valerian. A few minutes after drinking it, I could feel myself soaring. I forgot all my cares. I saw myself stretched out on my stomach on a hillside, a valerian blossom under my nose. I slept peacefully.

In the morning, the guard had to shake me by the shoulders to wake me up. In other circumstances, I would have been reprimanded. This time, he didn't say anything, but handed me the same drink as the previous evening. My head was still buzzing. From outside the cell, I could hear snatches of quarrelling. Their lousy medicine wasn't being enthusiastically accepted.

"Drink," said the guard. And to encourage me, he added, "Tomorrow is the opening of your trial."

The guard, who had been ordered to say nothing to the prisoners, told me it was June 8, 1958. Nineteen months and three days ago, Serov had arrested me, stamping my deputy's card under his boot. The guards made a tour of all the cells, exterminating the bugs that infested the beds. Other guards I had never seen before arrived with dark, carefully pressed suits and ties. These were hung up in the corridor, just outside the cells. Immediately after breakfast, I was taken to see my lawyer.

Bajor had a strange manner about him that I'd never seen before. As we were supervised by the same AVO guard who had been present at our first meeting, Bajor confined himself to confirming the official date for the opening of the trial: it was indeed for tomorrow morning. Several times, Bajor yawned conspicuously. I looked at him in astonishment. In an utterly urbane tone, the lawyer excused himself.

"Excuse me, dear friend, I'm not used to sleeping on camp beds."

The guard pricked up his ears.

"Confine yourself to the facts."

Bajor nodded in agreement. He had made me understand what he wanted me to know, He, like the other defence lawyers, had been confined since the day before, required to remain for the duration of the trial at AVO headquarters. Immediately, I understood that my wife could not be aware of the opening of the trial and that the country was unaware of the presence of Imre Nagy in this Budapest jail. I also understood that my death was imminent.

"Now, listen to me," said my lawyer.

I saw again on his face this strange expression, a combination of embarrassment and triumph, that I had noticed in the first minute of our meeting. The man looked at me closely and lowered his voice.

"We should plead guilty."

When you are alone, in solitary confinement, for a year and a half, the first human being that you meet makes such an impression that you would swear that you had known him from childhood. Laszlo Bajor was an honest man of noble ideas and he respected me. If he was now taking the initiative of suggesting to me so unexpected a change of strategy he must have very serious reasons for doing so.

The AVO agent was listening intently to our words. There was one question to which I desperately wanted an answer.

"But the others? What are the others doing?"

The agent got up and came close to us.

My defender gazed penetratingly at me and replied: "Be assured you won't be the only one. On the advice of their lawyers, Janosi — Nagy's son-in-law — and Donath, his close adviser, are also going to plead guilty. Comrades Nagy and Maleter will plead *differently.* But I know that they won't hold it against you, Janosi, or Donath if you plead guilty."

The AVO man intervened.

"I suspend the interview."

Bajor stood up.

"My friend, you are making an irreparable blunder. As Colonel Kopacsi's defender, I am charged by the party's highest leadership to communicate instructions to my client. Remind me of your name and position so that I can raise the matter *in front of Comrades Kadar and Munnich.*"

The guard turned crimson. I said to myself, "Bajor's going a bit too far," before it hit me that he wasn't talking to the guard, he was talking to me. Kadar and Munnich weren't interested in an AVO non-commissioned officer's blunder. I realized that, for a reason unknown to me, the two leaders of Hungary were concerning themselves with my personal case.

The unhappy guard didn't know how to undo what he had done. The interview was suspended. Bajor picked up his things, turned to me, and said before going out: "Don't worry: you'll see your northern homeland that you love so much...*and which loves you so much.*"

Then he left.

I didn't have to be a Sherlock Holmes to understand that something had happened in the north, in the industrial region where a good number of key positions were held by my old comrades from the Resistance.

In the Kopacsi case, a turnaround was in progress, independent of anything I had done.

Ten minutes later, I was taken to see Metelka, who looked at me knowingly.

"I told you that you would live."

I knew from long experience not to take anything the AVO said at face value. But still....*life.* Life. I was thirty-six and had been certain my days were over. Suddenly, I had reason to hope I'd been wrong.

The investigator told me what I had to do.

"Listen, Kopacsi. No one is asking you to accuse your friends. You would certainly refuse to do it. The only thing the party asks is that you recognize your guilt."

"But...guilty of what?"

"Of not having understood what happened in October 1956."

So here we were at the same point where Shumilin and his aides had left me. They had never asked for my answer; they simply assumed I would agree to their proposal that I play the idiot worker who, by mistake, had fought on the wrong side of the barricade.

I saw myself in Imre Nagy's place, in his cell in Romania. I heard the voice of the six-fingered man making him the same proposition. Nagy stroked his moustache and wiped his pince-nez. Calmly, he shook his head. "No. I am not going to lend myself to this shameful comedy. Tell those who sent you that Imre Nagy, Prime Minister of Hungary, member of the leadership of his party for twenty years, accepts his responsibilities. I've lived sixty years. I've always fought for the workers' movement. What I have done, I've done with full knowledge of the facts. You must stop trying to treat us all as if we were children."

"No. I'm not a child."

It was I who said that, sitting across from Metelka in the little office in Fo Street.

Metelka clasped his hands together.

"But who told you that you were? Hundreds, thousands of people make mistakes. All it takes is an ill-digested pamphlet, a poorly understood speech, and there we are in a state of total error."

He came close to me.

"*Give up the role of hero.* That's all we ask of you. And your life will be saved."

He had already pressed the bell. The guards appeared. I was led back to my cell.

"And your life will be saved." Did I have the right to play hero when my hero, my model, Imre Nagy, wasn't asking it of me? Anyway, my ideal was destroyed....

I was given the drink. This time I swallowed it without protest. I was back in the meadow on the hillside. I sank into sleep.

▌ "In the Name of the Working Class"

A commotion in the corridor awakened me. Voices I'd never heard before were barking orders. The bolt was pulled and two *police officers* appeared in my cell. Still befuddled by the tranquillizer, I thought to myself, "Sandor, they've revolted, they've come to liberate you!" I was dreaming of my guys at police headquarters with whom I'd passed so many harmonious years and who had followed me so faithfully through the harshest ordeals. But then I accepted the obvious, that I was in the presence of very carefully chosen AVO officers disguised for the occasion as regular policemen.

"Raus, raus!" bellowed the first in the language of the German SS during the war.

"Davai, davai!" roared the second, uttering the "Forward, march!" of the Soviet soldier.

But no, I was still suffering the effects of the liquid tranquillizer. The security officers, speaking my own language, were merely telling me to get up and get dressed. I shook my head and the imaginary SS cap and Russian shapska disappeared.

A third man entered and proffered the fatal cup of liquid. This time, disgust overwhelmed me and I refused. But the guard insisted.

"Drink it, or you'll get the same thing in a needle."

At a signal, a male nurse in a white coat appeared at the door carrying a syringe.

I chose the liquid.

Supported on both sides, I was pushed into the corridor, which teemed with more phoney police officers busy hauling the prisoners one by one from their cells.

I saw Paul Maleter, who had been in total isolation for months. He was the same as before, filled with energy, almost gay. He hadn't lost an ounce. During his imprisonment, he had asked for and always obtained double rations. I had once heard him explaining in a loud voice to a guard, "What do you want from me? I've always been a big eater and a big drinker and I will be as long as I live."

"Sandor!" he smiled, waving at me.

Paul was entirely at ease as we talked, as if the two of us had just met in the yard of a barracks or during some military manoeuvres. If the AVO officer hadn't stopped him, he would have grabbed me in his arms.

Despite the fog I was in, I was delighted to see everybody again. There was the poor editor, Gimes, who, for all his captors' attempts to fatten him up, was virtually transparent. And Nagy, who hadn't changed a bit. He looked encouragingly at us all.

The head of the AVO detachment bellowed, "Forward, march!" but the little procession wasn't ready to set off. Some of the prisoners were turning their heads this way and that, looking desperately for Joseph Szilagyi. For those who weren't up to date, sixty seconds was enough to understand. As with the earlier absence of the minister Losonczy, Szilagyi's failure to appear could mean only one thing: that he had been murdered.

We exchanged glances. Imre Nagy raised his head high and set off. There was nothing else to do. We were in the hands of people commanded by the Kremlin, the cruelest, most brutal power in the world. A mere two years earlier, these same people had made a show of wanting to correct the horrors that had sullied their history for the past forty years. A new world had seemed within our grasp. But they had changed their minds.

At the head of the procession, Nagy climbed the first of the flights of stairs leading to the upper floor where a courtroom had been set up. I followed, staring at his back; as he climbed the steps, he seemed to get bigger before my eyes. Here was someone who had passed from words to acts, who had written, with his pen and his life, a chapter of history. He knew he was going to die. But he moved vigorously none the less, perhaps taking solace from the certainty that, whatever the outcome of the trial, nobody could ever tear the pages signed Imre Nagy from the book of history.

Nagy arrived at the top of the stairs. His guardian pulled him lightly by the forearm toward that part of the labyrinth leading to the courtroom that had been set up for the secret trial. In the instant it took to smooth the ends of his moustache, he glanced at the rest of us climbing the stairs behind him.

His glance settled on me.

There was no doubt about it. Under his pince-nez, he was peering straight at me. His investigator, Ferencsik, had certainly told him that I was going to plead guilty. But on Nagy's face, there wasn't the slightest trace of reproach or surprise.

An instant later, Nagy recommenced his march and I followed him through the labyrinth of partitions.

The courtroom was a large investigator's office specially arranged for the occasion. It was empty. We sat down on benches, each between two AVO men disguised as police officers. For keeping their lips sealed about the proceedings, these security men would be rewarded later with promotions and cash.

"The People's Court!"

We stood up. At the same instant, in each corner of the room, powerful lights I hadn't noticed before were turned on and a movie camera operated by an employee from the police studios whirred into action. I knew this cameraman well because he had been on my staff for several years.

Now we understood why they had wanted to fatten us up: the trial was going to be filmed.

My attention, and that of my comrades, was riveted on the tribunal's president: it wasn't Rado this time, but Vida, the man also known as Tunis. With his tall, slim build, his tanned skin, and his finely trimmed moustache, he could have passed for a wealthy British planter in India.

As if the previous trial hadn't happened, everything began over again: establishing the civil status of the accused, and so on. I listened distractedly to the court clerk's murmurings. Half-blinded by the movie lights, my eyes searched the room for what my investigator had promised: "the presence of the entire leadership of the party." Where were they? Half an hour later, when Nagy was left alone before the court and I was taken to see Metelka, the mystery would be solved.

"Listen, Sandor, your turn's coming up, *the party leadership is gathered in the adjoining room and they're listening to you!*"

Most of these members of the new regime had been involved in one way or another in the beginnings of the insurrection that had taken place two years earlier in Budapest. Obviously, the Soviets expected that they would learn something from what was happening to us.

In my mind, I could see them sitting around the long table, equipped with notepads and bottles of mineral water. I could see a worried look on the face of Janos Kadar. He was glancing in the direction of Munnich, the deputy premier. During the insurrection, the two of them had been members of Nagy's government. As party first secretary at the time, Kadar had been a particularly fierce "Eurocommunist" before the term had even been invented. Lajos Feher, Sandor Gaspar, and Ferenc Nezval, all of them members of the Politburo, would be like cats on hot bricks. They knew they would be mentioned frequently by Nagy, who wouldn't hesitate to describe the events of 1956 in detail and to furnish the names of those involved. How they must have squirmed in discomfort under the gaze of Karoly Kiss and Antal Apro, veteran KGB agents in the Hungarian party, who were also present.

Of course, the Kremlin knew every detail in the history of each of the men it had put in charge of its Hungarian province. In fact, it was mainly *because* of their ambiguous role that these men had been chosen. But it is one thing to know the stains on the biography of a leader and quite another to invite him to the headquarters of the security police to attend a trial directed by Colonel Shumilin, the official representative of the Soviet KGB. Just hearing Shumilin's name was enough to make any of these leaders tremble in fear. Listening to these proceedings, they couldn't help but wonder about their future. Which of them would be in the dock next time? Who would be Shumilin's next victim? Moscow knew well that, for Kadar and his friends, this morning's examination of witnesses wasn't simply a recreational matinee. The air was filled, not merely with remorse, but with anguish.

"I call the witness Sandor Kopacsi to the stand."

This was the moment when, with no handcuffs on my wrists but with nineteen months of imprisonment on my shoulders and a much more serious verdict in view, I was pushed into the glare of the movie lights. My former operator was shooting, his face blank, preoccupied with his work, as if I were just another witness and not his former boss. Tunis questioned me the way a professor questions a student sitting for an exam.

"You will be heard first as a witness in the case of defendant number one, Imre Nagy. Describe the influence that the political views of Imre Nagy had on you and the influence of the manuscript that you received from him; describe how you were affected by your secret encounter with Imre Nagy one afternoon at the home of your friend and neighbour, Joska Szilagyi; finally, describe your intrigues during October [he used neither the term "insurrection" nor "counter-revolution"], in the context of the influence exerted on you by defendant number one."

Tunis, satisfied, sat back comfortably in his armchair. I glanced furtively at Nagy, seated between his guards. He looked calm. His personality radiated responsibility and commanded respect. He made no sign to me, but looked straight ahead, with the satisfied air of someone who has fulfilled his duty. His face was expressionless as I gave my testimony.

"Yes, from the time he was first president of the council, I was influenced by Imre Nagy. That is, since 1953. As a deputy, I was won over by his program as he explained it in his address to the assembly."

Tunis made a slight gesture of impatience, touching the left side of his narrow moustache. It was theatrical. He was playing to the camera.

"Never mind that. Let's talk about the period from 1955 to the fall of 1956 when you were busy hatching plots with Imre Nagy and his friends."

"During that period, I was deeply influenced by Imre Nagy. I found that it was Nagy and not the official party leadership who represented the genuine political truth. For me, it was Nagy's ideas that could lead the party and the country out of its crisis."

I refrained from adding, "Besides, I wasn't the only one to hold that view. Comrade Kadar, with whom I spoke several times, and other responsible comrades who today occupy important posts (and a seat in the adjoining room) thought the same way; you yourself, Tunis, I remember your warm congratulations to Joska at the time of his speech against Rakosi...."

But I kept those thoughts to myself.

Tunis found it necessary to inject some biting irony into the proceedings: "Oh yes. Imre Nagy's policies certainly saved the party and the country from crisis. Let's move on to the secret manuscript that defendant number one sent you."

He was referring to *Morals and Ethics*. I explained that it wasn't Nagy personally who had passed me the manuscript. The paper was circulated through the mail to all Central Committee members.

"Enough quibbling. Tell us what influence the manuscript had on you."

"A notable one."

"In what sense?"

"In the sense... of my later activities."

Tunis was happy. That was what he wanted to hear. He concealed his satisfaction and tried to look at me with a neutral air.

"And that's why you distributed twenty thousand rifles to counter-revolutionary bandits?"

But he couldn't draw anything valuable from the "secret meeting" at Joska's. With disgust, he pushed aside my version according to which we "talked about travels in foreign countries". But my story made Szalay, the prosecutor, prick up his ears.

"What countries did you speak about with Imre Nagy?"

"The Soviet Union where I had just spent my holiday."

"And what was Nagy's opinion about that country?"

Poor Szalay. Your questions were pronounced so triumphantly, as if you hadn't worked with me to soften the treatment of detainees on the instructions of the same Imre Nagy whom you were doing your utmost to destroy.

"Imre Nagy's opinion on the Soviet Union was: 'One has to have lived there to learn to appreciate it and to love its people.' He and his wife lived in the Soviet Union during the war."

There was an awkward silence. Everyone was thinking of the war, of the Russians, of Imre Nagy and Nagy's wife.

Then reality returned. At the suggestion of the proscutor, the president described my relationship with Nagy: "With the goal of seizing power, the former prime minister, Imre Nagy, made contact with persons holding key positions, including the former police chief of Budapest, one of the directors of the armed forces in the capital."

"Imre Nagy, have you any observations to make?"

"Yes. A question of the witness."

He rose, as he used to rise to speak in the assembly. Calmly, heavily, he approached the witness box. He looked at me solemnly.

NAGY: At the time you read the essay in question, did you find that its contents corresponded to the actual situation?

ME: Yes.

NAGY: Did you find in this text anything that suggested that I coveted political power and did so in an illegal manner?

ME: No.

NAGY: One other question. The minutes of the inquest contain a deposition from you to the effect that I ordered you to organize the National Guard and to include the insurgents in it. Do you still hold that to be the case?

ME: Yes.

NAGY: No, that's not how things happened. The minutes of the meetings held at that time prove that I received the delegation of the armed forces committee, and that on the government's behalf I approved the idea of organizing a National Guard of which the police would be one part.

Only then did I understand the meaning of his question and the error I had committed under questioning. The incident had taken place in Nagy's office, and a year later it seemed to me that it was he who had given the order. But he was right. We had proposed and he had only given his approval.

Nagy, who knew that he was finished and that his fate would be in no way affected by my testimony, wasn't searching for vindication. But this former professor was a man who set great store by accuracy. In contradicting me, his goal was to set the record straight.

That night, I was waiting for the nurse and his beverage. I drank it greedily. After a short wait, I felt the tension begin to leave me. I was flying high, drunk. I stood up on the bed, I started to hum. What was happening to me? I broke into the ancient songs of draft dodgers and highwaymen, I shouted and screamed. The guards came into my cell and tried to silence me, but I barely noticed their presence.

> The district is large enough
> To accommodate my wastrel ways,
> And I refuse to sign up in Kadar's Army.

In the original version, the last line was "the Kaiser's Army", not "Kadar's Army".

In a moment I heard people rushing down the corridor and "my" investigator, Metelka, burst into the cell, accompanied by officers I didn't know.

"Sandor! What's happened to you?"

"What's happened to me is that...I think you should all go fuck yourselves."

"Be quiet. Calm down." In a low voice, he added confidentially: "The Politburo comrades are in conference with Comrade Shumilin and the other Soviet comrades."

"Fuck the Politburo comrades, especially fuck the Muscovite pigs! Tell them that from me."

There was no question of leaving me in that state. The prison doctor arrived hurriedly with his bag. A short consultation followed in which, despite my intoxicated state, I understood that Dr. Bencze refused all responsibility for the drug I had swallowed.

"The liquid taken by the prisoner is experimental and it's impossible to predict all its effects."

Metelka grilled me on the subject of what I would like to have and, like a child, my response was: "Give...give me...some chocolate."

I had already had two pieces of cream pie during dinner, which had been first-rate as always.

A piece of chocolate in my hands, I soon dropped into a drunken slumber.

The next day, a series of witnesses were brought in against us. Most were themselves under arrest and awaiting trial. Some, under pressure, accused us of all sorts of crazy things. For example, one man claimed he had heard me planning to form a counter-revolutionary government. In reality, he had been party to a conversation in which several of us were speculating about the composition of the next cabinet.

(The "white book" published later by the regime said there were forty-seven witnesses in all. This book is the official record of the trial, issued to show how "legal" the proceedings were. Copies can be found in some Western libraries, including that of the University of Toronto. It lists Joska Szilagyi as one of the defendants at our trial, although by this time he had been dead for two months. The film taken at the trial proved useless to the regime because Szilagyi's absence revealed the falsity of the official version.)

For the most part, I didn't see these witnesses at all, neutralized as I was by the "experimental liquid". However, I'll never forget one of them, Colonel Mecseri, who had been imprisoned for the last two years along with many of his soldiers. This dark-haired, middle-aged man, commander of the thirty-third armoured Hungarian regiment, had taken seriously his duty to defend the capital. He had ordered his units to plant their tanks around Budapest and to fire when fired upon.

JUDGE: Were you aware of the fact that the Soviet units coming to the aid of the Kadar government [actually, Janos Kadar and his government had been *behind* the Soviet units and hadn't arrived in Budapest until forty-eight hours later] were fired on by your tanks and as a result suffered severe losses? These losses are properly called murders and you and your soldiers will share the responsibility with the defence minister at the time, Paul Maleter.

COLONEL MECSERI: My soldiers did nothing except obey their orders. They acted in accordance with their oath and the regulations. My soldiers and I were completely ignorant of the fact that the Soviets had formed a new Hungarian government.

JUDGE: I forbid you. . . .

COLONEL MECSERI (screaming, beside himself): We're being treated as criminals! We are not criminals!

After his deposition, the colonel of the Hungarian armoured regiment would be hanged along with several dozen of his soldiers, ordinary recruits, young men barely past their teens. These recruits proclaimed their innocence to the end. (In fact, the Geneva Convention expressly prohibits the execution of simple soldiers for acts of war, especially those committed against members of a foreign army.) One of them, a little fellow barely twenty years old, brave under fire but completely demoralized by his horrible situation, would collapse in front of the gallows, saying, "I'm only twenty, I haven't lived yet, I don't want to die."

The old prison guards, witnesses of many capital executions, tearfully recounted how this stripling was attached to a stretcher and transported to the scaffold.

The build and attitude of Mecseri corresponded perfectly to those of my friend Joska. A peasant like Joska and a veteran Communist, tough as nails, he died on the gallows like a man. Permitted to say goodbye to his wife, his last words were: "Tell my little soldiers that, no matter what these liars say, I wasn't a traitor."

The prosecution had the floor. Szalay, disgraced magistrate, was flogging a dead horse, trying to prove that Imre Nagy and the other defendants had been part of a *conspiracy* since 1955 and that, "allied to the forces of reaction, both within the country and outside", we had provoked the "counter-revolution" to re-establish the old regime.

This tone, these crude lies hadn't been heard anywhere but in *Pravda* for years. Now Szalay had scorned that newspaper. And how often I had heard him say, at meetings where we were seated side by side, "At least we're finished with Soviet-style denials of justice." Now, it was he who was asking the death penalty for Imre Nagy, leader of his country, for Paul Maleter, the best communist captain of his homeland, and for Miklos Gimes, that talented young journalist.

And for me, his colleague, friend, and confidant, he was asking life imprisonment.

After a short adjournment, it was the turn of Nagy's lawyer to speak. His name was Karman and he was more than seventy years old, with fifty years of struggle in the workers' movement to his credit. Finally, we heard statements worthy of a human being. We heard that Imre Nagy's role in the politics of Hungary was diametrically opposed to what the prosecution claimed. The armed insurrection was the fault of the maggoty clique of leaders headed by Rakosi and Gero; they were the ones who had blocked the new course recommended by the Soviet leadership and enacted in Hungary by Nagy.

We heard that after he was removed from office, Nagy had written to the party's highest forum warning of the danger posed by an absence of political solutions to the country's problems. When he had been reluctant to take the post of prime minister on October 23, 1956, Nagy was attacked by the Politburo: "You will have to answer to History if you don't take the leadership in hand."

During the insurrection, the highest Soviet dignitaries, Mikoyan and Suslov, came to Budapest several times to give Nagy their advice and support. As for Janos Kadar, witnesses had said that he was the first to countersign the changes introduced by the Nagy government under popular pressure. The Soviet government itself recognized, in its proclamation of October 30, 1956 (which was communicated to the whole world by the news agency *Tass*), that the relations between the Soviet Union and the popular democracies required important modifications.

JUDGE: I warn the defence representative that if he continues to denigrate the great Soviet Union and the leaders of our party, it won't be long before he finds himself on the bench with the accused.

The lawyer changed the subject. He evoked several opinions

expressed by leaders of the international Communist movement on the events of 1956 in Hungary. When he cited Togliatti, first secretary of the Italian Communist Party, and Ernst Fischer, a member of the Politburo of the Austrian Communist Party, the judge interrupted, bellowing his head off: "That's not the international Communist movement, that's the ravings of a few old revisionists."

The verdict in the Nagy case hadn't yet been pronounced and already Togliatti and Ernst Fischer were being condemned for a difference of opinion with the Soviet Union. The same fate would later befall the Czech Dubcek, the Spaniard Carillo, and all the "Euro-communists" in the world. The camera turned, the lights blazed, the microphone recorded — all to the satisfaction of comrades Shumilin, Serov, and Andropov.

It was June 14, 1958, a Saturday. After a long adjournment, the accused took the floor for the last time.

Imre Nagy spoke: "Twice I tried to save the honour of the word 'socialism' in the Danube River valley: in 1953 and 1956. The first time, I was thwarted by Rakosi, the second time by the armed might of the Soviet Union. Now I must give my life for my ideas. I give it willingly. After what you have done with it, it's not worth anything any more. I know that History will condemn my assassins. There is only one thing that would disgust me: if my name were rehabilitated by those who killed me."

Later, it was Paul Maleter's turn to speak. "I respected the oath of a socialist soldier," he said. "I went with the people through fire and storm. If you kill me, I will die at peace with myself."

Finally, as the sixth-ranking defendant, it was my turn.

Filled with emotion, I told how I had fought in the north with the Soviet Army. I said I had been a fair-minded chief of police. October was October but even then I never had a Russian uniform in my sights. And when I saw them die, facing my men... and mine, facing them....

I felt a pain of anguish. My voice became hoarse. Revolution isn't simple. Neither is what follows it, whether the revolution is victorious or otherwise.

In the loud-speaker, you heard a hiccup, on the film you could perhaps detect a tear. Don't draw too much satisfaction from that, Colonel Shumilin. It was nothing to do with you. I was thinking only of my country, my companions, of our lost cause, and of my ruined life.

Aided by a double dose of Dr. Bencze's cocktail, I slept. I had three more doses the next day, Sunday, June 15, which was a day of idleness and waiting. Then, at about 6:00 p.m., we were once again led through the labyrinth. We stopped in the anteroom of the courtroom. Weren't the verdicts ready? I was taken aside by Metelka.

"Sandor, if despite all our efforts we fail, promise me to enter a plea for clemency."

I promised and he went out. During several minutes when we were abandoned by our guards, my defender, Bajor, said rapidly, "Your wife is well, but she doesn't know the trial is on. My family and those of the other defence lawyers don't know either, we've been told to say that we're absent because of an out-of-town meeting." (But Ibolya knew; she later told me that a total stranger had come up to her at the zoo and urgently whispered: "The trial is on now.")

I spoke with Paul Maleter. This big kid was still his old self.

"Their 'high treason' in our two cases — Serov and company have a fat chance of proving it."

He was right. Military high treason would not be among the grounds cited in the judgement.

"What are you expecting, Paul?"

His only response was the well-known gesture of the edge of the hand across the neck. A big kid with a peaceful conscience.

He looked at me seriously.

"Sandor, you've got a chance to stay alive. Don't forget! Tokol, the Sashalom Barracks, the Russian Embassy, Fo Street... and *the rest*."

Imre Nagy, speaking solemnly with his friend, Ferenc Donath, and his son-in-law, Janosi, suddenly turned toward me.

"Sandor, I wanted to tell you. My wife and I, at the Yugoslav Embassy, we became very attached to your little girl, Judith. If you see her again, simply tell her this: 'Uncle Imre gives you a kiss.' She always called me Uncle Imre, who knows why."

The guards returned. Imre Nagy took off his pince-nez, then put it back, and said, his head half turned away from me: "You'll also kiss my wife for me. And my daughter. Won't you? Tell them how much I loved them."

"The People's Court! All rise! In the name of the working class and all the working people, the court condemns to death Imre Nagy, Paul Maleter, Miklos Gimes...."

Life imprisonment for Sandor Kopacsi.

Twelve years for Ferenc Donath, eight years for Ferenc Janosi, six years for Zoltan Tildy, five years for the journalist Vasarhelyi. We were allowed to sit down as the reasons for the judgement were read. Our thoughts were elsewhere; none of us was listening to the official claptrap.

"In the name of the working class," if you please. Nothing but that. What bitter irony for me, born and raised in the working class, to hear those words from Tunis, who so obviously was not.

"The judgement cannot be appealed," finished Tunis in a piercing voice. "Imre Nagy! Do you wish to introduce an appeal for clemency?"

"No, I do not."

Although Maleter's answer was the same, both his and Gimes' lawyers made appeals on behalf of their clients. The appeals were rejected.

Those condemned to die were the first to be escorted out. One last glance at their friends — a farewell — and they disappeared behind the door. Forever.

I was taken back to my cell. I collapsed on the bed. Although exhausted, I was alert to the slightest noise. They were gathering up the personal possessions of those condemned to death. I could hear the engines of trucks starting up in the courtyard. One, two, three, four, five engines at once. The prison van and four other cars filled with armed security officers: the cortège. The vehicles pulled out and the noise of the engines disappeared. Sunday strollers, people relaxing in the June sun on park benches or stretched out on the grass in Budapest's public gardens, didn't know that the convoy speeding by carried the former prime minister of Hungary, the former minister of defence, and a young journalist to their deaths.

Last station: the central prison on Kozma Street in the heart of the district I had represented as a deputy.

On the floor below mine, Maleter's lawyer was dictating his appeal to a secretary called in for this special occasion to work on a Sunday. "Paul Maleter, a courageous and effective former partisan...."

Night was falling when my cell door opened. Without thinking, I stood up. It was a guard. Sympathetically, he asked, "How many?"

"Life."

"No! That's tough."

"Well, you know. After all that trouble, they've given me a long vacation."

The guard looked at me.

"Good for you," he said softly. "If you take it that way, it'll pass quicker. I remember a case, a guy named...."

At that point, I fell asleep.

Once again, I saw the guard's sympathetic face. "Do you know how long you slept? Two days. We only woke you up to eat."

Eagerly, I asked the question: "Which of the three got clemency?"

He shook his head. "None of them."

At 6:00 a.m. on Monday, June 16, 1958, Nagy, Maleter, and Gimes were hanged in the yard known as the "little dungeon" at the central prison. Everybody in that prison was confined to the cells that day. The workshops were locked up. On this one day, the morning meal was distributed by officers. Everybody was ordered to keep away from the windows. Such orders were unheard of and excited extreme interest among the prisoners.

The grapevine works beautifully in prison. By noon, everyone knew that Imre Nagy and Paul Maleter had been executed along with "a third". The official executioner, Major Kovacs, refused to execute the verdict, saying that he had already had the experience of executing a minister and that it had caused him nothing but trouble. He was undoubtedly referring to Rajk. So the job was assigned to his assistant, Warrant Officer Karacsony, who later got drunk in the prison kitchen and bragged about it in front of the prisoners.

According to the prison "information agency", the Russians forced Nagy to be present while the others were executed. Along with two senior officers of the occupying army — probably Serov and Shumilin — he stood, tottering, at the entrance to the yard. If the report is correct, this was the second time he had had to witness the execution of an innocent friend. In 1949, Rakosi had forced him to attend the hanging of Rajk, who had been personally promised by Kadar that his life would be spared and who, before dying, cried out, "Janos, you tricked me!"

It was public knowledge at the prison that the Soviet officers took photos of the executions. They placed themselves at one of the windows of the prison hospital, and they were helped by technicians from the Hungarian security service. What would be the destination of these photos? Would they enrich the Kremlin's archives? Would they serve as proof to the Chinese? Or, shipped in an anonymous parcel, would they serve to appal Tito? A persistent rumour had it that a roll of film found its way to the West. It was only a rumour, but what was certain was that no further executions would take place in the yard. The next day, work started on a closed facility for executions next to the hospital. Many inmates refused to participate in this filthy job and were severely punished as a result.

The bodies were buried in the prison cemetery. There are no names on the gravestones, only numerical codes, so that the graves can be identified only with the aid of a secret register. The cemetery is under the same military guard as the rest of the prison.

The prisoners' accounts agree in their descriptions of the last night of the three condemned men. They were authorized to write goodbye letters to their families, which no one would receive. Nagy and Maleter wrote all night. Gimes chose instead to sleep; he was awakened in the morning by the guards.

The last words of Nagy and Maleter, spoken from the gallows, were the same: "Long live independent and socialist Hungary!"

Gimes guarded his silence until the end.

Their clothes were sent back to their families.

The Soviet authorities apparently were satisfied. *Pravda* termed the Budapest verdicts "severe but just". The Bulgarians wrote, "The dogs are dead." Peking's major paper carried the headline, "Good news from Budapest!" When Chou En-lai had visited Hungary some months previously, he had complained that not enough people had been hanged. Khrushchev had demonstrated to him and to Mao that his hand didn't tremble when dealing with "deviationists".

Serov was officially congratulated, but still he was bitter. He felt it had all taken too long. His original plan had been better. Almost two years earlier, on November 5, 1956, he had stationed sharpshooters in one of the tanks that surrounded the Yugoslav Embassy in Budapest. Their mission was to cut down Imre Nagy the moment he appeared at one of the windows. Nagy habitually stayed in the room adjoining the ambassador's office. Toward 3:00 p.m., a stocky silhouette appeared in the window. Nagy was easily recognizable by his large peasant's head, his moustache, and his pince-nez. One of the sharpshooters hit the bull's-eye. The silhouette collapsed. The man was dead.

But it wasn't Imre Nagy. Serov's sharpshooter had made an annoying error. He had killed Milovanov, a Yugoslav diplomat who resembled the Prime Minister like a brother.

Tito had protested. Khrushchev had had to repudiate his KGB

director. Instead of killing us all off like rabbits and deporting the country's youth to Siberia, Serov had had to agree to a long and delicate trial procedure, which was contrary to Soviet practice.

But he still felt that leaving Kopacsi and the others alive was a scandal. The day after the executions, Serov began trying to correct the leniency of the Budapest court. On the direct order of Rajnai, the Hungarian emissary of the KGB, two representatives of that same organization who were also members of the Hungarian Politburo, Antal Apro and Karoly Kiss, organized public meetings to gain support for cancelling the "overly lenient verdicts".

The large metallurgical factory, Ganz Mavag, was given the task of demanding that the sentences be cancelled and that everyone who had been in the Imre Nagy group be hanged. The two KGB agents went to the factory to prime certain workers to push this demand. The vote was going to be taken at a general meeting by a show of hands. The result seemed assured.

Happily, a fly dropped into Serov's ointment. Several former Resistance fighters at the factory decided among themselves to prevent the KGB from going too far. General Laszlo Gyurko, who knew me and the others, asked to speak. He had been sent by the Partisans' Union. He briefly described the Resistance background of those who would be the victims of the death sentences. Then he urged the meeting to reject the idea of "interfering in verdicts already pronounced". The workers pricked up their ears. Did this mean there were different currents of opinion? Despite it all, had something really changed in unhappy Budapest? Several workers spoke. The show of hands defeated the proposal for the death penalty, and Serov's initiative ended in a fiasco.

■ Seven Years of Darkness

In September 1958, I was transferred from Fo Street to the central prison where my friends had been executed six weeks earlier. I would have liked to see the neighbourhood we were passing through because it was my old fief as a deputy. On the outskirts of the suburb of Rakospalota, I might have glimpsed the retired mayor of the district, my father, staring at the passing prison vehicles. But the prison van in which we were travelling, handcuffed and with our noses pressed against a partition, wasn't intended for sightseeing.

I had a visit from my wife and child. Ibolya seemed distressed but did her best to hide it. Judith, by then eleven years old, looked at me with the sad eyes of an adult. I whispered in her ear: "Uncle Imre gives you a big kiss."

She began to sob.

As for the other message, the one for Nagy's family, Ibolya couldn't transmit it until much later. Nobody knew where the martyrs' families were. They were detained in Romania and didn't find out about the executions until three months later, thanks to some Russian and Romanian guards who told them.

In May 1959, we political prisoners were transferred again, this time to Vac prison, fifty kilometres from Budapest. A guard pushed me into the cell of the Sziklai brothers, who were serving life sentences. "Here's your boss cop, do with him as you like," were his words of recommendation.

The police had captured the Sziklai brothers near the end of 1952. They were a couple of tough characters, twenty and twenty-two years old, who had taken it into their heads to hold up a post office. They had pulled silk stockings over their heads, aimed two wooden revolvers at the employees and customers, and escaped with some mail bags and a cash box containing the equivalent of only a few hundred dollars. They had jumped into the taxi they had stolen and roared off.

Rakosi had been beside himself when he phoned me about it.

"It is intolerable in our socialist capital that workers must suffer attacks from gangsters worthy of Chicago. Either they are locked up within eight hours or you've got big trouble."

We set up roadblocks on every route out of Budapest. When a roadblock tried to stop a taxi on the road through the large suburb of Pesthidegkut, the vehicle smashed through the barrier. One of the policemen emptied his revolver into the car, which overturned. Inside we found the stolen postal bags and one of the brothers, knocked out by the shock. The other brother, who had also been in the car, got away. Young Laszlo Sziklai was brought to police headquarters where he was questioned, without brutality. His pistol was only a toy, but the brothers' intentions were serious. They wanted to use the proceeds of their stick-up to bribe the frontier guards so they could smuggle themselves out to the West.

Rakosi phoned again. He congratulated me, but he added that I had only eight hours to produce the other brother. Then he wanted to see the two of them hanged.

I was stunned by the dictator's ferocity. I immediately sought the help of my protector and minister, Hazi. "Stalinist" or not, Hazi was a reasonable man. Together we got up a plan to mollify Rakosi. Meanwhile, the other brother was captured. The minister went to Central Committee headquarters and, after several hours, came back exhausted but triumphant.

The Sziklai brothers got life sentences instead of the death penalty. During the events of 1956, they escaped from prison but were recaptured at the border.

In the cell, I found the eldest, Laszlo, surrounded by six other muscular types. He looked me straight in the eye.

"Even if the screw hadn't said anything, I would have recognized you in a crowd of a thousand people. Here's the police chief of Budapest."

I said to myself: "I've had it. I'm going to be put through the mill."

But that's not what happened. The boy thumped me on the back and turned to his companions: "Look at this guy. Without him, our bald father [Rakosi] would have hanged us, my brother and me."

"How did you know that?"

It was a naive question, the question of a novice jailbird. In jail, everything is known. The truth always filters through, although it's sometimes twisted along the way. Later, in this same prison, we were taking our walk when a delegation of officers passed. One of the cons started shouting: "There's the executioner of Recsk."

I looked up and saw Major Joseph Potecz, ex-commandant of the Recsk concentration camp where the mortality rate had sometimes been as high as six prisoners a day. Potecz turned as white as a sheet.

"I wasn't an executioner," he bawled, running off to take refuge in the central building.

From the time the convict shouted out his accusation, the former commandant's life became intolerable. Although he was head of the secret service for prisons, he was now discouraged from making inspections. An AVO captain named Fazekas arrived to replace him.

Fazekas's mission was to eliminate those who had got out of the trial alive. The old writer Tibor Dery was thrown in a cell with a murderer who beat him regularly. The great artist, almost seventy years old, had a nine-year sentence to serve; at the rate he was going, the murderer would finish him off within two weeks. My friends and I cornered the man.

"Who offered you this job and how much are you getting?"

He finally confessed. Fazekas was giving him a litre of booze a week and four packages of tobacco to do in the old writer. To save Dery, we had to up the ante. To find *two* litres of booze a week in a prison in central Europe and *eight* packages of tobacco is no small thing, but we succeeded. After he was liberated, Dery lived another decade and became president of the Writers' Union. During that time, this prolific author wrote another ten novels, which were translated into many languages.

Fazekas had a different plan to eliminate me and it required finding an excuse to put me in the "hole". He found one readily.

Ibolya and I could exchange only one letter every three months. Parcels were not permitted. But Ibolya had struck up an acquaintance with one of the guards and through him sent me periodic gifts of food better than the stuff I got in prison. It was in the guards' interest to keep the prisoners happy by whatever means necessary as a way of boosting their work output. The prison was also a factory, and the guards received a bonus if the prisoners were productive. Smuggling was therefore generally overlooked.

I was caught with some contraband ham and ordered to reveal the name of the guard who had brought it to me. This I refused to do. Fazekas threw me into the hold for fifteen days, in darkness, almost naked, with a quarter of a loaf of bread and a jug of water every two days. Having been weakened by this treatment, I was removed from the hole and put on "coal duty". Ten hours a day, without a break, running between the shore of the Danube and the boat, on a narrow plank, pushing a hundred kilos of coal in a wheelbarrow. At the end of three days, I realized that I wouldn't survive much more of this, that this regime was Fazekas's way of finishing me off. I knew that the prison commandant was a man named Beres, a Jew who had escaped from Auschwitz. I was counting on this circumstance when I asked to see him.

To ask to see the commandant was in itself risky: you were searched from head to toe and had to wait in the courtyard, sometimes for hours in the heat of the sun, facing the wall, hands on neck. Finally, I was led in to see the commandant.

"Would you be content if someone called you an Auschwitz executioner?"

He stood up as if someone had stuck a needle up his rear.

"How dare you?"

"I am here to tell you that you have a *kapo* working for you who is just as efficient as the ones who massacred the Jews at Auschwitz."

I told him what Captain Fazekas had been doing. He went red as a tomato, sent for Fazekas, and ordered him to conform to the rule according to which the coal teams were to be relieved every hour.

Fazekas gave a military salute. Afterwards, he took me by the arm to lead me back to the shore. Like a viper, he whispered in my ear, "Kopacsi, I'll get you in the end."

"Never, Fazekas," I whispered, like another viper.

"Think again. My hand is hard — and long."

"Even if it stretches from Moscow to Vac, you won't get me."

Obviously, he could have pulled out his revolver and killed me on the spot. But that was risky. He didn't have a mandate to exterminate his victims openly.

In 1960, the writers were amnestied. The rest of us "Imre Nagyists" as we were called, rejoiced; it was the beginning of the end. But most of the prisoners reacted differently. "Release everybody!" they shouted. A hunger strike quickly swept through the prison.

The AVO arrived in force. There was a total blackout, the workshops were closed, the prisoners were confined to their cells, and the informers were grilled. The Imre Nagyists were falsely declared to be the originators of the strike. I was working in the prison hospital and nothing could be proved against me — I had, in fact, persuaded sick prisoners to take nourishment — but many of our group were transferred to Fo Street and threatened with death. Several committed suicide. The Vac prison became an AVO hell, with the prisoners deprived of the most elementary rights. Even the guards were beaten. It would have been the end of us if our community hadn't been what it was, a team prepared for any ordeal.

It was in prison that I learned to respect strength of character, the last defence of a man in distress. Besides such eminent personalities as the political philosopher Stephen Bibo, former president Zoltan Tildy, or the leader of the workers' council, the young Sandor Racz, who became veritable oracles for me, I came to appreciate the friendship of such crooks as Joczo. He was a dispenser of justice capable of beating up a guard when cornered or of overturning rotten food on the head of an officer.

I'll never forget the one they called Roka ("The Fox"), another crook who became my friend. He came from Dzumbui, a tough neighbourhood of thieves and prostitutes in the suburbs north east of Budapest. Little by little, Roka had become the terror of the numerous informers in my part of the prison. Of course, he was nothing but a hoodlum. On the outside he had always carried a revolver, even under the Rakosi terror. "I pass the hat around — with a gun in my hand," he always replied whenever anyone asked his specialty.

But this didn't stop him from being hard on himself, from swallowing a steel blade in order to have himself sent to hospital on the trail of an informer, or falling down the stairs as a way of getting medicines to distribute to other inmates who needed them more.

What moved me most in prison was the ingeniousness and tenacity of the prisoners. Despite the dense network of informers, we manufactured radios that were good enough to bring in the news from Western stations. At any given time there was hardly a cell that didn't have its miniature receiver, the size of a coin and lacking for nothing, including levers to control volume and tone. During raids, we hid them in different places, in cracks in the walls or in pill boxes or even in the guards' jackets that sometimes hung in the corridors. Thanks to the radios, gipsy music played late into the night in the ears of the poor jailbirds dreaming of the bustling life outside the prison walls.

I said goodbye to the darkness after seven years, on March 25, 1963, thanks to the general amnesty decreed by Khrushchev to mark the implementation of the détente he had worked out with President Kennedy. Just hours before my liberation, my father's heart stopped. He died without my being able to embrace him one last time. I hadn't seen him since 1956.

■ *"Isten Hozott"*

A pair of eyes glared at me; I looked up and saw a Soviet general. I didn't know that it was Ichtchenko, the one who was called "The Memory". My father was loved and admired in the workers' movement and I found it natural that the Russians would be represented at his burial. I didn't realize until later that Ichtchenko hadn't come just to pay his respects. I was under surveillance; although I had been released from prison, my liberty was only provisional.

Several weeks later, the secretary of the Budapest party organization called me into party headquarters. His name was Lajos Mehes and I had known him before the revolution. After having inquired after my health, he told me of "the party's decision": "You must atone for your crimes."

I didn't ask in the name of what decree the party was inflicting an additional penalty on me. I listened to Mehes tell me that I had to "become a worker again" in a factory chosen by him. I took the address, thanked him, and left. Later that evening, an old friend, a metal turner like me, who was now a member of the National Assembly, came to visit me. He had helped my family throughout our ordeal.

"Don't let yourself be manipulated," he told me. "Come with me."

Early next morning we took a taxi. Thirty minutes later, I was hired as a turner in a factory that produced precision pieces for electric locomotives. The factory, in the centre of Budapest, was not the one Mehes had chosen for me. I started work the next day. Three days later, a co-worker came to see me at my lathe.

"You're not making much. At that rate, you're going to starve to death."

In Hungary, then as now, payment was by the piece. More precisely, a quota was established for each job; if the worker didn't meet it, his salary was reduced accordingly. If he exceeded the quota, he received a small bonus at first, but his quota was soon raised and he had to maintain the increased level of production just to keep his salary at the old level.

The quotas were usually set high so that only experienced workers were able to meet them, with the help of custom equipment they guarded jealously for their own use. They would keep extra pieces they produced as insurance against future shortfalls rather than claiming the bonus for them.

I replied that I'd undoubtedly lost my touch. He didn't ask why. He knew. News travels as fast in factories as in jails.

"You should have said who you were right away. We'll make sure you get what you need."

He took from his own box half a dozen modern tools that were indispensable for working more quickly. He gave me two pieces of paper: the first was a work order for parts requiring three hours of work and the second represented five hours.

"All you have to do is write your name on these. You'll find the parts to hand in for inspection above your head on the shelf. Everybody wants you to feel welcome."

After a few weeks, I had the hang of it again and was performing as well as the others. I spent a year and a half as a turner in that workshop and had some strange encounters.

One day, one of the draftsmen came up to me.

"Sandor, do you recognize me?" he asked.

"Vaguely. Weren't you in Interior? A lieutenant-colonel or something like that?"

"Shh. Shh. Not in front of the others."

He had been deputy to the passport director before he was caught red-handed selling passports valid for travel to the West. He was sentenced to two years, but was paroled under supervision after the first year. I took it as a healthy sign that in Hungary crimes inspired by an excess of ideological zeal were now being replaced by ordinary corruption.

"Sandor, I beg you not to tell the others that I was connected to the AVO, or they'll make it hell for me."

I promised — and kept the promise.

This lieutenant-colonel wasn't the one assigned to keep an eye on me. That was the job of a former Vac prisoner though, of course, I did not know it at the time. I had happened to remark one day within his hearing that on the outside I was surrounded by as many informers as I had been in prison. The remark was duly reported by the stool pigeon to his superiors. The next day, I was tersely summoned to the Fo Street office of the AVO. My wife and mother insisted on coming along as insurance. I was politely received by a major who confined himself to asking me to sign a paper saying I had broken the rule prohibiting a liberated prisoner from revealing anything he had seen in prison. I refused because signing such a paper would have made me liable for an additional ten years' imprisonment.

"Your report is false. Your agent lied."

"So sign a true report," he responded without hesitation.

"What sort of report should I sign? I'm not a member of your staff."

"Put on a piece of paper: 'I will not infringe the rule of secrecy on the subject of my imprisonment.'"

I wrote: "As I have not infringed, I will continue not to infringe...."

"Put down what you want and sign."

He turned away.

The next day, the little informer didn't show up at work; we never saw him again.

But Ibolya and I met dozens of others. It seemed all the spies in Budapest were now specializing in the Kopacsi case. I met them on foot, on the tram, in the bus, and even on the doorstep of our apartment. They all wanted "news" of me and especially to know which of my prison comrades I was keeping in touch with. It was so tiresome to have swarms of obvious informers hovering about that Ibolya and I decided to "keep" the least disagreeable of them. He was a fellow named Laci who had been fired by the AVO for obscure reasons. He was a modest, well-educated sort who was content to pass his Sunday afternoons in our company, sipping a cup of coffee. Besides the coffee, we fed him indoctrination, just enough so that he could write reports on my "pro-Chinese" or "pro-Albanian" ideas, which I invented and served up hot every Sunday.

We almost cried when we lost him. He was replaced by a former policeman, now a factory director, who took us for Sunday excursions in his car. As soon as we were seated in the car, I began my pro-Chinese stories. Nobody in the AVO could take this stuff seriously, and the informer was replaced. When we lost the factory director, a horde of agents was swarming around us once again. This time, we decided to consecrate our Sundays to excursions on foot in the mountains with only ourselves invited.

It was during this period that we succeeded in sending our daughter to Canada. Judith's life had become intolerable in Budapest. From the day I was imprisoned, the child was made the object of official discrimination. At school, she was put on the list of children deemed "socially alien". Ibolya went to see the principal.

"Socially alien to whom?"

"To the workers' state," the principal replied with a straight face.

"My daughter has nothing but working-class ancestors, on her father's as well as her mother's side, for four generations."

"Agreed," said the principal. "But her father has betrayed the working class."

It reminded me of *Mein Kampf* in which pure Aryans were transformed into Jews for having associated with them, thereby betraying the noble race.

Kids are kids. There were some horrible ones at the school who took advantage of the situation to tease Judith mercilessly. Were they encouraged by the teachers or the parents? At the age of fourteen or fifteen, when a youngster is at her most sensitive, my child was seriously thinking of suicide.

As in a fairy tale, the person who was to rescue Judith from this senseless persecution appeared in our lives out of the blue. He was an old social democrat friend whose life I had saved in the dark days of 1952. Back then, the man had been banned from the capital as a class alien and resettled in a damp, miserable stable in a small village in eastern Hungary. In such circumstances, people sometimes died of sickness and starvation. He came to see me.

"Help me, Sandor, it's *another* Laszlo Sarosi that the authorities are after. It's a simple case of mistaken identity."

I only half believed him until I made some inquiries myself. The evidence against him fell apart immediately, and I thought it would be a simple matter to straighten the whole thing out. But I crashed up against the bureaucracy, the same bureaucracy I had helped to create myself.

Nobody dared to take the responsibility for cancelling a deportation order, even a mistaken one. My minister, Hazi, preferred to steer clear of the case. "Sandor, don't get involved in these things, that's my advice. Or, if you prefer, that's an order."

This friend was the sixth child of a family so poor that other working-class families like mine were well-to-do by comparison. I took a piece of paper and typed out a phoney order according to which the man was authorized to live wherever he chose. I put a maximum of seals on the paper, which carried the letterhead of the chief of police, and gave it to him. Later, during the revolution, he became one of two hundred thousand Hungarian refugees to flee to the West. He settled in Quebec, becoming a shoe merchant and a Canadian citizen.

Now he was back visiting Hungary, accompanied by his wife, and he came to see me.

"Sandor, entrust your child to us. My wife and I will raise her."

"Thanks very much, Laszlo, but we will never part from our Judith."

The Sarosis left. A little while later, Judith was taken to hospital; she had swallowed some medicine in an attempt to poison herself. I wrote to Sarosi. By return mail, we received a letter of invitation for Judith and an air ticket. We applied for a passport for her and received it six weeks later. That same day, in tears, we put her on the plane. The next day she was in Quebec. We would not see her again until six years later, when in 1971 she came home for a brief visit. By then she was a Canadian citizen.

During our walks in the mountains, we noticed many changes. There were new houses belonging to the new ruling class. At Dobogoko and at Leanyfalu, the proud inhabitants were AVO officers. Elsewhere, there were many shacks belonging to ordinary people. At Alsoors, near Lake Balaton, we gaped at the superb homes of two of Kadar's deputies — Karoly Nemeth and Cseterki. They had arranged to have the road to their houses paved.

"If we had been wiser, we would be living here," Ibolya joked bitterly.

Between the two superb houses, we noticed a third, more modest one. It was an ugly, hybrid structure resembling a cross between a garage and a hunting lodge. We asked one of the locals who owned it. He crossed himself before answering.

"That's Bogar's ["The Bug's"] house."

The Bug was the public executioner, Major Kovacs. Bogar was the actual surname of one of his predecessors and the name has stuck to everyone who has plied this horrible trade since. "You see, Ibolya," I said. "We never could have lived here after all."

Major Kovacs was not any less busy for having refused to execute Imre Nagy. He exercised his profession every day of the week. We wouldn't have enjoyed seeing him come home from a hard day at the scaffold, take off his boots, put on his comfiest slippers, and sit down to relax on the terrace.

On December 6, 1969, I was authorized to finish the legal studies I had begun when I was police chief. I was graduated *cum laude.* But The Memory decided that my new degree wouldn't alter my situation in any way. Someone as guilty as I could not become a legal adviser to even the most modest enterprise. I had to continue labouring for a worker's salary, surrounded by informers.

One night in 1972, Ibolya and I were invited to dinner at the home of some friends. The lady of the house looked at us oddly and said, "Would it bother you if Szalay joins us for dinner?"

Szalay was the prosecutor in the Nagy affair, the one who had asked the death sentence for my friends and life imprisonment for me. The woman added in a whisper, "He begged me to ask you to meet him."

I said, "If it doesn't bother him to see me, it won't bother me."

He had become an old man. During the dinner, we spoke of insignificant things. We drank. As we went home in the same direction, he accompanied us on the tram. After we were seated, the old prosecutor leaned close to me and asked, "Sandor, can you forgive me?"

Because I wanted to be clear in my own mind as to his purpose, I asked, "In whose name do you ask that question?"

"In the name of He whom both you and I have denied: our Lord Jesus Christ, the Saviour."

I said that naturally I forgave him. But I asked how he planned to straighten matters out with those who were no longer around to grant forgiveness.

He watched the shadows pass in the night and replied, in a soft voice, "That is my affair."

Eight days later, we learned that he was dead. Having arrived alone in the middle of the night at a chalet near Balaton, he had collapsed in an armchair. The snow was so thick that it was three days before a horse-drawn dung cart could get through to remove the body.

One hot summer day in 1973, I was coming home from work, on

the tram as always. In the middle of the car, someone was sounding off. The Arabs and Israelis were at war, and this character was practically foaming at the mouth, repeating the official anti-Semitic line and adding embellishments of his own.

"They must be exterminated right to the very last one. There are too many of them. Someone has done a rotten job. . . ."

In Hungary, public opinion is strongly anti-Arab because the Arabs are supported by the Soviets. I don't claim that the public praises the Jews to the skies. But during the war in the Middle East, the average Hungarian took malicious pleasure in seeing the Russians' pets trounced by the Israelis.

A glacial silence greeted the fanatic's ranting. I was boiling with anger. But neither I nor the others dared open our mouths. Who would have been courageous enough to confront publicly the *official opinion*? Kadar's policy was officially termed anti-Zionism, but everyone knew that this was a euphemism for the same old anti-Semitism.

I returned home profoundly humiliated.

A Nazi bastard, and there is no way to shut him up, in a tram in the capital city of my country! From that moment on, Ibolya and I dedicated our lives to only one goal: leaving Europe and rejoining our daughter. I have already recounted, at the beginning of my story, how this dream became reality.

Before leaving Hungary, we visited Macza, Imre Nagy's widow, as well as Ella, my friend Joska's widow, and her children. The martyred prime minister's wife lived in a cramped lodging. Surrounded by part of her husband's library, with yellowing photos on the walls, she spoke of friends who had survived and of the families of those who hadn't. One day, Ibolya told her what Nagy had confided as his last message. A bright and sensitive country woman who had at a very early age become the companion of the serious and taciturn Nagy, she replied simply: "I know that he loved me and that I loved him and still do."

For almost twenty years, her husband had been resting in an unknown grave. She stood up, took a rag, and softly dusted one or two objects.

In Budapest, it's midnight. Here, at the Toronto airport, it's 6:00 p.m. Two little people I've never met before, my grandson and granddaughter, shout greetings to us in Hungarian: *"Isten hozott!*

[God brought you]," the Hungarian way of saying "Welcome".
My daughter Judith was bursting with health and happiness. We
would have had a hard time recognizing in her the little suicide
candidate of a few years ago. She hung around my neck and cried,
"I've got my daddy, I've got my daddy."

In the immigration office, George Egri, a Hungarian journalist
who had worked hard to help us get out of Hungary, translated.

"Ever been imprisoned?" asked the official.

Oh, my God! Is it starting here too? I broke into a sweat. Egri
saw that I was horrified. A short dialogue ensued.

"I refer only to imprisonment for acts that would be considered
a crime in Canada," came the clarification. I breathed more easily
and the immigration officer soon concluded the interview. "I hope
you like your new country."

A man of imposing appearance and wearing a skullcap greeted
me in the terminal. He introduced himself as Rabbi Zoltan Zagon.
Although I had never met him before, he asked permission to
embrace me. I didn't know what to do.

"But Father, I mean Rabbi. There must be a mistake. I was never
Jewish. You must be expecting some other refugee."

A kindly smile appeared on the patriarch's face.

"It's certainly you, my son, that I was waiting for. I was born
in your region in the north, and I know that during the war you
and your father gave refuge to dozens of my fellow Jews. I wanted
to thank you and help you if necessary."

After attending English language school, my next task was to find
a job. My wife found employment as a pharmacist's assistant in a
Hungarian drug store in the centre of the city. For me, the best solution seemed to be to try to continue as a metalworker or tool- and
die-maker, since I had considerable experience in these trades. I
turned to Pastor Adon Seres, who had earlier offered his help. In
two days, he called to say he had found out that Commodore Ltd.,
a computer manufacturer, might have an opening in a few weeks
for a tool- and die-maker but that at the moment they needed a
cleaner. He advised me to take the cleaning job while waiting for
the other to become available. I accepted the suggestion at once.

As the months passed, my chances of working in the trade I knew
best dwindled. An economic recession was under way and three-
quarters of the company's work force was laid off within a matter
of weeks. The cleaner was perhaps the only worker not threatened

with dismissal. Less than a year after starting my first job, I applied for a cleaning job at the provincial hydro-electric company and got it, since among all the applicants, I now had the most experience.

Meanwhile, I obtained my driver's licence and acquired a used car, having learned from my first job-hunting experiences that it's a prerequisite for many types of employment in Canada. As a cleaner, I no longer had the services of a chauffeur.

The year after our arrival, we celebrated Christmas with my mother. She had barely recovered from a broken leg when she stepped off the plane from Hungary. She was nearing her eightieth year and could not understand why her son had to live on this distant continent. But she was at peace with my decision when she left us after three months. The following year she died; of course, I could not be present at the funeral.

We use the weekends and summer holidays to explore our new homeland, and especially Ontario. From the icy seas of the north, south to Manitoulin Island, and down to Niagara Falls, we are astounded by the wealth of natural beauty in this vast land.

Like me, many of the Hungarians who fled in the aftermath of the revolution have adapted to their new homes and prospered. Bela Kiraly, my colleague in the command of the National Guard, did not wait ten years to leave as I did. After leading his troops across the Austrian border, he made his way to the United States and today lives in New York where he is a professor of military history and the author of several books on Hungarian and central-European history.

The Pongratz brothers, after defending their position at Corvin Alley for eleven days after the Soviet attack of November 4, avoided capture and led their units, still armed, over the Austrian border. Today they live in the United States. One of them, Gergely, is a past president of the Worldwide Association of Hungarian Freedom Fighters.

But many of those who led the fight for freedom in the streets of Budapest did not survive. After the second Soviet intervention, Joseph Dudas, occupier of the party newspaper, was hidden by workers in a factory in Kobanya, not far from Budapest. The wounded revolutionary leader rejected the advice of his comrades to escape to the West. A delegation of miners went to Kadar to urge him to meet Dudas to discuss an end to the hostilities between the rebels and the new regime. Kadar invited Dudas to Parliament, but his aim was treachery, not reconciliation. The AVO arrested Dudas during the meeting and, bizarrely, charged him with "conspiring to overthrow by force the legal government of Imre Nagy" — exactly what Kadar and the Soviets had just accomplished themselves. Dudas was executed on January 19, 1957.

Steven Angyal was also taken prisoner and condemned to death. His last wish was to be married in prison to his fiancée with whom he had conceived a child during the fighting. The wish was granted. His last words were: "Better to die than to live in shame like the rest of you."

Others who struggled in 1956 for a democratic Hungary are still struggling. Sandor Racz was arrested when the Russians crushed the workers' council and sentenced to life imprisonment. He was freed in the 1963 amnesty and now works in a factory and writes. In a samizdat (underground) publication on the twenty-fifth anniversary of the revolution, he reaffirmed his beliefs in the ideals of 1956. To mark the thirtieth anniversary of the uprising, his account of the trial of the workers' council is being published in Paris.

Of the eight defendants at the Nagy trial, three of us are still alive. Miklos Vasarhelyi was amnestied in 1960. He has been attacked by the party newspaper several times because of his unrepentant behaviour. In 1985, he took part in the opposition movement's conference in Monor at which forty-five members of the intelligentsia met to discuss the nation's problems. Another of my co-defendants, Ferenc Donath, also released in 1963, is today, at the age of seventy-six, one of the leaders of the human rights movement in Hungary. His political analyses have appeared in samizdat, and he was chairman of the Monor conference.

That conference took as its theme the political thought of Stephen Bibo, and in particular his book *A Compromise Plan for the Solution of the Hungarian Question*. This was the book the former minister of state and leader of the Peasants' Party was writing when I saw him during the siege of the Parliament building. The book proposes a "third way" to maintain a balance of power in Europe while safeguarding Hungarian self-determination. For calling on the United Nations to come to Hungary's aid, Bibo was sentenced to life imprisonment. Until he too was amnestied in 1963, he was frequently maltreated. His books are published in censored versions in Hungary today, but they circulate in complete editions in samizdat form. Although he died in 1978, his persecutors have still not succeeded in silencing him.

Even the man who admits to signing the request for the Soviet invasion — three days after it happened — is now counted among the enemies of Soviet domination of central Europe. Andras Hegedus, who was prime minister under Rakosi, openly condemned the invasion of Czechoslovakia in 1968. He was fired from his job as a statistician and expelled from the party.

Zoltan Tildy, the Protestant pastor who had been left in charge of the government after Nagy escaped to the Yugoslav Embassy, was sentenced to six years in jail, but was freed in 1959 and died two years later at the age of seventy-two. Ferenc Munnich who, but for the intervention of Tito, would have become head of government after the Russians crushed the revolution, continued as a cabinet minister until 1966. He died at the age of eighty-one.

As for Janos Kadar himself; as of this writing he is still in power at the age of seventy-four. He is given credit for the emergence over the last decade of a new, more tolerable form of Communism, "goulash Communism", under which Hungarians enjoy more plentiful and better food and consumer goods, less government interference, and more freedom of movement than citizens of the U.S.S.R. or any of its other Eastern-bloc allies.

Friends and acquaintances from Hungary visit us in Toronto from time to time and they tell us that life is much better now. I always listen patiently to these reports, since I am genuinely pleased that the atmosphere in Hungary has improved. Then I take out the Canadian passport that I received upon becoming a citizen three years after arriving in Canada. It looks very much like a Hungarian passport, but the resemblance is superficial. The Canadian constitution assures every citizen the right to possess a passport with which he is free to travel throughout the world. In Hungary, who is issued a passport and who isn't depends on the grace and favour of the state. Each time someone wishes to travel, he or she must reapply for the document. When I point these things out, my guests fall silent or sigh mightily.

During the last decade I have become friends with many people who were my former enemies. I feel sorry for the powers that be in Hungary who cannot heal the rifts of the past in the same way, who leave the graves of the executed martyrs of 1956 unmarked and unknown to this day, even to their families. Rather than being hidden, these graves should be national monuments because the increased liberties people now enjoy in Hungary were bought with the lives of the 1956 revolutionaries.

The man who supervised the destruction of the dreams of those revolutionaries came back to haunt me. In May 1982, a reporter from the *Washington Post* asked to interview me on the subject of Yuri Andropov. This paper seems to have been farsighted because it could predict that the ambassador who could string the Hungarians along so masterfully had talents that would take him far. And they were right; within six months Andropov became the leader of the Soviet Union.

Members of the media, both broadcast and print, trooped to my door. On the TV screen, I studied the face of the dancer I once knew. He appeared to be dragging one of his feet; his high office had come to him a little late. I was unhappy with the media coverage. The journalists showed Andropov as they would have liked him to be: an elegant dresser, a tippler of fine whisky, a cultured man who could speak good English. In short, a gentleman. The other side of the picture, the torture chambers under the dance floor of the Soviet Embassy in Budapest, had been forgotten.

I could never forget. After my imprisonment by General Serov, I dreamt of my own execution almost every night. These nightmares persisted twenty years later, even after my arrival in Canada. My wife could follow the unfolding of the nightmare very well. It started with a guttural sound resembling ambulance sirens and continued with thrusting about, cramps, and a series of terrible screams. Only after I wrote this book did the nightmares go away.

Ten years have passed in my life as an immigrant. As I near retirement, I am satisfied with the adjustment I've made. My father spent the first two decades of his working life employed at an electric generating plant; it's somehow fitting that I should end mine at Ontario Hydro, the electric power utility. Mr. Cleaner would not change places with any cabinet minister in Hungary, where a scapegoat must be found and punished for the regime's every failure. I thank God that I've found freedom, my peace of mind, and the joy of a new beginning.